Jefferson County
Reminiscences

By

MANY HANDS

Binford & Mort Publishing, Portland, Oregon

TO THE JEFFERSON COUNTY PIONEERS
In Gratitude, Admiration, and Remembrance

Pioneers–picturesque as our mountain-studded skyline; determined as the sage that covers our rolling plateaus; individual as the pungent juniper dotting our hills and valleys; generous friends, kindly neighbors, living or preceding us to the Great Beyond–Pioneers we salute you.

Sponsors
Walter McCaulou
Kenneth McCaulou
Harry S. Michael
Louis G. Kinkade

It is with much admiration and heartfelt thanks to the pioneer families and memories, that Jefferson County Historical Society has chosen to fund a second printing.
We want to thank the following people for their help:
Dave Horttor for the cover picture;
Sharon Dodge for the expanded index;
Jarold Ramsey for "furthering reading" about Jefferson County
The Jefferson County Library Association for permission to print.

HISTORICAL SOCIETY/MUSEUM BOARD
Beth Crow, Bill Dickson, Jodi Eagan, Luella Friend, Arthur "Bill" Grant, Reata Horney, Jack Watts and Museum Curator, Aloha Kendall

Jefferson County Reminiscences
Copyright © 1957, 1998 by Binford & Mort Publishing

Printed in the United States of America
Library of Congress Catalog Card Number: 98-72372
ISBN 0-8323-0529-4 (Hardbound)
ISBN 0-8323-0526-X (Softcover)

First Edition 1957
Second Edition 1998

ACKNOWLEDGMENT

At a meeting of the Jefferson County Library Association early in 1951 Martha Ross (Mrs. J. H. Ross) suggested that the group sponsor the writing and publishing of a history of Jefferson County. Those present agreed that the history would be an interesting and worthwhile project. Allie Farrell (Mrs. H. Ward Farrell) was appointed chairman of a committee to take charge of the project.

Grateful acknowledgment is made to all those people whose cooperation has made this volume a reality. To those who have written the articles, to those who have contributed information, to those who have solicited the given funds, and especially to the committee members who planned the volume, many thanks are due.

Most of all acknowledgment should be made to Allie Farrell, whose unfailing enthusiasm and tactful persistence have made possible the publishing of the book. Nor should her tireless and patient chauffeur, her husband H. Ward Farrell, be omitted from this roster.

FURTHER READING ON JEFFERSON COUNTY HISTORY

Abbot, Henry L. *Reports of Explorations and Surveys* [The Pacific Railroad Surveys]. Washington D. C. 1857.

Baehr, Russ. *Oregon's Outback: Tales and Legends from Beyond the High Cascades*. Bend: Maverick Press, 1988.

Brogan, Phil F. *East of the Cascades*. Portland: Binford & Mort, 1964.

Clark, Keith & Tiller, Lowell. *Terrible Trail: the Meek Cutoff, 1845*. Caldwell, Idaho: The Caxton Printers, Ltd., 1967. Reprint, Maverick Press, 1993.

Cornwell, Ethel Klann, *Rimrocks and Water Barrels*. Monona, Wisconsin: Lakeside Press, 1979.

Echoes From Old Crook County, Volume I & II. Prineville: Crook County Historical Society.

Foster, Teresa. *Settlers in Summer Lake Valley*. Bend: Maverick Publications, 1989.

Greenhoot, Gilma Endicott. *Rattlesnake Homestead*. Springfield: by Author

Helftich, Devere and Ackerman, Trudy. *The Schreek of Wagons, 1848 Diary of Richard M. May*. Hopkinton, Massachusetts: Rigel Publications, 1993.

Helm, Irene H. *School Days of Old Crook County*. Prineville: Prineville Print Shop, 1980.

History of Jefferson County, Oregon, 1914-1983. Madras: Jefferson County Historical Society, 1984.

Illustrated History of Central Oregon. Western Historical Publishing Co. 1905. Reprint UMI, 1998.

Monroe, Fred. *A History of the Grant and the Boone Families*. Charlotte, North Carolina: by Author, 1994.

Luelling, C. S. *Saga of the Sagebrush Country*.

Powers, Lelah Hall. *The Albert Moore Family by Goldie Moore Hall*. Anchorage, Alaska: 1991.

Poulsen, Earl C. *The Family of Neils and Dora Poulsen*. San Antonio, Texas: Dorthea A. Johnson Alvares, 1992.

Raber, Bess Stangland. *Some Bright Morning*. Bend: Maverick Publications, 1983.

Ramsey, Jarold. "New Era: Growing Up East of the Cascades 1937-1950," in *Regionalism and the Pacific Northwest*. Ed. William G. Robbins, Robert Frank, and Richard E. Ross. Corvallis: Oregon State University Press, 1983.

Rees, Helen Guyton. *Guytons Galore from French Huguenots to Oregon Pioneers*. Portland: Binford & Mort, 1986.

Rees, Helen Guyton. *Shaniko People*. Portland: Binford & Mort, 1983.

Stowell, Cynthia D. *Faces of a Reservation: A Portrait of the Warm Springs Indian Reservation*. Portland: Oregon Historical Press, 1987.

Turner, Clara Hoffman. *One Man's Family*. Seattle: 1978

Warren, Ruth Catherine. *The Memoirs of Ruth C. Warren-From Nebraska to Oregon*. Troutdale: Sharon Nesbit, 1987.

CONTENTS

Grizzly .... *Margaret Merrow* .... Page 1

Hay Creek .... *Eda R. Power* 9

Blizzard Ridge 46

The Culver District 54

Culver Postcript *Fred L. Rodman* 68

The Trail Crossing *Anna Merchant* Mrs. Melvin Byrne 70

Trout Creek *Jeremiah Carwin* 81

Ashwood *Gladys B. Keegan Phil Brogan* 96

Madras *Frank D. W. Turner* Martha Thomas ....

Lamonta *Euretta Harney Nina McGaffey* 174

Gateway and Lyle Gap *Ivah Tolbert & Allie M. Jewell*

Vanora *John L. Campbell* 198

Metolius *Clara H. Hoffman* 209

Grandview, Camp Sherman and Metolius River 217

Opal City *Wilma E. Ramsey* 239

Pony Butte *Lucile A. Thornton* 254

Mud Springs Valley *Mrs. W. J. Sterling* 259

South Agency Plains *Lela Ramsey* 282

North Agency Plains and Vicinity *Chester S. Luelling Cora Luelling* ... 316

Irrigation of Jefferson County 329

Transportation 350

Jefferson County Schools *June H. Fisher Ethel Hostetler* 350

Library Association and Pioneer Association *Helen Aring* 361

Warm Springs Indian Reservation 373

Index 381

Jefferson County Reminiscences

Grizzly

By Margaret Morrow

The earliest settled portion of Crook County was the area known as Willow Creek, located north and east of Grizzly Mountain. It is said that a Mr. James Blakely had been in the area with stock from the Willamette Valley and was very much impressed with the country. Upon returning home he discussed the possibility of setting up homesteads and in the year 1863 he and two of his relatives, Kennedy Montgomery and S. W. Wood, and a friend, Perry Read, settled along Willow Creek in what is now known as the Grizzly District. They were among the first settlers. One of the first was Fate Brown.

The country was very fertile. Wild flowers covered the hills and natural bunchgrass was very high and plentiful. There was little sagebrush and few junipers. The stream was filled with fish and the mountain was covered with a heavy growth of timber.

Running through the area was a trail that had been built in 1846, called the Jesse Applegate Trail. In 1869 Wm. Clark and Lew Daugherty were authorized by Wasco County Court to construct a toll road from the Steens Military road at Bakeoven, down Cow Canyon, Haycreek, Grizzly, and to Prineville.

1

The Dalles merchants wanted a better road into Central Oregon and especially to Prineville, which was founded in 1868.

In 1869 The Dalles to Prineville stage station was established and the Palmain Ranch was the first stage station in the Grizzly area. They would change horses there and then go on to Prineville. The entire trip took two days of travel.

Other homesteaders traveled to this area until every available homestead site was taken. The names Click, Chitwood, Edmonds, McMean, Fogle, Harper, Morrow, Warren, Newton, Brown and Compton are all remembered as some of the first families.

Perry Read was not married when he homesteaded, but in 1873 he rode 125 miles horseback to obtain a marriage license from the county seat in The Dalles. He then married Hattie Ellen Montgomery, the daughter of Kennedy Montgomery, in Prineville and they became one of the well-known families of the Central Oregon Country.

The homesteaders came with a few cattle and sheep but the gardens were good because the new land was always very fertile. There was an annual trip to The Dalles by wagon for yearly supplies of groceries and other necessities. It took two weeks to complete the trip. Friends would meet in town, not having seen each other since the previous trip for supplies.

It was possible to own over 400 acres in this section, besides the homesteads. They could own 160 acres preemption (file on it and live on the land six months and then buy.) Also they could take out timber cultures and set out Box Elder or other trees and cultivate them.

Grizzly

One reference states that a post office called the Willoughby Post Office near Grizzly, was established May 20, 1872, and was discontinued March 7, 1879. The first postmaster was Robert Warren. The next post office was called the Cleek Post Office, established west of Grizzly on the Dalles-Prineville stage run in 1881 and closed in 1883, with Harley Belnap as first postmaster. The post office was later moved to the Edmonds place and finally to the Grizzly Store.

A school was built in the 1870's on the Warren homestead and there were about 20 pupils. Some walked as far as six miles to attend and rather than go out to play with the other children they would stay and rest to be ready for the walk home after the day's studies were over.

At times there was no school in the early days and usually three months at the most. The grades ranged up to the eighth. One of the first teachers was a man named Dayton. He roomed and boarded among the homes of the pupils as did most of the teachers in the early times. He received about thirty dollars a month. The school increased as the years went by until there were over 40 pupils and a much longer school year when Warren Brown was the teacher in about the year 1901. His parents were homesteaders in the area and he attended school at Grizzly and later taught there.

The school was the center of the community activity. There was Sunday School and church, sometimes with a traveling minister, and during the bad weather the members took charge of the services. The Christmas program and party for the entire population of the Willow Creek area was a very special event

3

and the Thanksgiving dinner for everyone was always held there.

The winter of 1884 and 1885 was remembered as one of the worst of the early days. There was four feet of snow and sleighs were used on the stage routes. The ranchers with a good supply of winter feed for their cattle did not lose much stock but some of the ranchers lost all they had.

Almost all fences were built of rails and to this days several miles of rail fences are still in use. The homesteaders that stayed over the years gradually saw all the open range fenced.

There was, of course, a need for a cemetery and one was established about three-fourths of a mile from where the townsite of Grizzly is located. The caskets were made of pine by the Prineville Hardware Store which was the undertaking parlor at that time. The bodies were taken to Prineville and brought back for burial in the Grizzly Cemetery.

Almost everyone that remembers the early days can tell stories of the murders and killings that took place. There was no law in the area south of The Dalles.

In 1877, C. C. Mailing came to Crook County and located on the upper Willow Creek where he erected a steam sawmill, the first one in the county. He came from England and prospered in this area.

Charles Mailing was the first mill owner along the north part of Willow Creek. Jack Dee bought this mill in 1912 and Sam Compton was a partner with him. The Fronhoffer mill was on Coon Creek which comes down into Willow Creek. Harry E. Blackwell had a mill on Grizzly Mountain in 1919.

In 1904 the community had a ball team that played Culver

and Lamonta. Some of the members were Carl and Nova Newbill, Cecil McKenzie, Bud Smith, Joe Montgomery. Ernie Matson, George Hamilton, and Roy and Darrell Simpson.

The first store was built about 1900 by Ed Wills who later became the county judge of Crook County. John Lewis bought the store in 1913. It was a large building with a dance hall on the second floor. Dances were often held over the store, with a small orchestra consisting of organist Jack Church, violinists Jim Thomas, Lena Thomas and Charles McMean. The music was lively and the families attending brought children and grandparents, and all had a good time.

The store was the gathering place for the entire community, since the post office was there and the stage brought the mail every day but Sunday and all legal holidays except New Years. This was after the railroad came into Madras in 1911. Mr. Lewis had a good business because almost every piece of land was being farmed. As many as 150 families lived in the area and all did a part of their trading at the store. The supplies were freighted in by wagon. Sometimes they would have to wait because one of the wagons loaded with barrels of sugar or flour or other groceries would go over the grade at Cow Canyon. They would then have to wait for another wagon to come from The Dalles.

The first store building burned in the latter part of 1913 and John Lewis built a smaller but more modern building in the same location. Some of the various owners were Prentice Pitzer who took over in 1916, Fred Rufner, Judge Vincent, and Lou Hamilton.

One of the main stage stations, in the late nineteenth century, was the house built by Henry Cleek for a residence. It is said the logs for the home were cut in the Grizzly area and hauled to The Dalles by wagon and back to build the home. The large rambling house, while it stood in the same location, was in three counties, first Wasco, then Crook, and from 1914 on until burned in 1948 in Jefferson. The house was bought by Morrow and Keenan in 1900 and the stage station moved to the place now owned by Mrs. Fred Rufner.

Andrew Morrow and James Keenan bought the land from Cleek and ran sheep and cattle. The Morrow & Keenan herders of this period were Basques and they were very good. It wasn't necessary to count the sheep, they took such good care of them. The only trips necessary to the sheep camps were to take in supplies which consisted of flour, salt, coffee, prunes and bacon.

The following story is from the *Redmond Spokesman*:

"Early in the present century Mr. Keenan was an unwilling participant in the bitter range wars that found cattlemen pitted against sheepmen. The unfortunate struggle not only left thousands of sheep dead on the open range and on timber pastures but resulted in the death of a number of men and the mysterious disappearance of others. Mr. Keenan and his partner, Andrew Morrow, had first information relative to the range wars of 1904 and 1905. Their flocks on a number of occasions were targets for masked raiders.

"It has been estimated that 10,000 sheep were killed in the Central Oregon range wars. In the summer of 1904 Mr. Keenan

6

moved two bands of sheep to the Horse Heaven Creek range. Armed men rode the rang but Mr. Keenan and his herders moved their flocks at night and avoided corrals, reach a part of the country they believed to be outside the deadline. Mr. Keenan returned to his home only to learn that sheep killers had struck. Out of a flock of 2,400 close to 358 ewes and their lambs had been shot. The masked riders had tied the herder to a tree so that he could witness the shooting.

"In 1905 the Oregon Legislature passed two bills, one appropriating $10,000 for the capture of sheep killers and the other giving the Governor authority to punish persons found guilty of killing stock belonging to others. But the legislative action failed to awe the masked riders. When the Oregon Woolgrowers, meeting in Antelope, offered rewards for information leading to the arrest and conviction of sheep killers. The cattlemen formed the 'Crook County Sheep Shooting Association.' "

Some will say that many of those bitter cattlemen who took part in the slaughter of sheep had later become sheepmen.

During World War I several of the homesteaders sold out because they could get good pay in employment on the outside and could sell their land to the big cattle and sheep men for a good price. The Haycreek Ranch and Morrow & Keenan were buying many of the homesteads and their homesteaders who remained purchased additional land.

There were many good years when the homesteaders prospered but in 1929 there was a drop in prices followed by severe drought. In the early 30's the land became dry and barren, the only grass was badly overgrazed, and on much of the land only lupin and the green sage remained. When crops were planted the seed didn't even sprout except on the sub-irrigated land where a little grain, hay and grass were grown. This lasted five or six years. During this period most of the remaining homesteaders sold their land and moved away.

World War II brought some help to the landowners because they could get good prices for land, livestock, and grain.

Two of the outstanding things that have happened in the past few years, for the five or six families still living in the area, was the coming of electricity on November 20, 1950. The school was consolidated with Madras grade school in September of 1954, because there were only six students attending at that time.

The few remaining families still enjoy their Christmas parties and other social activities and also feel that they can call on their neighbors in time of need, just as the homesteaders did so many years ago.

Hay Creek

By Evada R. Power

In 1863 the Hay Creek community was in Wasco County, a vast domain of 200,000 square miles reaching from the Cascades to the Rocky Mountains and between the southern boundary of Washington Territory and the north boundary of California. It was the largest county in all of the United States. Seventeen counties in Oregon and portions of land in Idaho, Montana, and Wyoming have been carved from the original Wasco County.

In 1882 Wasco lost six million acres when Crook County was created. Jefferson with more than one million acres was formed from Crook County in 1914. Early settlers of Hay Creek had to file homestead claims in The Dalles. They in return traveled to four adjacent county seats as the distance was greatly reduced from first The Dalles, county seat of Wasco, then Prineville, county seat of Crook, and then Culver and Madras, county seats of Jefferson.

In 1863 Felix and Marion Scott of the Willamette Valley came to the Hay Creek country. They traveled over the McKenzie Pass, cutting their way over a faint trail made three years previous when Henry Spaulding, the missionary, and Jake Gulliford brought cattle to Central Oregon.

The Scotts were bound for the Salmon River Mines in Idaho, with a layout of eight or nine loaded freight wagons, about seventy yoke of work oxen and seven hundred head of loose cattle. Their plans were to open a road and they were aided by people of Lane County who donated labor and one thousand dollars. It took several months of arduous labor before the Scotts reached lower Hay Creek, late in the season, and plans were made to winter their stock

The Scotts have been called the earliest settlers of Hay Creek, though their winter stay could hardly be called a settlement. In 1865-66 they ranged 400 cattle on the same location. On March 16, 1866, when Presley and Marion Scott were there, with Charles S. Hardison, John B. Evans, his brother Thomas J. Evans. Lem Jones, and a man named Mills, they were raided by Indians, who got away with seven saddle horses and the camp equipment. The Scotts lived in a cave under the rimrock below what later became the Priday and Parrish and McPherson ranches.

John B. Evans settled on Willow Creek in 1866 and later in speaking of the winter he spent with the Scott cattle on Hay Creek, said "At this time the grass grew very high and rank. Hay could be cut almost anywhere in the Blue Mountains. Wild timothy and pea vine grew eighteen inches high. Bunch grass would make a ton of hay per acre. There were only a few settlers in the country and practically all of them were engaged in hunting. The game was very plentiful and the skins and dried meat were sold in The Dalles. The game chiefly hunted was deer, elk, and bear."

Williamson G. Allen, formerly of Lane County, settled on Hay Creek on a tract of land which he later sold to Dr. D. M. Baldwin.

Hay Creek

S. G. Thompson, the first judge of Crook County, and his two brothers, William and Duovery, were early settlers. William, better known as Bud, was once editor of the Roseburg *Plaindealer* and the Salem *Mercury*. He took a very prominent part in the early history of Central Oregon and was a colonel in the state militia in the Bannock War of 1878.

In his book, *Reminiscences of a Pioneer,* Colonel Thompson describes in detail the part he took in the Bannock War, including the friendship of Captain George, chief of the Warm Springs and Wasco Indians, who offered aid to the Thompson and Perry Maupin families, promising to take them and their horses to the reservation. Thompson selected the ranch of Dr. Baldwin as a rallying point in case of danger.

The Baldwin Sheep and Land Company was started in 1873 by Dr. D. W. Baldwin. He brought the first sheep from Vermont —registered Spanish Merinos—shipped them as far as he could by rail and then trailed them across the Blue Mountains to Hay Creek, a distance of one thousand miles from the railroad point. Dr. Baldwin had raised sheep in Vermont before coming west and he selected Hay Creek as an ideal breeding plant for Merinos.

The original ranch started with the purchase of one hundred and sixty acres, twenty-five miles north of Prineville. With the later purchase of homesteads, the acreage of the ranch increased to embrace several thousand acres. The doctor settled in this favored section with the idea of raising alfalfa to feed his flocks. In the face of ridicule he used all his fields and, with the possible exception of a southern Oregon venture, it was the

11

first alfalfa grown in the State of Oregon. At any rate, it was the alfalfa fodder that spelled success for Dr. Baldwin's enterprise, and his sheep became famous throughout the world.

The late Mrs. Mansel Wheeler, an early settler of Grizzly, said the good doctor was called on often to take care of the sick and sometimes traveled as far as a hundred and fifty miles.

Mr. and Mrs. Orlando Parrish settled on Hay Creek north of the Baldwin Ranch in 1876. Mrs. Parrish was the daughter of Mrs. Elizabeth Sager Helm, one of the survivors of the Whitman massacre of 1847. To Mrs. Parrish must go the credit for all the Lombardy tree plantings in this section. On one of her many trips to The Dalles, Mrs. Parrish (Mrs. Charles McCue after the death of Parrish) brought back tiny slips of the giant trees which took root in the virgin soil and multiplied until not only the Parrish Ranch but Dr. Baldwin's Ranch were criss-crossed and bordered with trees. The slips brought home in a buggy were shared and planted in the belief that they were needed as a windbreak. The Parrish Ranch, famed as an overnight stopping place for freighters and stage coach travel, later became a mecca for homesteaders who purchased their winter's supply of fruit and vegetables. During the fruit season it was not unusual to see 800 sacks of pears sold. The ranch became a part of the Hay Creek Ranch in the 1930's.

In 1884 Dr. Baldwin's health failed and he was compelled to sell his holdings to C. A. and J. P. Van Houten and H. Loneoy. In 1898 John Griffith Edwards moved into Hay Creek as half-owner of the Baldwin Company, assuming joint ownership of the ranch with C. M. Cartwright and J. P. Van Houten.

12

Hay Creek

Not until 1905 did Edwards gain full control or possession of the Baldwin Land and Sheep Company by purchasing the Cartwright and Van Houten interests. That year Louis Enderud, who now lives in Portland, arrived at Hay Creek and assumed the business management of the ranch.

Jerry Schooling, Oregon-born student of Oregon history, worked at the ranch for more than fifty years and helped build the three-story house for Edward's bride, the former Elizabeth Justice Bell Smith of Yorkshire, England, who married the English lord in 1903. This house became famous as a center of Oregon hospitality, and Portland society made it a rendezvous. To its friendly doors came governors and mayors, cultural and business leaders, and visiting celebrities. Sam Hill, noted road builder, was a guest as was E. H. Harriman of the Union Pacific Railroad.

One of the many stories Schooling saved in memory from his half-century residence on the ranch was in regard to the house. After a beautiful hardwood floor had been laid, Edwards grew alarmed lest the house would be cold. So teamsters were sent to The Dalles for more hardwood and a second floor was laid over the first. When this was finished Edwards was still doubtful and sent for more lumber and a third hardwood floor was laid.

Jerry Schooling and Ed. Dean, in charge of the show rams, made many a fair circuit in those days. The pure Spanish and Delaine Merinos bred at Hay Creek until 1898 were noted for heavy fleeces but were undersized for ranch and mutton. The first importations of full-blooded Rambouillets, both ewes and rams were from the French government flock at Rambouillet

13

and from flocks of Victor Gilbert of Wideville, France and Thirouin-Sorreau of Cherville, France. These were the only pure bred Rambouillet flocks in the world. These breeds were bred for size and mutton and eliminated both the grease and wrinkles of the Spanish Merino.

This cross made by Edwards of the Rambouillet with the Spanish Merino and Delaine produced much larger sheep, which kept the heavy fleece along with a larger and sturdier frame. The heavy fleece of the Spanish Merino and the long staple in the Delaine brought out a distinct type called Baldwin Sheep. They became known all over the world, for they were widely exhibited over the United States and foreign countries.

Ewes were not sold and thousands of dollars and time went to build up this breed. From this policy the ranch had a competitive advantage.

In 1902 the ranch bought prize-winner rams from the Paris Exposition, and many rams and ewes, prize winners, from lesser shows in France. Added to these were prize winners in shows from Vermont, Ohio, Illinois, Michigan and other states.

This careful selection produced 125-pound ewes which sheared 12 to 16 pounds, and rams weighing 200 pounds which sheared from 25 to 35 pounds of wool.

Twelve to fifteen thousand ewes were bred each year at Hay Creek. They were bred when two years old, and ram lambs were closely culled, especially cared for, and sold as yearling rams for range purposes to breeders everywhere.

One flock of registered sheep of each of the three classes were kept separate and registered with the American Delaine and

14

Spanish Merino Breeders Association at Delaware, Ohio, and with the American Rambouillet Record Association at Milford Ohio. This was to furnish rams to head flocks all over the United States. Many were sold each year into Natal and Cape Colony, South Africa. Many unregistered rams of the Baldwin type were included in shipments to South Africa and sold to Boer farmers.

During Edward's ownership the ranch built up to an average of 27,000 acres, not including leased or summer pasture in the national reserve. A working force of 70 to 100 men were employed to take care of the sheep and to put up hay for more than 50,000 head of them.

The decade after the turn of the century was profitable for the ranch, due to the activity of Edwards and his capable helpers—Louis Enderud, Ed Dean, and Jerry Schooling.

Four thousand rams were exported annually from the ranch which had built its breed by often paying as much as $2000 per head for rams from the French government, until the flocks at Hay Creek were the largest in the world. The government flock at Rambouillet, France, was established when King Louis Phillipi selected from Spain the choicest merinos. The sheep were named after the town.

Edwards sold the ranch in 1910 to L. B. Menefee, and Henry L. Pittock, one of the publishers of the *Oregonian*. The ranch was transferred by Pittock and Menefee to W. U. Sanderson in 1922 who, in turn sold it to Fred W. Wickman in 1937. In April 1952 A. J. Smith and sons of Big Fork and Kalispel, Montana, purchased the ranch. Wickman took the ranch back in 1954.

Old time employees still living in Central Oregon are Lyn

15

Nichols and John Aldrich, Prineville; Howard W. Turner, Fred Green, Jack Church, Judge T. A. Power, Madras; Frank Gill, Roy Newell, Redmond.

Lyn Nichols of Prineville has a memory stretch reaching back nearly three fourths of a century. When he was eleven years old his family moved to the Hay Creek country. His stepfather, Perry Maupin, homesteaded what is known as the Maupin Place. From the large springs on this place the Hay Creek Ranch pipes its domestic water supply. The stepfather was a son of Howard Maupin, the man who became famous as one of the killers of Chief Paulina. The elder Maupin was a veteran of the Mexican War under Zachary Taylor and from him Lyn heard firsthand stories about Chief Paulina.

Lyn worked at the Hay Creek ranch for 18 years, during the period when the ranch knew great prosperity because of an ideal combination of free government land and thousands of sheep and cattle, a common condition of the times, but a situation that will never again prevail in America.

Free land, unfenced and covered with bunch grass knee high, surrounded the ranch owned by Edwards when Lyn went to work there. Besides the sheep, 1500 to 2000 head of cattle were run. In the 18 years of his employment there, only once was it necessary to buy hay. Six thousand tons were almost a certainty. as the meadows were sowed to alfalfa and yields were large.

The sheep were ranged over what is now Jefferson County. Camps were on the Deschutes River and at Gateway, Frog Springs, Paxton, and Coleman; in fact every good spring in the county was a camp. At one time the ranch had five camps on

16

Hay Creek

Agency Plains when five feet of snow fell so that it took five days of trail breaking with teams and snow plows to get the sheep out. They were coaxed home with hay.

In the winter when hay had to be bought, the late Tom Boylen was foreman of the ranch. Several thousand head of sheep were trailed to Prineville where hay was bought at $20 per ton. When hay ran out, grain, shipped in but the storm broke before any grain was fed.

Hay Creek was a productive place and John Kraut as gardener raised vegetables for the home ranch and the sheep camps.

When Lyn Nichols and Florence Grimes, a daughter of early pioneers of Crook County, were married in 1902 they settled at Hay Creek. The house built for them is still in use and has been occupied by many different foremen and their families in the past 50 years.

Hay Creek was the first ranch to install a sheep-shearing plant. Lyn helped to install this machine and remembers that in its first year of operation 42,000 sheep were sheared. It would be interesting to estimate the total number sheared in the following years.

During Edward's ownership of the ranch it reached its peak in the ram business, becoming known as the largest fine-wool breeding plant in the United States.

In 1904 Lyn bought out his stepfather's homestead southeast of the Hay Creek Ranch. He had filed on a homestead of his own and, forming a partnership with another homesteader by name of Al Tipton, he left the employ of the ranch in 1906. In his long service at the ranch he had successfully filled every position

17

from chore-boy to foreman. His own ranch grew in size, and he availed himself of the free land reaching as far as the eye could see. The old Doak place, a landmark of the Hay Creek country was acquired. When Lyn decided to sell his ranch to the Hay Creek Company the ranch had grown to several thousand acres and 200 head of cattle. These holdings now are considered indispensable to the ranch.

In 1901 the price of sheep ran from two to three dollars and ewes $2.75. At that time wethers were kept for wool, prices on young ones was $2.50 and two-year-old wethers brought $3.00. Wool was around 13 cents a pound.

In March 1910 the Baldwin Sheep and Land Company, oftener called the Hay Creek Ranch, advertised a general closing-out sale of their entire flocks of sheep—special sales to be made at any time during the year, single or in lots.

A sale announcement quoted prices as follows—Ewes from $10 to $75; Rams $25 to $150; the highest range of prices being for the registered sheep. Delivery was to be made F.O.B. at Shaniko, Oregon, and shipment by freight or express as desired by the purchaser. Single animals or small lot for shipment would be properly crated.

The following is taken from the December 12, 1909 issue of the *Oregon Daily Journal*:

HUGE RANCH FORCED ON MARKET

The Famous Hay Creek Sheep Breeding Plant to be Sold Because Government Curtails Grazing Privileges in Forest Reserves

As a result of the conservation policy of the United States

18

Department, America's greatest sheep breeding plant is to cease business. It was authoritatively announced yesterday that all the flocks, numbering upwards of 20,000 high bred sheep on the famous Hay Creek Ranch, Crook County, Oregon, are to be sold immediately and the ranch closed down.

J. G. Edwards, manager and principal owner of the Baldwin Sheep and Land Company, who came to Portland to make arrangements for the closing out of his business, was at the Portland yesterday and confirmed the report of the contemplated sale of his sheep holdings. When asked for the reason, he said:

"The flocks of the Baldwin Sheep and Land Company have for many years required a certain grazing area in the forest reserve. From time to time the Forestry Department has reduced this area and each time we have been compelled to cut down the size of our flocks. We are now notified by the Department that another cut has been made and this will reduce our flocks to a number much below that we must necessarily have to run the Hay Creek breeding plant profitably. Our original grazing area permitted us to run 40,000 sheep; which practically puts us out of business. I mean no criticism of the Government, but the facts are as I have stated. Twelve months from the present date we expect to have our entire sheep holdings sold out."

In 1906 the Baldwin Sheep and Land Company's grazing allotment in the Blue Mountain Forest Reserve provided for 40,000 sheep. In that year the first cut was made by the Forestry Department and it took away 40 percent of the company's grazing area, reducing the flocks to 26,000 sheep. The Department's next cut in 1908 amounted to another 40 percent. This action was protested vigorously by the company and strong influence was brought to bear to have the order canceled. The Department finally modified the cut to 25 percent and this reduced the company's flocks to a little less than 18,000 sheep. In 1909 the ranch operations were held down to that maximum and no further reduction was expected, but late that year the company received notice that its range in the Forest Reserve for the coming year would be reduced 30 percent.

The Thirouin Sorreau flock was established at Cerville, France. This flock never exceeded 300 sheep and was now extinct. The government flock at Rambouillet was maintained with about 500 sheep. The Hay Creek flock of Rambouillet sheep was maintained at about 800, making it the largest in the world.

The policy of the ranch had always been to purchase the highest prize winners in this country as well as abroad, regardless of cost.

The deeded land of Hay Creek Ranch comprised about 27,000 acres south of Shaniko. Due to the enormous output of this ranch, Shaniko had for years been the largest point of origin for wool shipments in the Pacific Northwest. The ranch attained national importance in 1898 when it passed into the control of

Hay Creek

Lord Edwards, who for some years was recognized as the sheep king of Wyoming.

Edwards had been grazing flocks aggregating 100,000 head on the Wyoming range and was looking for a locality more perfectly adapted for the highest type of a combined wool and muton sheep. He selected Crook County, Oregon, and there built up the type known as the Baldwin Sheep, which is the only established and reproducing sheep known that is covered with long, heavy crinkly wool from its nose to its hoofs without wrinkles or grease, these latter objectionable perquisites having been eliminated in the breeding.

John C. Todd, son of John Y. Todd early day settler and owner of the Farewell Bend Ranch at Bend, recently recalled his first sight of the Hay Creek Ranch— "I was six years old and that was in the year 1884 when we were on our way home from attending the funeral of my grandfather who was Judge Campbell of The Dalles. We ate in the big dining room of the Hay Creek Ranch. At the other end of the room was a small table where the moguls of the ranch ate. The manager at that time was John Summerville who had formerly been a merchant in Prineville of the firm of Breyman and Summerville, and they had both bought an interest in the Hay Creek Ranch.

John Y. Todd with his family settled on the ranch in the Deschutes River in 1877 and about 1884 he obtained some alfalfa seed from Dr. Baldwin which had been threshed at Hay Creek. Todd planted it so thick it could not grow up but grew down and matted to make swell hog pasture.

The Hay Creek Ranch not only raised the first alfalfa in

Central Oregon and the State of Oregon but furnished the seed for the first alfalfa planted in what is now Deschutes County.

From the early fields of alfalfa the late Jerry Schooling used to cut the tender early tops for the cookhouse and the Edwards house where they were used for spring greens.

The younger Todd who makes his home in Lebanon, Oregon, believes that the construction of Sherars Bridge originally built by his father, John Y. Todd, in 1860, opened up Central Oregon. The stage route ran from The Dalles through Bake Oven to Prineville. Nearer home, the Cow Canyon road veered to the east, across Trout Creek, up Hay Creek, and over Grizzly Mountain to Prineville. All travel before the turn of the century from the north followed this route. In speaking of the Cow Canyon Road, Todd said:

"While no land grant was connected with it, somebody got a franchise and was allowed to charge toll for building a road, if it could be called a road, as it followed a creekbed."

"The last people to live there were the Charles Haights, after Shaniko and the railroad was built about 1900 and then a lot of travel by-passed Cow Canyon and went by way of Antelope until the present road was built by the state."

The stage coach and freight wagons lumbered through the valleys and up and down the hills brought an assortment of human baggage which spread over the vast expanse of millions of acres. To vision and reconstruct a living picture of this travel, all of which passed the Hay Creek ranch, must be described by an eye witness.

Hay Creek

In a letter written in 1948 John C. Todd described his first trip over this historic road 53 years ago:

"The burning of the house on Willow Creek, known to some later as the Morrow & Keenan Ranch and to people before 1900 as Cleeks, brought back memories of the first time I drove a stage coach on the Bake Oven-Prineville end of the line. The lay over drivers at Bake Oven were supposed to have gotten ptomaine poison, maybe too much sheep herder whiskey, and were unable to take the stages through.

"T. Burgess told me I would have to take the Prineville stage and another young lad The Dalles stage as the mail had to go through. We had worked in the harvest field all day and now had to drive all night.

"I forgot to fill my lantern so the driver's light went out going up the McPherson hill which used to be quite a pull, not much now. That's the divide between Hay Creek and Lower Trout. My team got out of the road and wound up astraddle of a big rock.

"A fellow at Heisler Station said you are an hour late and if you lose any more time you will probably be turned in for a fine on the contractor. He filled my lantern with coal oil and said you will get your very good horses at Cleeks and when you get to the top of Grizzly Mountain let them go down into Prineville. I sure did but could not make up my lost hour so the old postmaster started to roast me for being late but I had two old ladies on the stage who tied into him. They said they never had such a wild ride in their lives and that I came as fast as the horses could run. They exaggerated some as the horses

23

were not running only on the downhill curves. Those thorough-brace coaches rolled around considerable on rough roads, the only kind we had then.

"The part I regret is that there was supposed to be a lunch for the driver in a cupboard on the back porch of the old Cleek house at Willow Creek reached generally about daylight on the night drive which I did not find out about until the next day. The old stage road went up Hay Creek by Parrishes and the headquarters of the ranch, Cleeks and Grizzly. Route 97 through Lyle Gap was not built but had a good start in 1899.

"That morning at Prineville young Dick Garet, son of the contractor, asked me if I was equal to driving back to Bake Oven that day after having no sleep the night before as he did not want extra drivers piled up in the center of the run and figured the other two drivers would be over their stomach upset.

"I said yes and got along well until late in the afternoon when it got awfully warm going up Cow Canyon so I went soundly to sleep. I had a stockman's wife up on the boot of the stage coach with me so she took the lines and let the horses poke along up the canyon until we reached the top, then awoke me so we could make time. I sure was dead to the world or never could have slept on that old Cow Canyon road which followed the creek bed most of the way and the crime of it was they charged toll.

"I drove three months on the Bake Oven and The Dalles end that spring. It was mostly mud and sometimes I had to lay down fences to get past mud holes."

Claude Dunham who lives at Prineville, came to Hay Creek in 1884 with his parents, Mr. and Mrs. Amos Dunham. Claude was four years old and still remembers that the headquarters of the ranch owned by Dr. Baldwin stood on the spot now occupied by the building later used as a store for many years. The Dunhams bought the Thompson ranches from Bud and George Thompson and their home place became known as the Dunham Ranch, situated on the road to Ashwood, now partly covered by the lake made by damming Little Willow Creek. The ranch later became the shearing headquarters of the Baldwin Land and Sheep Ranch when sold to them in 1902.

Near the end of the vigilante days men knocked at their door late at night and asked if Thompson and Mills were there. They were told they were in the barn where they slept with loaded guns ready for any emergency. As they happened to be friends, all ended well. Right or wrong the vigilantes stopped cattle stealing in a country with law no closer than The Dalles. Some of them were heady with their succcess and were also feared. They organized, calling themselves moonshiners, but not in the sense of present-day moonshiners.

Before the Dunhams bought the Thompson ranches they figured in the Snake uprising. Bud Thompson heard of the trouble while at The Dalles and made a record-breaking trip, covering the 96 miles home, to find Chief George, a chief of the Warm Springs and Wascos, at his place. Chief George said, "if the Snakes come this way I'll know it in time and I will bring lots of Indians to help gather up your horses and your brother George's and Maupins' and we will take them and the women and children to the reservation and then we will go out and fight the Snakes and steal their horses."

Chief George went to the Maupins' home east of Hay Creek while Thompson organized the neighbors who had not fled west of the mountains. The ranch of Dr. Baldwin was selected as the rallying point in case of danger. George Thompson was judge of Crook County in early days.

Claude Durham, who now lives east of Prineville, as a boy walked four miles to Hay Creek where school was held. Later school was held in the Bud Thompson house half-way between the Dunham and Hay Creek Ranch headquarters. A. C. Palmer was a well liked early teacher.

Hay Creek School was later held at the Parrish Ranch and Rolla Parrish was one of the thirteen pupils. As the twelve others had to travel a considerable distance an election was held and the school was moved to the Lytle Place. Later it was moved further north. About 35 years ago a new school was built. Since World War II it has been hauled to Madras and rebuilt into dwellings. The site of this last school of the Hay Creek section was once called Whiskey Springs, then Yellow Jacket, and finally Box Springs when it was boxed up. It was said that it never was dipped dry.

In 1902 Claude Dunham and the daughter of the Reverend Wilsie were married. Mrs. Dunham's parents came to Hay Creek when she was 14 years old. Her father was probably the first and only minister to live in the Hay Creek Country. He also held services at Grizzly.

The favorite type of work was riding, which Claude did at Madras when Palmain had the only house in the basin as Madras was then called, and at Agency Plains when horse and rider were almost lost in the tall bunch and wild rye grass. He and Henry Cleek rode for weeks and several starved Indians hung around the cook wagon, sometimes killing a jackrabbit.

A new record for Hay Creek Ranch was set when W. U. Sanderson was principal owner and manager and sold sheep to Russia. This was the largest sale for export ever recorded in America.

It happened that the Soviet Government wanted to improve the wool and mutton qualities of the sheep which roamed the Russian Steppes. Experts from that government toured the world, visiting England and France and some of the great pure-bred flocks in America, finally coming to Hay Creek. Here was consummated the sale which resulted in the largest number of sheep, by far, ever to leave America.

The Russian envoys who selected the sheep checked every one of the animals and one day in November, 1927, the whole 10,000 sheep started from the little town of Madras in two trains of twenty seven cars on the long journey to Russia. Lee Curtis and Ralph Moore helped load the sheep.

The sheep arrived at their destination in good condition and with a small loss enroute. Windom Crosswhite, Frank Gill and Clayton Garrett delivered the sheep to the Soviet officials. On the sides of the train large banners announced: "This train-load of sheep shipped by the Baldwin Sheep Company—Hay Creek Ranch, Oregon U.S.A. to Soviet Government, Russia."

Mr. Sanderson told me that the hungry peasants of Russia killed and ate this high-bred expensive breeding stock in less than a year. That year, 1927, more than 15,000 sheep were exported by the ranch.

Roy Newell of Redmond is one of the oldest employees of the Hay Creek Ranch still living in Central Oregon. He was ranch foreman under Sanderson, leaving the ranch in 1924, the year the spacious Edwards' home burned to the ground.

Roy came to Central Oregon with his parents, Mr. and Mrs. Sam Newell, in 1905. He filed on a homestead on Teller Flats near Teller Buttes in 1906 and his father filed on a homestead in 1910.

Roy sold his homestead to Harry York in 1910 and bought the Walter Parrish Place—on the Madras-Ashwood road halfway between Madras and Hay Creek and a well known stopping place for early travel. Newell was road supervisor when the road from Madras to the top of Ashwood grade was built in 1912 and 1913, when Jefferson County was still a part of Crook County.

He sold this place in 1923 and bought the Garrett Ranch at Grizzly, which he still owns. The place on the Ashwood road is now a part of the Hay Creek Ranch.

When Edwards owned the ranch and Jim Rice was general manager, Newell was straw boss. During the years between 1906 and 1909 and at this period John Aldrich came to the ranch.

The marriage of Roy Newell and Clara Healy, daughter of early settlers of Culver, took place in 1915. Mrs. Newell died in 1925.

Among other early day employees were Tom Kaas, Lee Curtis, Lex Long and Jack Church. The store owned and run by the

Hay Creek

ranch catered to employees and early settlers. Shortly after World War I a newly married bachelor traveled eight miles by horseback to the Hay Creek Store to purchase a pound of pepper (the least he could buy). This became a subject for conversation and jokes for a month, even finding its way to the country newspaper published at Madras in a bright quip. It was a day of home-made jokes and one learned to take it even if not exactly appreciated.

Neighbors who lived from 20 to 50 miles away knew much more about each other, their families and business transactions, than do next-door neighbors of to-day.

Most popular manager was Charles Berkley, and no small part was due to his gracious and friendly wife. John Aldrich and his wife, the former May Lippe, shared in the respect and love of employees and settlers who came to Hay Creek for their mail and provisions.

The surrounding country was filled with homesteaders who worked at Hay Creek to feed themselves and their families while proving up on their own land claims, which in the course of a few years were sold to the ranch.

Fruit and vegetables were raised in abundance at Hay Creek and found their way to many a meager homestead board. When sickness and trouble came, the first thought was the Hay Creek Ranch and no request, however great, was ever denied.

The Aldriches are now living in Prineville and to their door come many old-time friends of Hay Creek days. In fact, the stock foreman who never lost his temper is a tradition which will live long after he is gone.

During the Berkley regime the ambition of every rancher and

29

employee was to own a "Lizzie Ford" car. When Berkley purchased a Ford, Mrs. Berkley was determined to learn to drive and under instructions from everyone her lessons started in an 800-acre hayfield east of their home. Amid the cheers of the haying crew she drove east, west, north and south, forward and back among the shocks of hay until she was master of the Model T.

Ralph Moore, a settler of 1890, was seven years old when his father, Seth Wallace Moore, a veteran Indian fighter in the wars of 1852, homesteaded south of Hay Creek. As a young man Moore hauled freight of salt, merchandise, and sulphur from The Dalles and worked on the Hay Creek Ranch. Ralph filed on a homestead south of Hay Creek, about seven miles from the headquarters of the ranch.

Moore's brother-in-law, George Lytle, drove from The Dalles with horses and filed on a homestead between Moore's and Hay Creek on the old stage road which ran from The Dalles to Prineville. Over this road Moore helped to haul the first sawmill to Bend. It was a portable mill and was set up right on the spot where the Pilot Butte Inn is now.

Early settlers around the Hay Creek Ranch were the Doaks, Maupins, Dunhams, Thompsons, Wilsie, Brewers, Nichols, Parishes, Pridays, Joslins, Wagonblasts, Gays and the Morris families.

Mrs. Eva Dunham Doak, daughter of Amos Dunham, lives in Redmond with his daughter, Mrs. Mable Renolds. She recalls that it was the first day of June in 1884 when she left Springfield with her family to settle at Hay Creek where her father acquired three ranches.

Hay Creek

The ranches were formerly owned by George and Bud Thompson. They joined the old Baldwin Sheep and Land Company Ranch on the west and reached the timber on the east. The nearest neighbor was two miles away and the post office was in the Van Houten House at the Hay Creek Ranch three miles away. Mrs. Doak rode for the mail twice a week on horseback and had several wire gates to open. Anyone who could ride a horse was expected to catch and saddle her own horse.

There were six children in the Amos Dunham family. The elder sister, Vina, taught school away from home. As there was no school in the neighborhood, the younger ones were taught by a sister. Later the younger children went to school in the old Bud Thompson House. Mrs. Doak says that after she left Springfield at the age of 14, she never attended school except for a short time in Prineville.

"At that time," she remembers, "all travel was with wagons and teams and it took a week from Springfield to Hay Creek. In our party there were two loaded wagons and a buckboard, a vehicle you never hear of these days. Four of us came on horseback and the road over the lava beds was very rough."

Mr. Dunham bought sheep and ran them for several years. Mrs. Doak often accompanied her father to The Dalles to sell his wool, and it was a very enjoyable trip, although it was a long, hard ride with the wagon and team.

Mrs. Doak was married in 1890 and lived in the State of Washington for three years, coming back to Hay Creek later, then moving to Prineville. She has lived in Redmond since 1930.

Another early settler was Albert James Priday who came to Jefferson County in 1880 from Westbury, England. In 1882 he was joined by his family, who waited in Portland for a short time for the railroad to be completed to The Dalles. The last lap of their journey from The Dalles to what later became Jefferson County was made by freight wagon.

The Priday family settled east of Madras on the Morris place, near the Perry Henderson Place. In 1885 they moved to the old Priday Place below the Parrish Place. The late Leslie Priday, son of Albert James Priday, herded horses for the Hay Creek Ranch and with the money earned he purchased his first calf. In 1889 the family moved to Trout Creek.

When the Pridays first came to Central Oregon, mail from England came addressed to them with the following description: "Mud Springs, Near Hay Creek, near The Dalles." All mail came through the Warm Springs Indian Agency. They lived in three different counties and received their mail at different times from seven different post offices while living in the same house.

The Charles McPherson Ranch below Hay Creek on the old stage road was a well known early day ranch and at one time was considered one of the best ranches in Central Oregon. Due to drought, lack of attention, and shortage of water, it has become a dry pasture. On this place is an iron fenced plot and gravestone erected in memory of Joshua Pearce, father of Mrs. McPherson who died in 1868.

The Hay Creek Cemetery was one of the first in Central Oregon. The first monument which the late F. H. Watts of The

Hay Creek

Dalles put in the Hay Creek Cemetery was in 1895 for Mr. Morris, a monument of stone. When Van Houten was manager of the Hay Creek Ranch he lost a son and for him was the second stone erected by Watts. However, there are grave markers in the cemetery dating back to 1874.

In 1920 Watts came to the Hay Creek Cemetery with Mrs. McPherson to move the body of her daughter to The Dalles to be reburied by the side of her father. The young lady had been buried at Hay Creek for six years and great difficulty was experienced in digging, as the soil is similar to that found in the Burns Cemetery, very hard to dig, but pulverizing when exposed to air. The outside box and coffin had completely rotted away. This made digging more difficult and as Watts carefully lifted the body he was astonished to find it petrified. It was a new experience, so with interest he noted the darker hue the skin had taken on, resembling leather. He considered this the only perfect work of sculpture he had ever seen.

The trip to The Dalles was a nightmare of fear, lest the body break. The body of stone was wrapped in a blanket and placed in the back of the pickup on a board. As he bounced over the rough roads he could hear the body rattle and he was sure that the fingers and toes would be broken off, but when he reached The Dalles he was relieved to find his fears were groundless.

As the Hay Creek Ranch changed hands, little care or thought was given to the graveyard. Fences were broken and trampled down as cattle roamed over the graves, tumbling and breaking headstones. Somewhere the records carried in books and in the

33

head of the late Jerry Schooling were lost. In recent years the fence has been rebuilt and some of the damage repaired.

G. W. Massamore and Preston Dunham were old settlers. Among later settlers were the Eatons, Richard and Clifford Winslow, William Delude, Bruce Shawe, Charles Brammer, Roy Powell, R. Banta, Mr. and Mrs. Edward Fox, Mr. and Mrs. Harry LaVein, Ray Goff, A. G. Duchein, Mr. and Mrs. Harvey Kemp and family, Josephine Hill, John Kosteliz, Mr. and Mrs. Fred Pederson, Mr. and Mrs. Andy Anderson, Mr. and Mrs. Frank Galloway, Pat Ray, Mr. and Mrs. Frank Morgan and family, Margaret Tandy, Charles McCue, Tom Eneberg, Fritz Haberstitch, Gene Goff, and Charles Farquarson. Others were Mr. and Mrs. Martin McInnis and family, Ed Allen, Charles Gibson, Mrs. W. I. Green family, Carlock family, McCumber, Shelley and Ovens families.

Mr. and Mrs. Edwin D. Allen and family settled to the southeast of the Hay Creek Ranch, choosing a location for their buildings in a spot the exact replica of a place Mr. Allen had seen in a dream before coming to Central Oregon. The homestead was named the Diamond A Ranch and soon grew to several hundred acres and was known for its products, especially butter and cream. Mr. Allen also had a sawmill and engaged in grain threshing operations, moving his threshing machine from ranch to ranch and averaging a crew of eighteen men on a work exchange basis.

Emil Stolte, Bert Turner, Jack and Harry Pitzer, Bert Richardson, John Martin, Ray Randal, and William West were also homesteaders. Jim Scates, Jim Connelly, and Jim Howell all

34

Hay Creek

settled on a creek leading up from the Doak place. The creek became known as Jim Creek.

David Gay and his daughter, Mary, located east of Hay Creek as did the Charles Lippe family and John Coyne, John Smith, Horace Kibbee, Gus Kibbee and their mother all filed on homesteads in 1903. Gus married Elizabeth Dee, daughter of early settlers of Grizzly or Willow Creek as it was oftener called. The actor, Guy Kibbee, often visited with his cousin and mother.

The Kibbee holdings were sold to T. A. Power in 1928. The David and Mary Gay homesteads, the William West and Charles Bramer, Winslow and Shawe places became known as the T. A. Power Tee PEE Ranch. Sheep Rock, the highest point in the Hay Creek area was also a part of the ranch.

When Central Oregon was opened for travel by the railroad, land-hungry people arrived and soon the vast domain of free land surrounding the Hay Creek Ranch was all homesteaded.

School was held in a little building in the timber on Blizzard Ridge. Later the school was held in the Horace Kibbee house. In 1913 a standard country school of one room was built on the Power Ranch by William West and T. A. Power. A large barn was also built, as the pupils, sometimes numbering 32, rode to school on horseback as far as from seven miles away. The school and community became known as Fairview. In its day it was considered the best country school in the county.

The OK Ranch was settled by Mr. and Mrs. John O'Kelly and their family of three girls and two boys. Their daughter, Leona, taught school in the Blizzard Ridge school house. She and Jim Garrett were married and homesteaded in the com-

35

munity in 1911. Later the OK Ranch became their home.

Jim is a son of the late Harlan Garrett who came to Central Oregon from Missouri in 1864. He had cattle and camped out as he ranged over the free range. In the winter he moved to Crooked River for winter feeding. About 1880 he filed on a homestead still known as the Garrett Place at Grizzly, now owned by Roy Newell. He also took up a preemption claim.

T. A. Power tells in the following words how he came to settle in Central Oregon:

Power's Narrative

"I was in Alaska in 1910 and 1911, working on a railroad that has since been abandoned. While there I heard talk of Central Oregon and its opportunities. When I came back to Seattle I had a chance to go back on my old job on the Sante Fe as head of the signal maintenance department, but Central Oregon interested me. I had visions of a homestead expanded to a ranch filled with grazing cattle.

"At Portland I was further intrigued by the entrancing pictures and descriptions several different real estate agents gave me of Central Oregon. Always in the back of my mind was the story I heard Pat tell in Alaska, as he rested when he spit on his hands to get a better grip on his shovel. He said two railroads are racing to get tracks laid up the canyon and if a man missed a stroke in hitting a spike he was left behind and never could catch up. One agent had a relinquishment to a homestead which I could obtain by paying $500 for the improvements which consisted of a one-room typical homestead

Hay Creek

cabin and a fence around 40 acres which had been indifferently cultivated.

"With my Alaska stake, mostly in gold, in a money belt I came to Central Oregon with enough enthusiasm to conquer all obstacles. The trip was made by four-horse stage from Shaniko. As the coach was crowded, several young men rode on top. It was a ride that I will never forget. Speed, handed down from the times when Indian and bandit attacks were common, continued to be the proper way to drive a stage coach. I had great fear of being dumped off and left behind as the stage coach shook, rattled and wobbled over ruts, rocks and sage brush. Going down Cow Creek canyon was a breath taking thrill, as the horses rushed on at an unusual rate of speed. The driver never relaxed his whip or urging until it seemed the horses must die of exhaustion. I held on to my hat and tried to ease myself gently in the same spot from which I was forced with each surge of the coach. I finally got the spirit of the thing and let my imagination picture our get-away from bandits or Indians. I felt a pity for my family in the East who could not know this West I had adopted for my home.

"Well, the first night I stopped at the old Parrish place on the old stake road from The Dalles to Prineville. The place was well kept up. The tiny slips Mrs. Parrish had brought from The Dalles when she came there as a young bride had grown into stately trees that gave a look of permanence and endurance to the place. Mrs. Parrish was a daughter of Mrs. Elizabeth Sager Helm, a survivor of the Whitman massacre.

"We passed by the Hay Creek Ranch of which I had heard in

the East. Dr. Baldwin of Boston who established the ranch in 1873 had been an acquaintance of my family, and so I felt a keen interest in the place.

"When I saw the place I had come to take, I lost interest in a homestead. The place was between the Hay Creek Ranch and Grizzly in a poor alkali belt that even to my inexperienced eye held few settlers there, I decided to go back to my job at Las Vegas.

"At Madras I met an old settler who persuaded me to go out and look at a place near his which he said was open for homestead entry. If I liked the place I could pay him $50 and if I did not like it I need pay him nothing. The place was all that he represented and fulfilled a city dweller's dream of independence It was situated at the foot of the Blue Mountains with a western view of the Cascades, with sometimes 13 snowcovered peaks plainly visible. I decided to become a homesteader. There was grass and water in abundance with fairly level fields, just waiting for the plow. I became indeed, 'Lord of all that I survey.'

"Although it wasn't as easy as it sounded, I have never regretted my decision. I have found health, the one thing I lacked when I lived in a crowded city. I have found peace of mind and happiness and a modicum of this world's goods in Central Oregon.

"Large trees made an inviting place to build a cabin. Years before the place had been settled by a squatter who had planted these trees. A creek fed by a large spring 600 feet away ran by the place. An old cellar dug in a bank to serve as a dwelling place had caved in. It seems as though these squatters had been

Hay Creek

horse thieves and at that time one of the two partners was serving a prison sentence. In times past when the law became too hot on their heels they retired to a rendezvous in the deep timber. One day, years later, I came upon their hideout. It was a crude shelter of logs built in a deep thicket. They kept provisions concealed there and it was a known fact that they often disappeared for months at a time.

"Hardly had I set the wheels in motion to file on this place when I received a most threatening letter from the man who was serving a prison sentence. I answered and offered to give him a hundred dollars. He refused it saying he would be back to get the place.

"By the time I had built a cabin and had some fencing and plowing done, and bought a team my little stake was depleted.

"A neighbor, an old carpenter helped me with my cabin. One day he had to go to Shedd. He made the trip by horseback and was back in less than a week. I decided to put in the windows while he was gone. I put them in upside down and the old fellow had a good laugh when he got back.

"On another day when I was shingling my two-room cabin I had a funny experience. In those days the Indians camped on my place on their way to the timber where they hunted deer and in and out of season.

"I saw a squaw going to their camp and I ran out and hollered at her asking her if she had any gloves to sell. I had never owned any buckskin gloves, and I was anxious to have a pair like my neighbors wore. But at the sound of my voice she ran faster and was soon out of sight.

"I thought her actions strange, but I was little used to the ways of Indians and soon dismissed her from my mind as I climbed on the roof and became interested in shingling. When the day was nearly done I climbed down and when I reached the bottom of the ladder I found a large Indian coming toward me in a most menacing manner. In his hand he carried a large knife. Involuntarily I stepped back against the ladder, my hand still gripping the poll axe I had used in shingling. He said in a guttural voice, 'Someone insult my wife and I gonna kill um.' Had I shown the least fear I know I would not be here today. I looked him straight in the eye and I said, 'Just wait a minute, there's some mistake. I'm the only man here and I know I didn't insult your wife.' He talked all around the subject, and finally I guess I convinced him that I wasn't the man he was looking for.

"When the seriousness of the situation had eased and I was able to take my eyes off this burly buck, I looked up the creek to see eight or nine Indians emerge from behind trees. Each had held a leveled gun pointed at me. My concern changed to anger as I realized how much good my poll axe would have been to me.

"I was still a little shaken from my experience when a half-breed who was camping with the Indians came down. He said, 'Cripes, I didn't expect to see you alive. The Indians fully intended to kill someone.' It seems that when the squaw had gone for the horses one of the sheep herders had made improper advances and had frightened her. When she arrived without the horses she was scolded and told to go back after them. She refused and cried, 'Poor squaw has no one to take her part. If

40

Hay Creek

Indian bother white woman, white man kill Indian!' She kept up her wailing and crying until it got under the Indian's skin. Finally they held a council and a war dance and set out to protect an Indian maiden's honor.

"I said to the half-breed, 'The Indians came very near making a great mistake and I will not allow the Indians to camp on my place. Tell them I will give them one hour to move and you also tell them never to come to my place again.' I showed him the lines and he hastened to the camp with my orders. And that has held good to the present day. A trail they formerly used was abandoned and they go around my place.

"I walked over to tell the old carpenter my experience that evening and he was quite concerned. He urged me to stay with him as I had neither doors or windows in place. I felt that I should not give in to the first fear that came my way. As I got close to my cabin I realized that I should have followed his advise. It was the fall of the year and I could plainly hear someone walking on the fallen leaves that surrounded my cabin. Crunch, crackle, and then quiet, and then a few more steps, around and around my cabin. To be sure I thought the Indians had come back to kill me. When the footsteps stopped I crawled forward on my hands and knees to get a better view as the moon came up from behind the hill. So intent in my scrutiny of the cabin before me and my ears keyed to the faintest sound that I had forgotten about the caved-in cellar. I raised up to get a better view and as I took a step forward I stepped off the bank into the cellar. I landed on the back of an old cow who was lying there. She was as frightened as I was. She gave a loud bel-

41

low and threw her tail up over her back and lost no time in getting to her feet. Before I had a chance to realize what was happening, she was running away with me. When she stopped long enough for me to fall off she had carried me nearly two miles. Was I mad? The old cow had made the footsteps that had raised my hair in fear.

"I scarcely had my cabin finished when the old urge to move on took possession of me and I had about decided to throw up my homestead when I received a threatening letter. It was from the convicted horse thief squatter who was now out of prison. He wrote that on a certain day he would take possession of my homestead, and that I had better pull out before that day. That decided me to stay and I waited in trepidation as the day arrived with no sign of the man. A month later he strolled into my place about dusk. The brave front he had paraded in his letters was gone. He said he wanted to be friends and that he would now take the $100. I told him that he was too late. He said, 'I was a fool not to take your offer but I'd like to stay all night with you.' I hated to turn him away but I could do nothing else with a man who had threatened me. So I watched him walk out of my life. Later I heard that he died in prison. He was a bad egg.

"I worked at the sawmill at Grizzly and I helped put up hay at Hay Creek. It was there I learned how to harness a horse and the difference between wheat and rye.

"Gradually I was building up that herd of cattle that I had dreamed of owning some day.

Hay Creek

"When I had less than 20 head I fell in love with a girl visiting at an adjoining ranch. I had lots of competition but I owned the best saddle horse in the whole country, so I got the inside track when I let her use my horse.

"However the boys on the ranch did everything to discourage my suit. They even went so far to tell her I was a cattle thief. They had seen a large cow with a Grizzly rancher's brand and the calf with my brand on it. In high glee they had sent for the Grizzly rancher to convince him that I had stolen one of his sucking calves. When Sunday came the rancher arrived and he was taken by the would-be suitors to see the proof, where my cattle grazed on the hillside. In disgust he turned back. The cow, 'Old Spot,' was the first cow I had bought to start my cattle herd. I bought her from the Grizzly rancher's sister and paid $80 for her. I had never bothered to brand her as she was better known than I was. I worked all summer to pay for that cow, and her progeny formed no small part of the herd I eventually built up.

"To be sure I married the girl and together we saw some of those cattle die of old age."

To the northeast of the Hay Creek Ranch, homesteaders took up every available acre. Earliest settlers were the Jim Clarke family who were relatives of the Clarke wagon train of 1851 which camped on the Deschutes River near the present city of Bend and named Pilot Butte, and the Frank York family who came in answer to an appeal in a religious paper put there by Mrs. Clarke for settlers as she was lonely in an empty expanse of sage brush and bunch grass.

When the Clarkes settled on their homesteads an indifferent road ran up through the Gap from Gateway and the nearest post-office was Ashwood where the mail was carried in from Antelope by team. Clarke and his sons, Day and Bert, helped to build the present 28-mile road from Madras to Ashwood, with muscle, brawn, and their horses. In 1916 when the road was finished the mail was carried from Madras to Ashwood and as many as sixty families received their mail along the route. Today one family receives this service.

Clarkes kept the travel and Mrs. Clarke's skill with sour dough became known far and wide. Her biscuits were the kind that melted in the mouth and always kept a hunger for just one more.

To late comers with their one and two room cabins the Clarke homestead with its wall to wall rag carpet, three bedrooms and the hospitable board seemed like an oasis in a desert. Many a weary traveler and homesick homesteader made it a point to stop at the Clarke place at meal time, finding replenishment of both body and spirit. The orchard set out by the Clarkes is a well known spot on the Ashwood Road.

Ora Clark married Marvin Elkins and they homesteaded near her parents. Johnny Jones, Jim Philips, Harrison and Glen Versaw, John Thacker, Alvin Bowman, Glenn Stockton and Phil Rheinhardt were later homesteaders.

G. W. Richards homesteaded what is known as the Richards Hill. Early day motorists became stuck in the adobe mud and had to be pulled out. When weather was bad and the roads became slippery Richards kept a team harnessed in the barn and was on call day or night. For this service he made no charge and for the two winters he was there one dollar forced on him by a grateful motorist was all he ever received.

G. E. Richards, his son, homesteaded Samson Butte seen for miles and known as land mark called "Old Baldy," as the top looks bare and brown at all seasons of the year.

Dan Trolan and family settled near Saddle Butte. They turned off the Ashwood Road at Jump-Off Joe, which is a jumping off place as the road makes a turn to wind down one side of a canyon.

Jump-Off Joe got its name when two riders came along an early cow trail there and one horse started to buck at the very edge of the rim of the canyon. The watching rider called out, "For God's sake jump off Joe." Joe did and the horse plunged down the canyon and broke his neck. This spot had a similar tragedy on Thanksgiving day, 1917, when John Yost, the first mail carrier on the star route watched as a team of horses his father was driving started over the rim. Just as they plunged over the top the front of the light wagon gave away and the elder Mr. Yost tumbled out to land on a little ledge below the rim. One horse was killed instantly and the other was so injured it had to be shot. Mr. John Yost, Sr., said, "I have a great deal to be thankful for this Thanksgiving day."

The Ashwood end of the road was the worst and many times the mail could not have got through if a team wasn't used on that end. For nearly a half century the road has been graded, graveled and regraded. In some places count has been lost on how many times a layer of gravel has been dumped.

Blizzard Ridge

By Milo Elkins and Joe McCollum

East of Hay Creek and south of Blizzard Ridge the second sawmill to be set up in Jefferson County was owned by Charles Durham, an Englishman who came from England to Central Oregon in 1877 with Mr. and Mrs. Charles Mailing and Charles Cooper.

About 1890 Durham and Jack Dee's father, who was a brother of Mrs. Mailing, picked out the site for the mill on a tributary of Trout Creek which later became known as Durham's mill.

This mill and its employees have played an important part in the settlement of all Central Oregon for from this mill went lumber in four- and six-horse teams to the established Hay Creek ranch, to Shaniko, Antelope, Ashwood, and Madras, besides to homesteads far and near. Among early buildings in Madras built with Durham lumber is the old Sanford building, the two-story wooden building on Fifth and C Streets and the house now owned by Walter McCalou which was built for the Max Luddleman family.

Durham and his mill have become a sort of tradition and former employees spin many a yarn when they chance to meet.

Milo Elkins, now living in Redmond, came to Durham's mill

46

with his parents more than half a century ago and the following is his story of those early days:

Narrative of Milo Elkins

On Monday morning, October 29, 1898, my folks loaded all of their belongings and children, an organ and five head of cattle, three milk cows and two yearling steers and one saddle horse, on a steamboat named *The Dalles City* at Camas, Washington, and started to Central Oregon via The Dalles. There things were transferred to a wagon with a California rack with four head of horses owned by Hall Bros. of Grass Valley, Oregon, and driven by Art Hall, arrangements having been made beforehand for the team and wagon to meet us at The Dalles and haul us to Durham's mill, nine miles east of Hay Creek in Crook County. My Dad had a logging contract for Durham.

Tuesday morning my Mother went up town and bought herself a new range, and was she proud of it. It was delivered down at the dock with our other things and then the loading started and it took all day. Of course the bed rolls and grub box were left off and we camped there that night. During supper it was decided that maw, Cora and Arthur were to ride in the seat with Art Hall, the driver. Eunice had to ride as she was only four years old but I don't remember where she was put, probably in the jockey box; Roy, age 8, and the rest were to walk. Of course Dad had the saddle horse and drove the cattle.

The first night we camped at Fifteen Mile Creek, east of The Dalles about 15 miles. The next day we came to the head of Sherrar's grade. Maw and Cora wouldn't ride down the grade,

47

it was dangerous, narrow and no turnouts so Dad left the cattle for us boys to drive down, and he rode down ahead so that he could stop any wagon that should happen to come along. Everything worked out alright and we camped on the Deschutes River that night.

The next day we reached Will Hall's Place south and east of Grass Valley, about 10 miles drive. Will had a large house with an upstairs and we laid over there one day and visited as my folks and Halls were old friends and neighbors in Washington. Next day we started on and went through where Kent built up later and camped that night just south of Shaniko at Cross Hollow Springs, there wasn't any Shaniko then.

Next day we hit Antelope and bought baker's bread, the first some of us had ever tasted, thirteen loaves for a dozen and camped that night at Cold Camp south of Antelope about eight miles, and then the next day we hit Trout Creek and camped at Columbus Friend's ranch. They ran sheep at the time. Mrs. Friend came out and got acquainted and insisted Mother come in and cook on her stove and I think she did.

Next morning we were out early, it was to be our last and hardest day. Columbus Friend said we never would make the grade from the creek to the Chet McCorkle place, but he said if we couldn't to come back and get a team and stretcher and when we got on top we could bring his team back. Dad thanked him and we started out. Well, we made it, but how!

We nooned at the Chet McCorkle Ranch, it had taken about five hours to make about six miles, climbing that ridge road

48

out of Trout Creek, heavily loaded as we were. It was no small feat.

The last day my brother Marvin rode the saddle horse and drove the cattle and Dad told him to stay with the wagon so if we had to have help we would have him and the saddle horse. The road was badly washed and worn down to rocks, some of them was a lift of twelve and fourteen inches straight up. There were a few times the team couldn't do it and Dad, Marvin and I would get hold of the spokes and spoke it over excepting once, and then the drive would back the wagon down and we would throw small rocks and dirt in below the big rock and build up a gradual slope and tamp it down then Dad would tie a rope to the wagon and get on his horse and take his turns around the saddle horn. Art would start the team and with Dad pulling with his saddle horse and Marvin and I pushing from the rear we made it. Of course the family were all walking by that time.

We reached the edge of the pine timber just at dusk. Dad said it was only two and one-half miles farther and a safe road mostly down grade so we went on and got to Durham's mill about six o'clock, just before dark. After a little supper the beds were rolled out and I think everyone slept well.

Next morning we were up early to have a look at this new country, and it wasn't much to look at, it had been logged off pretty close for about three-fourths of a mile, and then it was beautiful, just like a park with no underbrush. You could have seen a jackrabbit running for a half-mile. There were many miles of open range in the timber as this was the edge of the Blue

Mountain range. Also on the prairie there were miles of tall bunch grass.

There were a few neighbors, the John O'Kelly family with six children lived northwest about three miles at the edge of the timber on the Hay Creek road and the Tobe Crocket family three miles east with their two small children. The George McCoy family lived north and west about four miles, with their five girls who were very popular young ladies.

Now our school consisted of three months each year: May, June, and July. Laura McCoy was our first teacher. She later married Logan Black who worked for Dad. He was a brother of Stanton and Ad Black. There were eleven pupils from three families.

I am not sure of the date, but I think it was 1901 that Dad filed on 160 acres at the edge of the timber where he built a large house. The upstairs was used for a dance hall and people would come many miles to attend dances. There was no admission charge, no supper tickets, no music charge, and no gas or oil charge for transportation. The old time fiddlers played for sheer joy and the midnight supper and breakfast was pioneer cooking at its best, seasoned with generosity and friendship.

Now back to school teachers, our second year Leona O'Kelly taught, later she married Jim Garrett. The next teacher I remember was Katy Storts from Woodburn, Oregon.

Now all of this country from the Chet McCorkle ranch to the Pine timber was known as Blizzard Ridge, including Samson Mountain. Alex Friend was quite an old timer, he lived on the east side of the ridge, a bachelor. Clyde Gay, another bachelor lived at Windy Gap. Others were the Wade Huston family southeast of the ridge and his brother, Dean Huston, another bachelor. This was in the gold old days of sour dough bread and brown beans.

(Milo Elkins thus concluded his engaging reminiscences—but not quite, because he added to the historian who asked him for his narrative, "Evada, it will take a younger and better looking lady to ever get me started on anything like this again.")

John O'Kelly, one of the first settlers on the ridge, home-steaded the ranch known for more than sixty years as the OK Ranch. He named Blizzard Ridge shortly after the turn of the century when, as he was driving home from Ashwood, a Blizzard forced him to retrace his steps instead of facing the storm.

Eighty-seven-year-old Joel McCollum worked at Durham's mill around the turn of the century shortly after he and Lydia Dunham were married. Joe worked there for six years logging with horses. Other employees recalled were Howard W. Turner, Lees and Gus Kibbee, a cousin of the movie actor, Guy Kibbee, and Ad Black. In fact Joe stated he was the one who encouraged Kibbee to file on a homestead over 50 years ago. Durham was also in partnership with Jack Dee's father in a sawmill at Grizzly. Once Durham entrusted Joe with $1500 to deliver to Dee to pay the help.

Durham always had cash on hand to run his business and often buried it. One day Joe dug up a baking powder can in front of the blacksmith shop less than eight inches deep, with more than one thousand dollars in it. When he turned it over to Durham the latter gave him two twenty-dollar gold pieces.

Durham decided to move his mill to Cowle's orchard. Shortly

after the mill was moved Durham was found dead in bed. He was buried in the Mailing plot in Prineville.

The marriage of Joe and Lydia Dunham in 1896 was a gala affair attended by more than 235 people who came from far and near to dance at their wedding. Joe was then working at the Hay Creek Ranch and Van Houten said if the boys would clean up a store house they could use it for the dance. It later became the machine shed.

Employees of Durham's Mill and Hay Creek Ranch, including Jerry Schooling, were at the wedding. In the same year Joe filed on a homestead between Wilson and Teller creeks. He built a house and partly fenced his 160 acres. Enough hay was raised on 18 or 20 acre to feed his horses and two cows.

Joe's middle years were a happy existence with never a thought of getting rich in land or money. He was rich in health and happiness. His wife's people owned the Dunham ranch, and he could always get a job there or at the Hay Creek Ranch or Durham's Sawmill. In the fall he would drive his four-horse outfit to The Dalles and bring back food supplies for the Hay Creek Ranch and at the same time he would bring back his own supplies, sometimes enough beans, flour, sugar, and dried fruits to last a year. His children were growing up in a sugar age instead of the molasses spread of his own childhood. Often he would start the winter with thirty dollars and would have some left in the spring when he prepared to earn a grub-stake for another year.

Dancing, visiting and riding, with the accompaniment of sour dough biscuits, is not an unhappy memory of Joe's, spend-

Blizzard Ridge

ing three score and ten, plus seventeen more. Enduring friendships that have lasted more than three fourths of a century are the riches that Joe now possesses and his dividends are the hours spent with friends.

Shortly after the beginning of the twentieth century Joe sold his homestead to Chuck McCorkle for $900. Later the place was sold to Bert Clark who in turn sold it to the Hay Creek Company.

Mr. and Mrs. Stanton Black were married in 1900 and moved to Blizzard Ridge. Mrs. Black, the former Elizabeth Boyd, daughter of early settlers of Summit Prairie. They rented the Reppa Hamilton place where they lived for several years. Later they bought the adjoining Sawler place where they lived for 30 years. Ronald Black, born in 1906, now lives near Baker.

Growing up on the "OK Ranch" south of Blizzard Ridge, 1898-1908

*by Birdie O'Kelley Mahaffey Palmateer
and given to Martha Stranahan*

My father and mother [John Harrison and Mary Hamilton O'Kelley] were married 3 Aug 1877, in Lakeview, first couple to marry in that city. They lived in Paisley where they had four children: Leona, [Mrs. Jim Garrett] was the first white child born in Paisley. The next two baby girls died as babies. They had a little boy named Johnnie. While he was very small they sold the shop and home and moved to Prineville where my father ran a blacksmith shop for a year.

It was a rough, tough town—lots of shooting scrapes, vigilantes hanging men every little while. My mother wanted to get away from that. Father sold his shop, took up a timber culture near Ashwood, Oregon. They lived there a year or so. Johnnie got blood poisoning from a cat scratch and died.

A son named Grover was born to them. While he was very young, they sold that place, loaded all their belongings in the wagon pulled by four good horses. Leading a cow, they left for California–drove twelve miles and camped at a spring at the head of Hay Creek. Liked what they saw. Father rode into Prineville, filed on the place as a homestead. They built up the place, planted lots of trees, lived there 19 years, and had four more children: Bart, Georgina, Martina, and myself, Birdie O'Kelley. I was born May 1, 1898.

The first ten years of my life were wonderful, growing up in

Blizzard Ridge

that beautiful place, with timber near by, lots of bunch grass, wild-flowers of every kind on the hills. We children would put in hours gathering wildflowers and picking up pretty rocks. Nowadays the rocks are called agates and fire opals. To us they were just rocks.

There were all kinds of wild animals, which we saw occasionally.

My father ran horses over the range–had around 300 or 400 head. In the last years of the ranch he also had 50 or 60 cattle, some hogs, chickens, a big garden which we had to help take care of.

We children had saddle horses and saddles and rode many miles over the hills. We had to ride seven miles to the post office at Hay Creek Ranch for our mail. I made my first trip alone at the age of seven. My father wanted a letter mailed and said if there was a letter for him from a certain address to hurry back with it, so in three hours I was back–14 mile round trip. He said it was a good time as I had four gates to open and close going both ways, and a sucking colt following who would run down the fence instead of going through the gate when I took the mare through. I'd have to chase him to get back with his mother.

My sister Martina and I would go for the mail about every two weeks, bring back all the neighbors' mail, usually about two 50-pound flour sacks full, *Oregon Journal, Oregon Farmer, Hearth and Home*, and a few other old-time magazines.

My sister Georgina liked to cook and sew. Brother Bart was usually helping in the fields.

We had two three-month school [periods], three in the spring, three in the fall, so the children could help their parents in the summer and there was too much snow in the winter. The teacher got $30 per month, boarded with some of the school directors for free. When we'd get home from school, which was 1½ miles, we would change our dresses and go to hunt the cows. Sometimes they would be with Hay Creek Co. Cattle and we'd be afraid, so we would send our old cow dog after them. He would separate them and head them for home.

We would get the calves in from the calf pasture. They would take part of the milk and we would help Mother milk the rest. We carried it to a nice sawdust cellar where it was strained into pans. A couple of days later we'd skim the cream off into the churn. Sometimes we'd have eight to ten pounds of butter per churning. Mother would take care of that, mold it into pound molds, sell it to the Hay Creek Sheep Co., for fifteen cents per pound, eggs ten cents per dozen.

When the sheep at Hay Creek Ranch lambed there would be some lambs the ewes wouldn't claim or they would have twins, and not enough milk. They would give them (the bummers) to us girls. We would go on horseback with grain sacks. We would cut holes in the sacks, put the little lambs in and hang them over the saddle horn to take them home and raise them. They were known as "bummers." We would raise them up to 70-80 pound lambs and sell them for $3 to $5 per head. We always got new calico dress material for our work; the material was only 8 cents a yard, new hair ribbons for school for 25 cents, and Mother took the rest of the money and bought us shoes and whatever we needed for winter.

Sometime my father broke and matched up a team to sell. We would have to raise a colt from one of the mares, feed him milk two or three times a day. If you went out with a pan and it wasn't for the colt, he would wheel and kick at you—some of them got pretty mean. . . .

When I was 10 years old, [1908] my happy days began to fade. My father sold the old home place [to Jim and Leona O'Kelley Garrett] and moved to Culver, where he rented 1200 acres of wheat land from George Rodman. He ran that place for two years, had several hired men, also bought a G.I. Case threshing machine. He threshed for lots of people, including new settlers in the Opal City, Redmond, Powell Butte, and Sisters [areas]. . . .

Later my folks decided to move to Silver Lake, where the government was opening up some homestead land—125 miles south of Powell Butte. . . .

[This is as far as Birdie's diary goes as she had a stroke and could not finish her life story. This was given to Martha Stranahan and thanks to her we include it with Blizzard Ridge.]

The Culver District

By Anna Merchant and Fred Rodman

One is mystified beyond words as he looks down over the beautiful Culver Valley of today and on to the west to those snowcapped mountains, where stand that towering giant Mt. Jefferson and majestic Mt. Hood, and farther south Three Fingered Jack and that formidable Black Butte which was used by the pioneers as a weather prophet—knowing by the amount and location of snow on it whether it was safe to cross the mountain range or if spring had come and it was safe to plant the potatoes and corn.

Bounding this district on the south is Juniper Butte and farther to the east Haystack Butte, joining on the east with the Lamonta and Red Rock districts. To the north was an almost level valley until it breaks over the rise into the Metolius and Madras districts.

As we gaze on this panorama we try to visualize those days long gone by, when those sturdy pioneers came into this country now so well populated and with verdant fields watered from irrigation ditches running everywhere. It is hard to realize there could have been such hardships—those long snowbound winters, Indian uprisings, and the many other trials they experienced in their struggle to establish a home for themselves and those to follow.

Perhaps the skyline was just as beautiful and the sunsets just as gorgeous then as now but to those of you who never saw those miles and miles of hot dry sagebrush and Juniper covered lands it would be almost impossible for you to understand what the pioneers were up against. However, they found an abundance of bunch grass for their cattle and horses, and many acres of fertile soil that could be tilled.

Water was their main concern. So many of the earliest settlers chose their lands near the foothills where there were springs or where wells could be dug without going very deep. It is thought Ben Beeman and his wife and daughter, Esther, were the first to come to this section. And they located on the slopes overlooking the valley and the mountains.

In 1872 Aaron Thomas and Mary Melinda Jenkins settled to the east of the Beemans on a preemption claim. This place is where they are now constructing the Haystack Dam for a storage reservoir for irrigation water from the Wickiup Dam.

Mr. and Mrs. Jenkins had five sons, all born after they came here—Alvin, Virgil, Delbert, John, and Tom. Their first cabin was made of Juniper logs but in 1882 they built them a real house and this was one of the few remaining landmarks until it burned just recently.

The son Virgil was born at Halsey, Oregon, in 1877. The reason for his being born there instead of at home was that the Snake Indians were causing trouble and the women folks had all been sent across the mountains. As the story was told to Virgil by a Mr. Barnes who was a Home Guard at the time, a bunch of Snake Indians came across the Warm Springs and stole several horses and girls from the Indians there. They moved on above Prineville across Coombs Flat and camped on Crooked River. The Warm Springs Indians followed through and in the night attacked and burned their camp and recovered their horses and girls.

Virgil grew up on the ranch and in 1898 he homesteaded one and one-half miles northeast of where Culver stands today. In 1900 he and Martha Banta were married and they had seven children. Virgil is still living and just recently disposed of the last of the ranch.

Virgil's Mother died in 1885 and Mr. Jenkins later married Addie Carson. They had one son, Aaron. After Mr. Jenkins' death, Addie married Frank Hoffman and the Jenkins' place was known as the Hoffman Place and of late years the Dick Tate Ranch.

In 1890 George and Ella Osborn settled a preemption claim adjoining what was later to be Old Culver. They also had a timber culture claim.

The Osborns raised ten children—Frank, Robert, Maude, Fannie, Lula, Winnifred, Lois, Floyd, Gertrude and Rex. Their place was a popular boarding house and stage stop where passengers and horses could be put up for the night. After the Osborns left the ranch their son Robert farmed it until his death, then his son Clair carried on until the land in this section was purchased by the Government and designated as marginal, and is now used for summer cattle range.

The Culver District

William H. and Mollie Peck took their preemption claim just east of Juniper Butte in 1881. They later homesteaded adjoining land. They had four sons and three daughters—Vena, Dave, Hattie, Lee, John, Euretta and Ralph.

Mr. Peck was a blacksmith and had his own little farm shop where he did much of the blacksmithing and horse shoeing for folks for miles around.

Among their varied pioneer stories, they told of the double winter of 1883 and 1884. They had withstood what should have been the winter. Then in March there was a terrific storm. The snow fell so deep and lasted so long that they suffered great hardships and their stock on the range west of the Butte got very hungry because they could not get feed to them.

Mrs. Peck had typhoid fever that winter too, but the neighbor woman helped nurse her through. Mrs. Peck, Mrs. Osborn, and many other of those brave pioneer women were always ready to go and help in case of sickness or trouble, and they helped many of the babies into the world, often without the aid of a doctor.

Grandma and Grandpa Peck later moved to the town of Culver and were very active in the early development of the town. She died in 1925 and he in 1937.

Clark Rogers filed what was called a squatter's right on what is now the Cove in 1879. He also filed on a homestead soon afterward. The deed to this land was signed by President Cleveland on January 9, 1886.

The first house built by Mr. Rogers was made of logs hauled from Grizzly and dropped over the rim of the canyon and dragged on down by team. As he was a very short man, he built the ceiling to fit himself and a taller person had to bend over to get around.

Clark was the father of Bill, Dave, May and Ella. May married Jerry Schooling and Ella married George Osborn.

Just south of the Cove there is a high perpendicular cliff of rock. From its base to the river is a wide rock slide, so rough that the only animal that would be likely to try to cross it would be a mountain sheep.

In the early days when antelope and deer were plentiful in the Deschutes and Crooked River canyons the Indians would drive them up to this shut-in, where they were trapped and killed in large numbers.

In 1888 T. F. McCallister traded a house and lot in Prineville to Mr. Rogers for the Cove. Ferd, as he was known, planted quite a peach and apple orchard and this was practically the only source of fresh fruits for years.

In 1890 Mr. McCallister built the first road down the deep canyon wall to his place. This was just a trail wide enough for a team and sled. Later it was widened for a wagon but not too many people drove down; they preferred to walk or go horseback .

Mr. and Mrs. William Boegli bought the Cove in 1905 for $10,000. Mr. Boegli was born in San Francisco in 1876. When he was very small he was put in an orphan's home in Salem. At the age of 12 he was brought by the McCallisters to live with them. All the education he had was purely the Abraham Lincoln type. He became a very good school teacher and in later years

The Culver District

was Crook County school superintendant and later the first judge of Jefferson County.

He married Amanda Adams in 1905. Both he and his wife belong to the Christian Church and have given freely of their time and knowledge to the cause of christianity.

The Boeglies sold the Cove in 1941 to the State Highway Commission for $16,000. It is now a very popular State Park known as the Cove Palisades.

Elijah and Elanor Barnett homesteaded in 1882 north from the Jenkins Place. Mr. Barnett originally came from Ireland. They had four children—Benjamin, David W., Margaret, and Viola. Ben was an early-day school teacher. Dave remained a bachelor and in later years was treasurer of Jefferson County. Maggie married Orace G. Collver who had homesteaded near the Barnetts and for whom the town of Culver was later named.

Mr. Barnett started the Haystack Post Office at his place in 1890. The mail to this office came by stage coach to Prineville, then to the Haystack Post Office once a week. Up to the time of this office it was necessary to go to Prineville for mail. Some one of the families would ride in once a week and bring every one's mail.

In 1900 a post office was established at Perryville but it was designated as Culver and to us now is Old Culver. Mr. Collver was the postmaster. He ran a general merchandise store in connection with the post office.

Maggie Collver died in 1900 and Mr. Collver later married Virginia B. Prentiss from Virginia. Mr. Collver's niece, Ruth, came to make her home with them in 1904.

59

Quite a town sprang up around Mr. Collver and the post office. Some establishments which we remember are Clines General Merchandise, Dr. Snook, Charlie (High Pockets) Wilson's Barber Shop, Read's Hotel and Stage Stop, Joe Breeden's Blacksmith, Osborn's Boarding House and the school. Times were changing fast and the railroad had been built to Shaniko. So Culver had daily mail by stage coach operated by Max Cornett.

With the coming of the railroad to Central Oregon Mr. Collver moved his store and post office to the New Culver and continued to be post master until his death in 1939.

Perry and Hattie Read with their family—Lilly May and the twins Pearl and James P.—came to this neighborhood from Grizzly about 1895. Lilly filed on the homestead and they built their home with several extra rooms and ran a hotel and stage coach stop. Lilly was one of the early-day school teachers. For several years this community was known as Perryville, named so after M. Read.

Mr. and Mrs. J. H. Healey were early settlers in this eastern section, as were the Windoms, Lant and Henry or Hen as he was known.

H. A. Belknap, the Hays family, Guyon Springer, and Joe Nickles were among those coming early. Alf Allen homesteaded just north of Jenkins but did not stay and Campbell bought his right.

In 1886 Mr. and Mrs. W. S. Hale homesteaded some two or three miles east of what is now Culver. Their daughter married Claude Hinton who came here in 1899. The son Orlie homesteaded near his father. He set aside two acres of his place for a cemetery and his mother was the first person buried there. Now many stones are marked with pioneer names.

In 1894 George Rodman homesteaded about two miles south of Culver. Mr. Rodman was born in Sacramento and was one of the nine children of Wm. H. Rodman. George came with his folks to the Bear Creek country where they raised sheep and freighted. His father was very active in the early-day government of Crook County and especially the vigilante committee.

George married Sarah Ellen Eagen in 1895 and to them was born Fred, Iva, George Jr., Adrian, Lelia, Millard and Dorothy.

Over a period of years George acquired several hundred acres of land, including the Beeman Place left to him by his mother. He was a very successful dry-land wheat farmer but did not live to see the coming of irrigation. George died in 1940 and she in 1951. Their children each have their share of this land. George Jr. lives on the original homestead.

Mrs. Rodman was born in the Territory of Washington. Her father, James Eagen was born in Ireland. He was in Custer's Packtrain at the time of the Custer Massacre but was several miles behind the main army, so managed to escape.

About 1900 and the next few years the flat was homesteaded very fast. The very first to file on homesteads near where the New Culver was to be, were Dave Rogers, son of Clark Rogers, and Dave Peck, son of William and Mollie Peck.

Soon came the Tuckers, who with their daughters, Pearl and Francis, each homesteaded west of what is now Culver. Later Pearl married Jack Peck and Francis married Lee Peck.

The Andrew Limbaughs, Jones Evans and his sister, Louella; Bill, Frank and Wiley Hunter all came about the same time. Also the Killingbecks, John O'Kelleys, Frank Loveland, the Gomer Youngs, Carl Stevens, and Bill Richards were among those who settled in the early 1900.

With the limited amount and kinds of tools to be had and with no caterpillar tractors or mechanized machinery, it was amazing how in a few short years the country changed. All those miles and miles of sagebrush and juniper trees had to be grubbed and burned, and, oh, the tons and tons of rock to be moved.

One of the first things was to get water for the house and stock. So a cistern was dug and cemented and water would be hauled in tanks or barrels and stored in the cistern. The water was usually drawn from the cistern with a bucket on a rope but sometimes there was a pitcher pump. Most of the water for the surrounding country was hauled from the Osborn or the Hoffman Place. A few wells were dug. Many melted snow or caught rain water from the eaves for their stock in the winter.

Many cattle and horses were run on the range and to supply water for, these several trails were built to the Crooked River. In addition to the trail to the Cove, was the Rattle Snake Trail sometimes called the Barkley Trail; the Barnett Trail, built by Elijah Barnett, Hen Windom, nad William Peck, the Boone Trail, built by Luther Boone. The latter was built to take material down to the river to put a heavy wire to and anchor in a big spring, where it was stretched to the top of the rim and a pulley with a five gallon can was run on this and water pulled to the top by a hand wrench.

The Culver District

The trail to Opal Springs was built in 1898 by Frank Rodman who contracted the job for $110. It was also to take cattle down for pasture and water, but there was so much wild parsnip near the river that many of the cattle were poisoned and died. So the cattle had to be kept out of there. Then Geo. Rodman, Henry Windom and Guyon Springer formed a partnership and installed the first pump on Crooked River. This was a ram type pump and furnished water for large herds of cattle. Above Opal Springs was the Pike Trail built by Ed and Aaron Pike and Earle Noble.

Schools also presented a problem. The first school house in this section was built shortly after the Jenkin's family came, and was located just southeast of their house a short way. This building was later moved to Old Culver, but as the need grew a larger building was put up. Some of the children toward the eastern part attended the Red Rock School while others went to Grey Butte.

These were all one-room schools, with one teacher for all eight grades. Many of the children walked several miles to school but some of the more fortunate rode horseback. The school term was usually three or four months of the year.

Some of the earlier teachers were Addie Carson, Warren Brown, Ward Lampson, and Lilly May Read.

Another first for the settlers were fences to protect their crops from the range cattle and horses that roamed the country at will. Juniper posts were cut and set in the ground and two to four barbed wires were stapled to the posts for fences.

Fuel was another item for the winters were very cold and the

63

thermometer often went several degrees below zero and perhaps would stay so for several days. Snow several feet deep was no uncommon occurrence. Wood stoves or fireplaces were the only means for cooking or heating. Large piles of juniper wood were gathered from the surrounding country, or some hauled pine wood from Grizzly. Much thought had to be given to feed and shelter for stock.

All their supplies they could not raise were brought from The Dalles for a number of years and later from Shaniko by freight wagons. An outfit usually consisted of two wagons coupled together, with six or eight horses drawing them. Many of those pioneer men were known for their skill in driving these freight outfits, their teams being guided by a jerk-line on the near lead horse. Or possibly each team had a set of lines, making six or eight lines for the freighter to manipulate.

The lead team were usually adorned with a set of arched bells fastened to their hames. However, these were not for adornment but served to let other freighters know of their whereabouts on those treacherous curves and hills, as the tingling of those bells could be heard for miles. Many the anxious family that shouted with joy at hearing the sound of these bells for they knew their father was again nearing home safely. The trip to The Dalles and back, usually took 14 days. The freighter always carried his own grub-box and bed-roll and what grain he could for his horses, stopping for the night at those places where he could have feed and water for the horses and roll his bed in the hay mow.

Pioneering sounds like work and work it was but those brave

peoples were not without their lighter moments. They were as a whole sociable and visited among their neighbors. They had their churches and Sunday schools, probably held in the school or someone's home. Many were baptized in the water of Crooked River at the Trail Crossing. They had many school programs, spelling bees, literary societies, pie and basket socials, and many other forms of entertainment. Those who danced would load their families and a basket supper in the hack or wagon early in the evening and drive for miles, maybe to Lamonta or to some one's house where they would dance until the break of day. They danced the good old round dances, with an occasional quadrille. Dave and Ralph Peck and Jim Read were much in demand as callers. Dave and Ralph are gone but Jim still loves to dance and he and his wife Belle never miss their square dance club.

Everyone knows since the beginning of time there has been "love". Romance blossomed all along the way. Many of the gallant sons of those hardy pioneers came riding across the sage-brush on their noble steeds to woo and win the hearts and hands of the neighbors' daughters. Many of the young folks of this and the surrounding districts were married and started homes and families of their own, and many of the descendants of these pioneers still can be found around here.

All these years, the neighbors were few and far between. About the only way of communication would be to saddle your horse and ride over. But in the early 1900's a farmers telephone line was strung among a few of the farms and later this extended to Lamonta where one could be connected with Prineville.

One must admire the courage and bravery of those pioneers. They came into this new and unknown country with perhaps all they had in the world in a wagon drawn by a team of horses, and sometimes trailing a few cows. They had no modern machinery or motor-driven tractors. Just some crude plow and maybe a one horse harrow. Much of the brush and trees were grubbed by hand. They had little to do with. Their women folks had very few articles of furniture or cooking utensils, yet they did all the baking, churned the butter, washed the clothes in a tub with a washboard, and even made their own soap. A flat iron heated on the stove was used for ironing. They still found time to sew and knit for all the family and were never too busy to help a neighbor if the need arose. Their only source of light was either tallow candles or kerosene lamps or lanterns. The first electricity came to this country about 1905. But tonight as I sit and look over that same valley and see those hundreds of electric lights twinkle and hear the roar of the automobiles and trucks as they zip by right through the heart of the Culver district on our very modern highway—U.S. 97 that extends from Canada to Mexico—I realize it could never have been had not those pioneers had the foresight and determination to stay and conquer.

From 1905 on, the country made many changes. Rumors of a railroad were in the air. W. C. Barber, J. C. Cockerham, and Harold Lawrie saw the need for a townsite. So they platted Culver in the heart of this lovely valley, on land that was Dan Swift's homestead. With the coming of the railroad, Culver became a thriving little town with the post office, school, two churches, two hotels, two general merchandising stores, a drug

The Culver District

store, a weekly newspaper, a lumber yard, and grain warehouses. The depot was a busy place every evening when the populace all turned out to watch the mail and passenger train arrive.

The first passenger train arrived April 15, 1911, and the first freight a few days afterward.

Jefferson County was set aside from Crook County in 1914 and Culver was named the county seat by Governor Walter Pierce. The first court consisting of Wm. Boegli, J. M. King and Harry Gard met December 28, 1914. But, alas, in 1916 by popular vote Madras was chosen for the county seat and on that notable Sunday morning Madras came in a caravan and moved the records away. This caused much controversy between the two towns for many years.

Earl Thompson invented and installed a pump in Opal Springs, and pipes were laid to Culver and the surrounding country. Thus the domestic water situation was overcome and the first water was delivered through these pipes to Culver on August 22, 1916. This water is now piped over much of the county, to Metolius, Madras, and as far north as the Agency Plains. Up until this time the water for the town came from a railroad well drilled 700 feet deep.

Those of us who are priveleged to live in Jefferson County today and enjoy its many beauties and peaceful surroundings should stop and pay homage to those brave and noble pioneers who gave so much that we could have this golden opportunity. May their memories remain as long as the sun still sets over those glistening snow-capped mountains and creates those glorious sunsets, unsurpassed anywhere on earth.

Culver Postcript

By Hazel L. Laird

James Henry Windom was born in California in 1857. Rebecca Leach was born in Brownsville, Oregon in 1864. These two people were united in marriage in 1885. They came to Central Oregon to settle in a community called Haystack in Wasco County. Later it was taken into Crook County which was a part of it for many, many years before being divided into Jefferson County to which it now belongs.

Windom was probably the first man to till the soil in that section. When the newlyweds moved there they brought boxes of canned fruit packed in oats. These oats were saved and used for seed to plant, which yielded an abundant crop. This gave him the idea of growing wheat which also produced a good yield. He was the first settler to bring in a horse-power threshing machine, which he bought in the Willamette Valley. Mr. Windom and his two brothers, Jess and Alonzo, brought a thresher over the Santiam pass by wagon.

Mrs. Windom said she was alone much of the time while her husband was at work. She was often frightened by passing Indians who stopped for water or to beg for food. If she saw them coming she would push the furniture against the door and try to hide, but they never molested her, as they were the friendly Warm Springs tribe.

To this union were born five children—Winifred, Harry, Carl, Hazel, and Pauline. The Windoms had only two very distant neighbors, the George Osborn and William Peck families.

Mr. Windom, Jim McMeen, and G. Springer were the first to utilize the water from Opal Spring. It was in 1898 that, with several other stockmen and farmers in that community, they installed a water wheel and pump to raise the water to the first bench, a distant of about 500 feet and used it to water cattle. Then in 1914 E. A. Thompson installed the Thompson water engine which forced the water through pipes to the residents in Culver, which was then a thriving town in Jefferson County.

The Windom Ranch was known all over Central Oregon and was farmed by his sons until 1934, when the land was bought by the Marginal Land Co.

The Trail Crossing

By Anna and Vern Merchant and Mrs. Melvin Cyrus

The sun shines on many lands east, west, north, and south, but I'm sure when the pioneers came into the Central Oregon country and stood at the foothills of Gray Butte, they knew that they had found the best place on which the sun ever shone.

As these early settlers looked upon this new country with its mountain skyline, the sky above so blue, many juniper trees standing guard so majestically, fine lush bunch grass waving in the cooling breeze, and many springs of clear, cool water, there must have come to them a vision of a home for me, a home for you.

Thus the first settlers came into the area later to be known as the Trail Crossing District.

Homesteads were filed on, lines were established, and homes were built. Then arose the need for schools, churches, and better roads.

The southern part of this fertile valley was bounded on the south by Crooked River with its rugged, mystifying canyon many feet deep. A narrow cattle trail wound down its side, the river was forded, and the trail wound up again on the other side. And from this crossing the locality became known as the Trail

The Trail Crossing

Crossing District. Later a wagon road was built and about 1890 a bridge was constructed across the river. The timbers for this first bridge were hauled many miles from the Maling Mill at Willow Creek. Also the lumber for many of the houses was hauled either from this mill or mills on Grizzly Butte.

One of the first settlers was the Foley family, who homesteaded at the head of the trail that crossed the river.

The Ruble family were among the very first. Mr. and Mrs. Andrew Ruble, Lucy, Walter, Claude, and Katie homesteaded their home-place in 1885 near the Gray Butte foothills.

There were good-water springs which they developed, and from which homesteaders for miles around hauled their water in barrels or later in tanks constructed for that purpose. Most of the homesteaders made a cistern in which to store the hauled water. They would dig a hole in the ground, then tightly cement it, and cover it over.

In due time, the Rubles acquired several hundred acres near by. Their first house was built of logs. Katie, their youngest daughter, with red hair in long braids typical of the miss of those days, and riding side saddle on her little pony, was admired by all.

Not long after the Rubles settled, the families of John, Bill and Abe Banta homesteaded in this valley. The first school house was built on land donated by John Banta. This was a small one-room school, and all eight grades were taught. However, school had been held a few terms in a small cabin east of this site.

The Ase Coles, Carpenters, George Dodson, Montieth, Rycraft, and Ketchum families were there quite early also.

Charlie Thompson will be remembered by all who knew him, a bachelor who lived for many years in a dugout in the ground. He became known as Badger. He later built himself a one-room cabin.

Seth Crawford and his family homesteaded in the southeast corner near the foothills. Just east of the Crawford home was a section corner which was one of the main correction points of the original survey. Mr. Crawford caused quite a stir of excitement when he discovered a vein of coal on his place, but it was never found in paying quantities. It was near where his house had stood that the huge cut was made through the hill for the canal to bring water to the 50,000 acre North Unit Irrigation Project of which the district is now a part.

The Crawfords had moved away years before as had so many of the older homesteaders. Most of the older ones have passed away, and their families are scattered far and wide. I have deep feeling of regret that this history was not written years ago. Then names, places, and dates could have been more accurate.

C. L. Lowthers came sometime around 1900. He sold organs over the territory. He was also a minister and preached many fine sermons.

Billy Keckler and Mr. Waldorf were bachelors.

In 1897 the Morris family homesteaded at the top of the grade on the south of the river, their place being a stage stop for many years.

Dwight Roberts was the first mail carrier. He peddled fruit

trees when he first came, then homesteaded, and later drove the R. F. D. The route started from the original Culver Post Office, came down through our valley, then went north through the Gray Butte district. He had a little white mail cart drawn by two small ponies. However, there was no mail route until 1905 so the homesteaders went to the Haystack Post Office or later to Culver for their mail.

Ralph Peck, L. L. Nichols, Jesse South, and Edgar Barnes were later carriers on the mail route. Edgar began in 1916 and was the first to use an automobile for carrying the mail. Edgar also filed on a homestead.

In 1906 my father, Isaac Martin, and family homesteaded toward the western part of the district, and later the railroad crossed our place.

The L. L. Nichols family came in 1907. There were seven lovely daughters and one lonely son. Mr. Nichols carried the mail one year.

Sue Barnes, a relative of Edgar Barnes, was the first school teacher in the Trail Crossing District School which was held only about three to five months each year. The children of the very early settlers went horseback to the Gray Butte School. Ida Rodgers and Grace Robinson, now Mrs. Glen Ridgeway, were early-day teachers.

Some of the later homesteaders, I remember, were Simon Peter Burgess and his sister Martha who were school teachers. Charlie Loring and H. O. Montgomery were bachelors. Colby Fleener and family, Carl Schreiber and family, L. L. Hobbs and son Harry, and Ed White and I. A. Talbert with his family all homesteaded in the northeastern part. Mr. Talbert was also a school teacher. If I have left out anyone, it has been unintentionally.

The life of those early homesteaders was far different from what we enjoy today. There were no tractors, no motorized farm machinery, no television, no radios, automatic washing machines, nor the hundred other luxuries we have now. The homesteaders made their own entertainment, and, oh, the good times they had at picnics on the Fourth of July or other holidays with their well-filled baskets, at spelling bees, sleighrides, debating societies, and school programs. Occasionally there was a dance at Lamonta or Willow Creek. Many attended church at Culver or Gray Butte, and sometimes there would be services at the school house, conducted by some minister of the community or a visiting minister. Many were baptized in Crooked River near the Trail Crossing Bridge.

They found time to dress up in their Sunday best and have Sunday dinner with a neighbor, and no one was ever too busy to help in case of sickness or trouble. Doctors were miles away. So the old fashioned herb teas, onion poultices, and varied home remedies saved many a life.

The crops were the dry land sort, the main ones being wheat, oats, barley, and rye. Much rye was raised for hay.

Poplar and locust trees, yellow roses, flags, lilacs, and matrimonial vines were among the plants found at nearly every home. Gooseberries, rhubarb, and currants were in nearly every garden. These, along with dried applies and prunes, were practically the only fruit available.

The Trail Crossing

As the farm work was all done with horsepower and the same was true of transportation, many acquired perfectly-matched teams and a fine buggy or hack. Many fine saddle horses were seen, and last but not least, were the very necessary work horses.

The days of hauling water from a spring are perhaps almost gone, but we remember the clear ice-cold water. We cherished each bucket full, and I'm sure we gave inward thanks for each drop. There were many places where water had to be hauled for use on the homestead, but a few had wells with windmills. And how those windmills would whirr and race when the wind blew hard, and also how they could shock you when a thunder shower came up and you took hold of the crank to stop the wheel from turning so frantically in the high wind!

The wood used was mostly precious juniper from the surrounding country. Some burned the sagebrush if they could find it in large enough pieces. Many made the annual trek to Grizzly Butte to cut pine for the winter's fuel supply.

Washtubs, wash boilers, and washboards were standard equipment, and most folks made their own soap, using the fat or tallow from butchering and purchasing a few cans of lye. This made a cheap supply of very good soap, and since money was nearly always in short supply, it was indeed an item in the budget worth considering. Some even made their own lye from ashes.

Everyone kept a milk cow or two and a few chickens.

Cottage cheese, potatoes, and dry beans were among the plentiful foods, and almost everyone raised a garden.

Every family baked its own bread and churned its own butter. An annual trip would be made to Prineville with enough wheat to be ground into barrels of flour for the year's supply. And, oh, those delicious sour-dough biscuits! How I'd like to have some once again.

And vinegar was made in the cellar of nearly every home. The last spoonful of honey, jam, or jelly went into the crock which already contained the mother, or starter, and the jar rinsed out with water and poured into the crock. In due time, enough vinegar was produced to put up the pickles and to make vinegar pie which was a real treat in those days.

Then, too, we recall the meat preservation. Just the thought makes us wish we could have some sausage like Mother and Dad used to fix. Sausages were made into small cakes, fried gently, and put into crocks with layers of lard completely covering each layer of sausage. In later years the sausage was fried as before and canned with the gravy added. The hams, shoulders, and bacon were cured by salting, then hung and smoked. Men would butcher their own beef, pork, veal, or mutton and go from house to house selling it or dividing with neighbors who would in turn divide when their time came to butcher.

I remember the old coal-oil lamps and lanterns. If you have never filled them, washed the chimneys, and trimmed the wicks, you have missed something. The coal oil was brought in by freight in five-gallon cans. I remember especially the kitchen lamp on the wall with a reflector behind it. It cast a lovely light on the walls and ceiling.

And the old wood range with its reservoir for hot water was

a heavenly place, with frying pan sputtering and kettles bubbling and the tea kettle just ready to boil to make coffee for the men soon to come from the fields.

Many jackrabbits, coyotes, and bobcats roamed the country, and in the very early days herds of antelope could be seen. Many horses and cattle grazed on the open range.

Rattlesnakes were a source of fear, for there were many. They would hibernate in large bunches in the rocks for the winter, and people tell of blasting out great dens of them near the Ase Cole Place.

The cook house for the harvest crew, although now gone out of existence, was a never-to-be-forgotten experience.

Stealing watermellons was a pastime, lark, or prank, however the mood might be.

As I mentioned before, there was quite a lack a utilities such as we have today. Hence there were no refrigerators or deep freezers. So the task of putting up ice for summer use was quite an art. Men armed with ice tongs, saws, lunch, and plenty of warm clothing would hitch their four- or six-horse teams to their wagons and go to the river long before the winter daylight. There they would saw the ice into blocks and load their wagons and drive home to pack the ice into a bin filled with sawdust. A picnic in the summer was never complete without freezers full of that delicious home-made ice cream.

In 1910 and 1911 the railroad was extended from Madras on south. In order to cross the Crooked River Canyon, a bridge was necessary. The narrowest place was some two miles below the Trail Crossing. Mr. Howard Turner, of Madras, who was

U. S. Commissioner at that time, tells of the rivalry between the Harriman and Hill interests for this particular spot. He tells that one night in February of 1910, he was rudely awakened by a delegation of men, one of whom was Matt Clark, right-of-way agent for the Oregon Trunk Railroad. They asked that he go to his office and prepare papers so they might script the forty acres of land needed. This he did and they drove to the Dalles yet that night. How they did it, he says he never could understand, for it was stormy and the roads in those days were not built for automobile travel. Of course, their car, like all others in those days, wasn't built for speed. However, they were at the land office when it opened the next morning, and as they finished their transaction, the men arrived from the Union Pacific Railroad or the Harriman interests to script the same piece of land but too late. So the bridge was built by the Oregon Trunk Railroad. It was a magnificent piece of work, being 340 feet long and 320 feet above the water. It was constructed from both ends simultaneously. The steel for the south half was transferred across from the north on cables, and when all was in place, the two ends were riveted together in the middle.

The bridge, at that time, was the third highest and seventh of its kind ever to be built. Many times we watched the workmen, six or eight at a time, climb or descend a rope ladder suspended from the rim of the canyon straight down to the bottom.

Reference was previously made to the building of the road across the canyon at Trail Crossing. Considering the tools and machinery they had to work with, this road was a masterpiece

78

The Trail Crossing

in itself. But, of necessity, it was narrow, very steep in places, and with many sharp curves. It, of course, became quite slick in the winter. One winter Mr. N. A. Burdick, Mr. Max Cunning, and another man from Redmond, slid off the road, and their car plunged many feet down the hillside. Mr. Burdick and Mr. Cunning were only injured, but the other man was killed.

Another time, two couples with a small child stopped near the rim on the north side to view the gorgeous sight. They left the child in the car, he shifted the gears, the car rolled into the canyon, and of course the child was killed.

Naturally, with the coming of the automobile, the need for better and faster roads arose here as everywhere. The State, in conjunction with Jefferson and Deschutes counties, in 1926 built a highway bridge near the railroad bridge. Thus the old Trail Crossing was abandoned.

This bridge is also a beautiful piece of work. It is built on concrete pillars at either end, and the bridge itself reaches gracefully across. Thousands of tourists each year stop to view this magnificent sight.

The land adjoining the bridges on the south was given to the State by the Oregon Trunk Railroad, and it has been set aside as the Peter Skene Ogden State Park.

In 1825 Ogden led a Hudson's Bay trapping party on the first recorded journey into Central Oregon. They crossed the Crooked River a short way above this spot, and so it is the park was named in his honor.

One could ramble on for pages about the good and bad experiences of those early homesteaders, of their hardships and disadvantages, but we marvel at their courage and determination to make a home for themselves and their families here. We know they found much happiness in so doing.

Trout Creek

By Verna May Corwin

Trout Creek begins as a small stream, and some springs, up in the Blue Mountains about 17 miles above the small town of Ashwood. It is added to on its winding way to the Deschutes River by innumerable small streams, each one with its own individual name given it by an elderly settler. History and interesting events have occurred all up and down the length of the creek, and branched out on each of its sides, much farther than its tributaries. Much of its history has been lost for the lack of recording and in the passing of the early settlers who actually lived the history.

My primary concern is the part of Trout Creek known as the Willowdale community, but first I would like to mention a few of the settlers who helped make history beside the creek.

All along the length of Trout Creek are innumerable former ranches and homesteads of early settlers, some just abandoned, others sold to large landholders, whose only memory is the first owner's name on a spring, creek, a hill, or a canyon. Each one added to the life and doings of the time, events long since forgotten.

One of the earliest settlers was Tom Hamilton, who came to Trout Creek in 1878. Mr. Hamilton's daughter, Beth McDonald, and her sons Tom and Ronald, still run the original homesite as well as a lot of land acquired in later years.

Tom Hamilton was the first to breed and raise Shorthorn cattle. In fact he introduced purebred Shorthorns to this part of Oregon. His daughter's family is interested in sheep, a continuation of the purebred sheep introduced by Mr. Hamilton.

A few miles below the Hamilton Ranch lies Ashwood. It was a booming community in the last part of the 19th century and the first part of the 20th century as the cinnabar (mercury) and silver mines around it prospered. There are still mines being worked near Ashwood, though not on the large scale as in former years.

James Wood, whose family helped name Ashwood, also helped to discover and develop mines near the town. Mr. Wood was postmaster of Ashwood from 1862 till his death. A brother, Lee Wood, lived near there on a ranch. The boys were sons of W. A. Wood and Martha J. Rush, both of whom lived to be 101 years old.

Below Ashwood lies the old Friend Place. The home place is now run by Aaron Hale, a son. Various grandsons farm portions of the original land.

Aaron is a true Oregonian, having been born on his grandfather Hale's homestead on McKay Creek near Prineville in 1884, the year oldtimers refer to as the year of the heavy snow. The snow was four feet deep on the level and it completely covered a band of sheep. Settlers lost lots of stock and many are the heroic deeds of rescue that went unsung.

It is said the Mr. Friend, Aaron's stepfather, found most of

Trout Creek

his sheep after 21 days and that most of them were alive because they were in good condition when they were covered up with the snow. Mr. Friend and Perry Maupin worked the jaws of the sheep to take out the numbness. They also pulled grass and put it in the sheep's mouths, working the jaws with their hands until the sheep could handle it themselves.

When the snow started, the livestock, especially horses, stayed together. So the snow was tramped down and melted until they were trapped in pens surrounded by high walls of snow. When the snow walls melted the horses were left on a high cake of ice. It was necessary to drive them off by horseback. They were a sorry sight, because in their starving conditions they had eaten each other's manes and tails.

On a portion of this ranch is Paulina Basin where Howard Maupin killed the renegade Indian Chieftain Paulina.

Trout Creek enters a deep gorge now, and on both sides are ranches and hills, but along the creek there are none until the gorge opens out onto the old Cartwright Place. This place was originally homesteaded by Nunns and sold to Cartwright and then to John Priday, who still owned and operated the ranch until his death in the fall of 1956. It is here that Trout Creek begins to open out into the meadows and hay lands that are the backbone of cattle raising.

Just below where Ward's Creek joins Trout Creek are the old Sanford Schultz holdings. Trout Creek jogs up into Wasco County here and it is just over the county line that the old Schultz home stands. At one time the family kept travelers, as so many did in those days. The old toll road up Cow Canyon

Jefferson County Reminiscences

begins here and many people would stay the night at Schult's so that they could get an early start up the steep narrow grade.

About half way up the Cow Canyon grade was the toll gate, kept by Lige Haight. It was along this road that all freight and travel went from Shaniko to the Inland Empire, Bend, and Burns.

Mrs. Schultz was a daughter of John E. Bolter who kept a stopping-place several miles below. The Sanford Schultz Place is now owned by Warren Priday, a son of John Priday.

The original John Bolter Place is operated by his son John and grandson Edward. A portion is farmed by a granddaughter's family, the Harvey Woods, who also owns a part of the Garret Place. Bolter's was one of the main overnight places on the long road from Prineville to Shaniko and it was known far and wide for the excellent and plentiful food set before the travelers by Mrs. Bolter. They also have the distinction of living in three counties but still living in the same house, the county being divided three times since the land was taken up by the Bolters. At first it was Wasco, then Crook, and then Jefferson.

Below the Bolter Ranch, part of the old Teal and Coleman Ranch, is the Robert Cram Ranch. It is run by the heirs of the late Robert Cram, a son of Bidwell Cram and Kate Bolter, a daughter of the J. E. Bolters.

The ranch of Bidwell, or Bud Cram, as he was known all over Central Oregon, was the first place owned and developed on the creek and most likely the first in the central part of Oregon. This place was also a part of the original holdings of the large cattle barons of early history, Teal and Coleman. The

84

Trout Creek

Cram Ranch was the home of Henry Coleman, from whom Mr. Cram bought the start of his ranch, Cram's holdings were estimated to be 3,000 acres when he sold out to Ernest Alexander in 1946.

At one time it is said that Mr. Cram owned and operated 20,000 acres. Besides this his cattle roamed over a great portion of this vast Central Oregon country where they could go for miles without finding a fence.

Mr. Cram was born in Texas and came to Oregon from Yreka, California, in 1880 with his family who at one time ran the toll gate in Cow Canyon. He worked as a young man on various ranches, including the Mays Ranch, till he bought his home on Trout Creek.

What is known as the Priday Ranch and is now owned by Glen Fulton was also a part of the Teal and Coleman holdings. It was sold to John Stuart and then to Albert Priday who homesteaded and bought additional lands. At the time of the death of A. J. Priday's widow the holdings were purchased from the heirs by the son, Leslie Priday, who had operated the ranch since his father's death. To this was added more purchased and homesteaded land until, when the ranch was purchased by E. W. Williamson of Bend in 1945, it had grown to about 72,000 acres, parts of which were in Wheeler County.

On this ranch are found the famed agate beds with agates of every description and color, which are seen on display all over the world. The Glen Fultons now own and operate this Trout Creek Ranch.

On a part of the Priday Ranch, near the home and on the

highway, is the Episcopalian Church. The building was originally the railroad depot at Paxton, near Madras. It was bought, moved, and renovated by the people of the community with generous help from Episcopalians everywhere. This was truly a community project, as people of almost every faith gave generously of their time as well as their money to help in the project of making this a beautiful and serene place for the traveler or native to stop and worship. Prior to this, churches of various denominations had been held in the school house and in various homes.

Below the Priday Ranch, on still more of the Teal and Coleman holdings, is what is known as the Harrison Place. It is on this ranch that Hay Creek enters Trout Creek. It was purchased from Harrison by Bidwell Cram, and became a part of his vast holding. In 1944 Lester Horigan bought it and later sold it to Henry Lever.

A short way up Hay Creek and considered a part of the Trout Creek community is the old V Z Ranch, owned at one time by Lyle and Veazie. A. L. Veazie, the son of Edmund F. Veazie, a Portland lawyer, has been very much interested in Oregon history and has contributed a great deal to the history of Central Oregon and of Trout Creek. W. H. Lyle had a toll gate at the gap between two steep hills and to this day it is known as Lyle Gap. This road was found to be the best grade out of Trout Creek when it was surveyed by engineers in 1923.

The VZ Ranch was sold to Mr. Cram and later he sold it to his daughter and son-in-law, the Chester Kennedys, who still operate it as well as considerable more land. Mr. Kennedy is now joined in these operations by the daughter and son-in-law, the John Richardsons. It is interesting to know that a part of the Richardson house is the original old log house and the old VZ brand is still used.

It is believed that it is on this place that Teal and Coleman first set up their headquarters. They had a contract to furnish beef to the government posts in Oregon and Washington and they maintained supply posts in the Klickitat, Yakima and Tygh Valleys. In the fall of 1868 William H. Gates, with Harmon Simpson and Richard M. Williams, drove in 750 head of cattle. Mr. Gates was the foreman for the company which consisted of Colonel Joseph Teal, his brother-in-law Henry Coleman, and Barney Goldsmith of Portland. In February, Coleman came with another band. He and his brother William both took up claims and Gates settled about a mile above the Veazies. His house was about where the modern home of the C. M. Kennedys now stands. Mr. Gates burned out a large beaver dam to drain a swamp and the firm's operation grew to a great size in the next 10 years. The local markets could not absorb the cattle. Mr. Gates told Edmund F. Veazie in 1917 that in 1878 they sold 5000 head of cattle to Land & Ryan, Texas men, who drove the cattle out. Teal and Coleman themselves made drives to Council Bluffs and Cheyenne to reach the railroad. One of Col. Teal's sons, Joseph N., afterwards a leading lawyer of Portland, spent several years on the Trout Creek Ranch and went on some of these drives. The last one of 3000 beef cattle to Cheyenne, and thence on to Kansas, was the ill-fated drive that almost broke Joseph Teal.

Just above the VZ Ranch is the old MacPherson Place. It was sold to a Mr. Hunter and then to Leslie Priday. It is now owned by the Hay Creek Company. One of the first graves in Central Oregon is on this place, that of Mrs. MacPherson's father. The old wooden headboard has on it the date of 1876.

A part of the MacPherson Ranch was once homesteaded by a Mr. McCoy, one of the feuding McCoys whose conflicts with the Hatfields of Tennessee made the mountains a dangerous place to live. He had married a Hatfield girl and to escape the ire of both sides immigrated to Oregon.

To go back down on Trout Creek—just below the Harrison Place the creek narrows down for a mile or so and then begins to broaden out again, though never into quite such broad meadows as the Willowdale portion. Here is found the old Monroe Place, now owned by Lester Horigan, and a little farther down is the old Kampher Place. The Kampher brothers Godfried and Albert, were Swiss immigrants. It is now farmed by a daughter and son-in-law, Mr. and Mrs. Leo Hatch. Mrs. Hatch was a daughter of Gotfried.

No one has ever been able to find out for sure just why the old post office on Trout Creek was named Cross Keys. The post office was first established in 1878 as Trout Creek and was changed to Cross Keys in 1879. It was closed in 1902. Mail has been received on Trout Creek at seven different addresses—Trout Creek, Ridgeway, Cross Keys, Youngs, Heysler, Gateway, Willowdale, back to Gateway, and is now on a mail route out of Madras.

The first school started in 1886, just above where the Willow-

First sawmill on Willow Creek, 1877 owned by C. C. Mailing of Grizzly,
the source of much pioneer lumber often hauled long distances.

Headquarters place of the Baldwin Sheep & Land Company, popularly known as the Hay
Creek Ranch, a vast-sized layout famous as a breeding center even more than for its bigness.
The average owned acreage was 27,000, plus great areas of free grazing land; the number of
sheep 50,000; the working force 70 to 100 men.

dale Service Station now is on the Robert Cram estate. It was held only for the several winter months when the young people weren't so urgently needed at home. Miss Etta Wrenn was the first teacher and her school consisted of a fairly large group of pupils. Some of them were 2 Bostwicks, 3 Johnsons, 3 Bolters, 2 MacPhersons, 3 Heights, and 4 Nunns. The young people would gather at the school, as would the older people, for all social occasions. They met here for church when an occasional minister came through the country and they met here for their dances. An oldtimer has said to me, "Be sure to put in your story about the fun we had at the dances, with little old Joe Stuart playing on his fiddle."

The telephone wire from The Dalles to Bend went through Trout Creek in 1904. When the telephones were installed in the homes it gave the community a quick service to the outside world.

In 1923 the modern paved highway was finished and it was found that with the exception of a few places, like Cow Canyon, the early pioneers who first came to the territory started their roads where the grades were best.

It is hard to find out exactly when the earliest settlers first came to Trout Creek, but in reviewing histories it seems that this inland community didn't begin to settle extensively until after the Indian wars were settled.

General George Crook, for whom the settlers, out of gratitude, afterwards named Crook County, took command of the troops engaged against the Indians in this region late in 1866 and brought the troubles to a successful end in June 1868.

Jefferson County Reminiscences

Some people seem to think that this area was explored as early as 1824 but there seems to be nothing mentioned of Trout Creek. Later in 1843, John C. Fremont and Kit Carson, with 25 men, passed through what is now the Warm Springs Indian Reservation and out by the site of Bend and on to the Klamath country. In 1845 the lost and wandering immigrants, led by Stephen Meek, came through Trout Creek. They came down Crooked River, part of the way in the channel of the stream, after being led astray and deserted by Meek. These were the discoverers of the famous Blue Bucket Mine which no one has been able to find again. On September 22, 1845, they were on Crooked River where a rescue party met them. They made camp on the Deschutes, northwest of Madras, at Sagebrush Springs and on Hay Creek, then double-teamed and pulled up Cow Canyon onto Shaniko Flats and on into The Dalles. Twenty of the party perished between Boise and The Dalles. Some returned later and settled in Crook County.

Due to the Indian trouble and discouragement by the United States Government, settlement was late and slow. In fact, settlement of all the territory east of the Cascades was discouraged. On August 7, 1856, General John E. Wool, commander of the Department of the Pacific of the U. S. Army, issued an order to Colonel George Wright at The Dalles forbidding immigrants to locate east of the Cascades. These mountains were considered as a wall of separation between the Indian and the whites. This order was revoked by General Harney on October 31, 1858.

When at last people started into this territory they followed either of two routes. One part of them came through on the old Oregon Trail, past Fort Dalles, or through Southern Oregon and across the high desert. Very occasionally some hardy souls would come acrosss the McKenzie, the lava beds, and the mountains between here and Lane County. All of these immigrants were bound for the lush green valleys of Central Oregon where it is said bunch grass grew as high as one's head. Of course there were the earlier trappers, fur traders and the miners who in their search for virgin fields were always the first into new wilderness territory. But the early settlers, the ones who came in search of homes, didn't move in until around the middle of the 19th century.

P. L. Veazie says that Felix and Marion Scott made one of the first roads into this new territory in 1862. It was a crude road at the best, it being said that in places in the lava beds some of the large rocks had to be crushed by hand with sledge hammers to get the 8 or 10 loaded freight wagons, 70 yoke of oxen and 600 or 700 loose cattle over. This party was headed for the Salmon River Mines in Idaho. The people of Lane County had raised a subscription of $1,000 and donated some labor to help open this road into the territory. When the Scotts reached Trout Creek with their wagon train and large herd of cattle it was late in the season. So they decided to winter their livestock in the protected Trout Creek Valley where feed and protection were for the having.

They built a cabin, site of which can be located on the NE¼ of the NW½ of Sec. 34, T. 8, SR 15E. Until recently the remnants of the cabin that marked the location of Central Oregon's first settlement were still visible, and stumps of junipers cut then were in evidence.

As far as can be determined this was the first "settlement" in Central Oregon, although it was hardly large enough to be called a "settlement." It was on Trout Creek and was the first time white people had lived in this territory for any length of time.

The Scotts returned with about 400 head of cattle to the same location in 1865-66. A man named Ritchie also bought a hundred head and a man named Cunsil followed with 100 heifers which he held on Wilson Creek, a tributary to Hay Creek which is itself a tributary of Trout Creek.

In 1866, when Marion Scott and his companions were on Trout Creek, they were raided by Indians, who stole seven saddle horses and took the camp equipment.

John B. Evans who came in 1865 with the Scott cattle to Trout Creek and who settled in 1868 on Willow Creek, says:

"At this time the grass grew high and rank. Hay could be cut almost anywhere in the Blue Mountains. Wild timothy, pea vine, etc. grew three feet high and pine grass 18 inches high. Bunch grass would make a ton per acre. There were only a few settlers in the country and practically all of them were engaged in hunting. The game was very plentiful and the skins and dried meat were sold in The Dalles. The game chiefly hunted was deer, elk and bear."

In the pioneer days an enormous number of deer, both mule deer and flag-tails, were killed for market within the territory, which afterwards became Crook County, many for the hides or hams alone. Antelope, sage hens, prairie chickens and grouse were plentiful and as for trout, my brother Clarence got 50 that averaged a pound in one day's fishing on the Deschutes. Even the small streams abounded in trout. By the heavy growths of vegetation on the hills and slopes and the rye-grass, tule swamps, natural meadows and willows in the valleys combined with the beaver-dams the floods were brought almost to a standstill and the erosion, such as has since damaged so many meadows, was prevented.

The largest cattle drive was by Joseph Teal and Henry Coleman, his partner. At Bend they were joined by the cattle of John Y. Todd. In 1880 the country was overrun with cattle. Markets were poor in the west, range was deteriorating and shipping points were distant. From Trout Creek the settlers had to drive their cattle on the long tortuous route to The Dalles and thence to take them by boat to Portland.

Joe T. Deal decided he would sell most of his herd and talked other ranchers into going in with him on a big cattle drive to Cheyenne, Wyoming. John Y. Todd, operator of the Farewell Bend Ranch, which is now the city of Bend, decided to go along with Todd. Each got together 3000 head of cattle, including their own and their neighbor's. On these drives they would hire the pasture as they went along, paying by the head. They tell that at one of these places the counter was standing on a plank over the gate when one of the riders thought it would be a joke to throw an empty coal-oil can amongst the cattle. This stampeded the cattle and they took the man right along with them. They tell that he rode right along with them for about 100 yards and then they spread out and let him down. It was a wonder the poor fellow wasn't killed.

As drive boss, Todd took the lead with his own 1500 head of cattle, and Henry Coleman with the Teal herd followed. There is no written record of that long drive, some 1200 miles, or the route they followed. It is assumed they headed the herd directly for Cheyenne, by-passing the mountain ranges. The big Teal herd was assembled on Trout Creek from all of the surrounding pastures which went all over Wapinitia, Shaniko Flats, Warmsprings, Agency Plains, and in fact the whole surrounding territory for hundreds of miles. The Todd herd was assembled on the Deschutes. The herds may have merged in Eastern Oregon, no one seems to know.

It was a treacherous drive at the best and this drive was not of the best. Disease struck and there was a heavy loss.

At the Cheyenne railroad Teal had formed a firm, the John T & Co. to market the cattle. At Cheyenne, Todd turned his cattle over to Teal for marketing and returned to his home at Farewell Bend. When Todd failed to get any money from his herd he returned to Cheyenne the following spring, there to find out the final chapter of the ill-fated drive.

Todd learned that in Cheyenne the cattle had been sent to Kansas to fatten. Many of the animals, Todd was told, had broken through the ice of the Missouri River and were lost. The drive leader went bankrupt and Todd received nothing from his 1500 head of cattle or pay for the overland drive.

The ranchers from whom Todd had gotten cattle to make

94

the drive filed suit against him. The suit was eventually carried to the Supreme Court where Teal and his brother-in-law lost. This broke them and they sold off their holdings on Trout Creek to some of the newcomers. This started a new era.

The pioneers settled in their homes and were soon welcoming the coming of the homesteaders. Soon these pioneers where there had been so much open country began to feel crowded by the nearness of neighbors. Some of the homesteaders were rolling stones and soon moved on to what they always hope are greener pastures, selling their land to their neighbors.

It is interesting to note what was originally Wasco County, created in 1854, including the full present width of Oregon from north to south and from the summit of the Cascades to the summit of the Rockies with its northwest corner about where Butte, Montana, now stands. It had an area of about 130,000 square miles. Out of this was carved Crook County in 1882 and in 1914 Jefferson County was carved out of Crook County. A goodly portion of Jefferson County is covered by Trout Creek and its small tributaries.

Ashwood

By Mrs. C. Keegan and Phil F. Brogan

1

*Told here is the story of the Ashwood community and
its environs from pioneer days to the present,
with special mention of mining work*

The search for gold and, in later years, the quest for that
silvery metal known as mercury played important roles in the
early day history of Jefferson County, from Trout Creek to the
Horse Heaven Hills.

But even before gold was found in the sulphide ores of a gul-
ley that slopes west towards Trout Creek and the distant cove in
which the renegade Indian chief Paulina died under gunfire on
a summer day in 1867, this region had a history—a history largely
concerned with stock raising.

Grassy hills, green in the spring, and abundant water from
timbered mountains in the southwest that flowed through Trout
Creek, naturally attracted stockmen in pioneer times. Long
before the discovery of gold the valley was homesteaded, from the
pioneer Howard Maupin ranch at the junction of Trout and
Little Trout Creek to the pines of the Blue Mountains in the
southeast.

96

Ashwood

First stockmen of the area made only an over-winter stop. They were Marion and Felix Scott and members of their party who in 1863 crossed the McKenzie Pass lava fields en route to the John Day goldfields with a large herd of cattle. They spent that winter in a cave in the Hay Creek area. Their cattle grazed on the surrounding hills and, it is presumed, found their way to the lush valley of Trout Creek with its fine flow of water.

Among the early permanent settlers was Thomas S. Hamilton, who settled on Trout Creek above the present site of Ashwood in 1874. Once he grazed as many as 7,500 sheep and 200 cattle on his extensive holdings and was the first to introduce blooded stock into this part of the region. His daughters Beth, Mrs. Alex McDonald, and Joea, Mrs. Johnson, own and operate the ranch at the present time. On Lower Trout Creek, near where the stream starts its race through towering walls of lava, Columbus Friend also settled in the late 1870's. He was a native of Iowa, who came to Oregon in 1870. His grandson, Byron Friend, and his stepson, Aaron Hale, each own and operate parts of the ranch today.

First settlers on Lower Trout Creek, also in the 70's, was Howard Maupin, who had earlier lived in the Antelope Valley, on the trail from The Dalles to Canyon City, and was first postmaster there, at the old location of Antelope. It was while Maupin was still living in the Antelope Valley that he joined in the pursuit of Chief Paulina and killed him in Paulina Basin, which overlooks the early-day Maupin holdings from the west. The town of Maupin on the Deschutes bears the pioneer's name, as does a butte on the divide between the John Day and

97

Deschutes watersheds, east of Antelope. It was in 1867 that Maupin obtained his Trout Creek holdings, but apparently he continued to live in the Antelope Valley, to care for his stage station.

In the late 1860's Henry Coleman of Lane County, one of the large group that joined in the backwash of immigration across the Santiam Divide, settled on Hay Creek, near the Trout Creek junction. The Jones Place and others on Upper Trout Creek also bear the names of oldtime settlers.

The village of Ashwood came into existence in 1898, on the banks of Trout Creek, a stream that was flush and high in the spring months. This was in Crook County in that year, and trading points were Prineville and The Dalles, end of the rails. The Columbia Southern did not reach Shaniko until 1900, then the hamlet of Ashwood was only about 25 miles distant from a railroad. Shaniko early in the century was recognized as the world's largest wool-shipping point. Wool from the Ashwood area moved slowly up Little Trout Creek on freight wagons, through Antelope, and up the grade to Shaniko.

The townsite of Ashwood was platted on June 16, 1899, by James Woods and Addie Woods and consisted of 15 blocks. The town took shape on the James Wood homestead. Overlooking the village is Ash Butte, one of the ancient Clarno volcanoes, which in earlier eons was entirely buried, then exhumed in a general uplift of the region. Gray and serene the old volcano still towers, unchanging, over the village this writer saw take shape more than half a century ago.

When the postoffice was established in 1898 the word Ash

was combined with Wood to form the name Ashwood. This was done to honor Whitfield T. Wood who settled in the vicinity in the late 70s. His son, James Wood, was the first postmaster.

The first building on the new townsite was erected by John W. Robinson, a pioneer merchant. Soon other business houses took shape. These included the Grater Hotel. The O'Neil Brothers of Prineville opened the Ashwood Saloon in 1898, and later sold it to Benton & Grater.

On the discovery of gold in the area, Ashwood took on new life, and for a time was in the news spotlight of the Pacific Northwest. A school was erected in 1900, and this remained in use until replaced by a modern building in 1953.

It was on March 30, 1901, that the first issue of the Ashwood *Prospector,* a weekly paper, published by Max Lueddemann of the Antelope *Herald* first appeared. A copy of Vol. 1, No. 1 is on this writer's desk as he prepares this history of the hamlet of Ashwood. It was a four-page paper, half of which was "boiler plate." Most advertisements were from Antelope. The *Prospector* was discontinued in April, 1905.

The history of the Ashwood "gold rush" dates to about 1896, when a man named Wilson, herding sheep at the Jones Ranch, picked up some pieces of float quartz. He took some of the samples with him to his home in Walla Walla, had them assayed, and found they held $35 to the ton in gold, with silver also present. After the find, the location was known as the Silver King. Soon after the discovery Wilson organized a company of John Kirby, Thron Thronson, P. T., John Hubbard,

John Knight. The operation was known as the Oregon King Mining Company, and through the years the mine was known as the Oregon King.

But even before Wilson found the quartz float, as early as 1884, W. T. Wood, while digging a well, discovered sulphate ores holding valuable minerals. He organized a company to develop properties and was one of the leaders in the opening of the Ashwood mines. He had a heavy amount of stock in two companies.

The original company formed by Wilson, after sinking a shaft to a depth of 100 feet, sold their 12 claims to the Oregon King Mining Company, organized by P. J. Quaaly of Kemmerer, Wyoming, and J. G. Edwards and C. M. Carthwright of Hay Creek. The original company retained control of the stock. By 1901 the shaft was down to a depth of 430 feet, with drifts. From the foot of the hill a tunnel was run to intersect the main shaft. W. S. Thomas was supervising the development in 1901, the year when the first litigation of a long series was started. The litigation resulted from a suit by T. J. Brown of Roseburg, who claimed the mine by right of discovery.

The Oregon King was closed over a long period of years but was reopened in 1925 by Jack Edwards, with a shaft sunk to a depth of 600 feet by miners who lived in the hotel at Ashwood. After being operated for less than two years, the mine was again closed by a lawsuit. In 1933 the mine was reopened by the Alaska Juneau Mining Company, with new buildings erected. The site had every appearance of a thriving mining town, with a hotel and dining hall. A huge diesel was installed in a cement structure at the opening of the shaft. Then the operations again ended, with more litigation believed to be the cause. Except the power plant, buildings were sold.

In 1942 the mine was again opened for Fenton and Custer Young, who leased it from Edwards. The mine was operated for a number of years, then work ended because the shaft reached into other claims. More recently the mine was opened by Anderegg of Portland, also under a lease from Edwards. The power plant was destroyed by fire in a later year.

Because of the Oregon King gold strike it was only natural that interest in mining should extend over the entire region. Hundreds of claims were filed and there was some extensive stock selling promotions, such as in the Morning Star claims and others. But through the years there were no rich fields, despite the fact that the sulphide ores held gold and silver.

In the search for gold in early days none of the miners paid much attention to the ore of mercury—cinnabar. Yet it was this ore that in later years resulted in extensive mining developments in the Donnybrook and Horse Heaven areas. One of the mercury developments was near the location where the Red Jacket Mine was sunk in the days of the quest for gold.

It was in the Horse Heaven region that one of the outstanding discoveries of mercury in western America was made. In the summer of 1934 two schoolboys, Ray Whiting Jr., and a chum, did some prospecting in the area. One day while eating lunch upon the hill near an outcrop of co-called ribbon rock one of the boys kicked off a piece of rock and found cinnabar. However, before that time, Art Champion and Grover Keaton of Prineville localized the mercury outcropping in 1933. They worked up westward from Cherry Creek toward the final location of the Horse Heaven mine, on the divide between Cherry and Muddy Creeks. Champion and Keaton sold their claims before locating the cinnabar in place. Ray Whiting and C. C. Hayes purchased the claims. Hayes and Whiting associated themselves with Robert Betts and Captain E. W. Kelley. They organized the Crystal Syndicate, which later became Horse Heaven Mines, Inc. It was in 1936 that the Sun Oil Company purchased the property. This new organization was financially able to improve equipment and speed development.

A slump in the mercury market and the difficulty of obtaining miners eventually slowed operations. In 1944 the Horse Heaven furnace had been operated for 11 years and in this period about 100,000 tons were furnaced and something like 15,000 flasks of quicksilver were produced.

Operations at the Horse Heaven Mines, under a new firm, were resumed in 1954, with furnacing of already mined ore as the price for mercury soared.

By 1955 Ashwood had again become a quiet village, in a region where history was made half a century ago. It was the range country that first attracted settlers in this region, and it is this range, with its stock, that is now paying the taxes as it did in pioneer days when Henry Coleman settled on Hay Creek and when Jim Grater built on his land the log cabin that still stands just south of the Ashwood townsite. Those were the days when A. B. Orfitt lived on Upper Trout, and was joined in the late 60's and early 70's by John Atteburg and James Cox.

Ashwood

The Jim Grater of pioneer days was James M. Grater, whose ranch was immediately south of the site where Ashwood was founded. He ranged his stock up Trout Creek into the Blue Mountain timber.

There was a rush of homesteading in the Ashwood country between 1908 and 1916. One of the first homesteaders was Tom Bradford, who filed on land on Pony Butte. Every 160 acres of good land was filed on in that era, with springs and creeks placed under fence. The result was trouble for the oldtime stockman.

Of the many who homesteaded in the Ashwood country, Charles R. Keegan, whose ranch is near the historic Oregon King holdings and the place known to residents of half a century ago as the "Jack-the-Ripper" cabin, is the only stockman living on his original claim.

The mining and mineral history of the Ashwood country cannot be passed over without mention of the Priday agate beds in the Pony Butte area just south of the gorge of Trout Creek. In the past quarter of a century the value of precious stones removed from that locality, now known as the Fulton Agate Beds, was greater than the value of gold removed from the Oregon King and other mines of the area, with the quicksilver claims excluded.

Such is the sketchy history of a region this writer knew as a boy long years ago. They were years when ranches were far apart, and the ride from the Axehandle highlands to Ashwood, now a matter of half an hour in an automobile, took half a day on horseback. It was a long ride from the John Day slope west past the Gamble and Creegan places, with the Morgan place off to the north and the "Red Alex" McLennan Ranch to the right.

Then, in Long Hollow, there were the pioneer Red Jacket Mine and the Dan McCarthy Place.

That ride was past the "Jack the Ripper" cabin and none of the youngsters of the rangeland knew the story of the origin of the name.

Newcomers call that region a rangeland. For oldtimers it is a land of memories.

2

Presented here is the history of a segment of Jefferson County, covering the Donnybrook, Kilts, Currant, Muddy and Cherry Creeks, Burnt Ranch and Horse Heaven areas.

Now off the beaten path and detoured by major highways, the rangeland region of eastern Jefferson County, from the highlands that overlook Ashwood, to the colored hills of the John Day Valley, was in the spotlight of pioneer history .

Battles between Indians and whites were fought on the grassy hills, when horns of mountain sheep and antelope were still abundant. Miners, on the long trail from The Dalles to Canyon City, died there, and Paulina and his raiders just prior to 1870 left their trail of burned ranch homes and haystacks.

And in a sheltered cove facing the lava-walled gorge of Trout Creek, not far downstream from Ashwood of the present, the mongrel chief of the Piutes, variously known by the whites as Paulina and Panina, died under the rifle fire of J. N. Clark,

Howard Maupin, and William Ragan. That was on a summer day in 1867, when Paulina and his braves were moving toward the Deschutes country with cattle stolen from ranchers on the John Day River.

The cove where Paulina died under gunfire is now known as Paulina Basin, near the junction of Trout and Little Trout Creeks, where Howard Maupin in later years made his home, and where the scalp of Paulina was lost in a fire that destroyed the ranch home.

But long before Paulina, responsible for the death of miners, trappers and early-day settlers, blazed his bloody trail across eastern Jefferson County of the present, history was in the making in the area.

No one knows when the region east from Ashwood past Donnybrook to Cherry Creek and the John Day was first visited by white men. Possibly a member of Nathaniel J. Wyeth's party made a detour into the region in 1834, when Wyeth, trader and patriot, moved up the Deschutes River in search of a group of South Sea Islanders who had left a camp and, presumably, headed south. Possibly John C. Freemont, "The Pathfinder," explored a part of the area in 1843 when he headed south through Central Oregon. However, if there was any such exploration of the region east of the Deschutes and north of Trout Creek at that time it was by Captain Fremont's men, not by the Pathfinder himself.

When gold was discovered at Canyon City, in the upper John Day Valley, in the fall of 1861, there was a heavy eastward movement of travel across the region now in northwestern Jefferson County. In the first sweeps of travel, along routes from The Dalles eastward, the trails were undoubtedly widely scattered, with each party taking the trail of its choice after crossing the Deschutes in the area of Sherar Bridge and moving inland via Bakeoven and the station a short distance northeast of Antelope of the present where lived Howard Maupin, already mentioned. Antelope Post Office was established at that station in 1862, the year following the discovery of gold at Canyon City. Maupin was the first postmaster.

The first recorded trip of a party across northeastern Jefferson County was in 1862. It was in that year that Joseph Sherar, who had mined in California, started with passengers and freight by packtrain to the John Day mines. On that trip the party named Antelope Valley, Muddy Creek, and Cherry Creek. It was in 1871 that Sherar became operator of the toll bridge across the Deschutes, at the Sherar Bridge site, first visited by white men in 1826, when Peter Skene Ogden passed through that area. At the falls, on the "River of the Falls," the Deschutes, Ogden found an Indian camp of twenty families.

The exact route followed by the Sherar party is not definitely known, but it is presumed he took his pack string past the place known as Bakeoven, then over the rim into the upper Antelope Valley and east past the place later known as Cold Camp and on across Currant, Muddy and Cherry Creeks and on past the Mitchell site and into the John Day country.

Shortly before the 60's there is a possibility that a member of a party of army explorers, Lieut. Bonneycastle, visited part of the Jefferson County region. In 1856 Capt. D. H. Wallen had been instructed by the military department to make a reconnaissance for a road from The Dalles to Salt Lake City, and to determine whether such a road could be constructed up the John Day River, then over to the headwaters of the Malheur. Capt. Wallen crossed the Deschutes at the mouth of the Warm Springs River, then dispatched part of his command east of the route followed by himself, which was inland by the way of the head of Crooked River.

Such is the history of the early exploration of the northeastern Jefferson County region, but even before Wyeth, Ogden, and Fremont touched the western part of this area, and long before the miners blazed trails over rangelands in the wild rush to the John Day gold fields, Indians made their homes in this part of Oregon. Proof of this is in a low cave on Currant Creek. As late as forty years ago, this writer recalls, the walls of this cave were covered with Indian pictographs, some of them possibly more than a thousand years old. Arrowheads and artifacts scattered over the range country in early days, also told their story of hunting parties, in quest of antelope, deer and possibly bison.

After Paulina died under the fire of settlers in 1867 and the army rounded up renegades, more peaceful conditions came to the range country and the stock era had its start. In a great backwash of immigration, pioneers of the Willamette Valley, around Linn County, moved eastward over the Santiam divide to establish ranch homes in the Ochoco Valley, to establish a school on Mill Creek, and to found Prineville, where the post office of Prine, later changed to Prineville, was established in 1871.

In this new era, all of Central Oregon was still in Wasco,

107

mother of counties. It was in 1882 on October 24 that Crook County was sliced from Wasco. Settlers of the Ashwood-Donny-brook area were in Crook County, and transacted their official business in Prineville, until Jefferson was created on December 12, 1914.

But much history transpired in the rangelands northwest to Trout Creek prior to the break-up of counties and the establishment of Jefferson. This history largely deals with the stock era, when settlers moved in to file on lands where cattle, horses, and sheep were grazed. In that earlier homesteading era, long before the mad rush for enlarged homesteads prior to World War I, The Dalles was the main trading point. The Dalles remained the shipping point for interior stockmen until that day on May 13, 1900, when the Columbia Southern's line to Shaniko was opened for traffic.

Before 1900, supplies for ranches was freighted from The Dalles.

The task of tracing the earlier homesteading era history in northwestern Jefferson County is difficult, despite the fact that this writer, as a boy, lived part of that history, on a 160-acre ranch that faced the distant John Day River from rangelands of the Donnybrook country. The writer's father, John C. Brogan, settled in the area in 1896, but long before that day there were homesteaders in that part of Jefferson County of the present. And far down on Muddy Creek the big Prineville Land & Livestock Company Ranch had already taken shape, with its holdings consolidated.

To settlers at the turn of the century the P. L. & L. holdings

108

were generally known as The Muddy Ranch. Cattle and sheep belonging to "The Company" ranged over the hills. Fences stretched along lush creeks. Occasionally "Muddy Ranch" herders grazed thier flocks to the edges of homesteads and there was an occasional conflict.

One of these occurred in 1901 when Tom Reilly met a "Company" herder named Breuner on a rocky ridge north of the Black Rock homestead. Reilly died in the gunfire that followed. It was after the death of his brother that Pat Reilly came to the present Donnybrook country to take over his brother's holdings, and to enlarge the ranch later known as the Donnybrook Livestock Company.

There is a story in the naming of the community as Donnybrook, a story with a rangeland flavor.

It was early in the century, around 1905, that a group of stockmen met in a cabin in Calf Gulch. The occasion for the meeting is no longer recalled. Possibly it was the tailend of the lambing season, and possibly a member of the camp dropped down the slope to Ashwood and returned with a gallon of liquor. At least a fight took place in the cabin. One man was shot in the leg. Amiable Joe Bannon, one of the early-day ranchers who had settled on Little Trout, saw some similarity to the fracas in the cabin to certain disturbances at the Donnybrook Fair in his native land, Ireland. Bannon called the place Donnybrook.

Gradually the name replaced an older name, Axehandle, given for a big spring on the old Wood road between Antelope and the Blue Mountain timber.

Incidentally, the first school ever taught in the present Donny-brook area was within a stone's throw of Axehandle Springs, in an old sheep cabin on the bank of the creek that carried the runoff from the Springs into Currant Creek.

This historian was a member of that first school, opened, if memory serves us right, in 1904. Laura Harvey, a neice of Mrs. Dan Crowley, was the first teacher. Pupils who studied that first year, on hard benches in a dark cabin, were Howard and Gertie Eades, Elvie, Hazel and Ellen Crowley, and Dan and Phil Brogan. Later Ruth Crowley and Celia Brogan attended classes there and in the new school built just across the road. This school in later years was moved over a hill on rollers to a location near the original Crowley home. Dessie Eades also attended one of those earlier schools.

Before the first school at Axhandle, the present Donnybrook section of Jefferson had a homestead history that goes back beyond the days when Sandy Finlayson, later killed in a team runaway, filed on a ranch on Currant Creek for years known as the Finlayson Place at the turn of the century. Another of the early-day homesteaders was J. R. Morgan. Jack Brogan filed on a homestead near Axehandle Spring around 1895, and later this claim was in extensive litigation in connection with the Lewis mining claim. Earlier the pioneer stockman Phil Brogan, who was stabbed to death in the old Silvertooth Saloon in Antelope by a former employee, homesteaded on Little Trout Creek. John Creegan, whose original homestead later became part of the Fenton Wharton holdings, filed on his claim after 1901. Earlier, Dan Crowley, his wife and their younger children, came in from the Wamic country to live on a claim high in the Frog Springs area, on the road leading into the pine country of the Blue Mountains. It was later that the Crowley family moved down to the Axehandle country.

Southwest from Axehandle is the region known, in early days, as Tompkins Gulch, where an early settler named Tompkins died in a range fight. Adjacent to the John C. Brogan homestead was the ranch of Horace Gamble. There Horace, Hardy and Simon Gamble lived.

North of the Brogan ranch was Skull Hollow. The origin of the name of this locality is lost in the mist of time, but youngsters of 1900 heard a story of skulls having been found in this valley, where John McLennan later had a sheep camp. Possibly they were skulls from old Indian graves. Possibly soldiers clashed with Indians there in the days when patrols searched for tribesmen.

To the east of Donnybrook, in the Cherry Creek region, is another "pocket" of history, in an area that also includes Upper Muddy Creek. Stockmen attracted by abundant feed and plenty of water in the creeks that flowed north to the John Day River, settled there. Among the old-timers were Grant and Polk Mays, names well known in pioneer range times. The Mays ranches were on Muddy Creek, as were the Hinkle holdings.

Among the early settlers of the Cherry Creek Valley were members of the Shrum family. Andrew Jackson Shrum, who came to the Willamette Valley with his father in the migration of 1844 from Missouri, settled on Upper Cherry Creek. At the junction of Cherry Creek and the John Day, where a broad basin was farmed, ranchers settled even earlier. Among the old-timers there was James Connolly, and nearby, in a canyon of Cherry Creek frequently swept by floods from cloudbursts, was the Pat Fagan Ranch. Some of this area borders on or is within Wheeler County of the present.

In the junction area was the pioneer Burnt Ranch Post Office, which migrated through the years, depending on the home of the postmaster. The post office was on the military road between The Dalles and Canyon City, and the locality was named by Joseph Sherar on his pack-train trip up to Canyon City in 1862. It was so named because there was in the area a ranch home that had been burned in an Indian raid. The Burnt Ranch Post Office was established in 1883 through the change of name from Grade. Addie Masterson was the first postmaster.

Along Muddy Creek was another area of early settlers, and among the first was Jacob Kaser, who expanded his holdings in 1903 by purchasing land from Volney Schrum, on nearby Cherry Creek. North on Cherry Creek shortly after the turn of the century was a Portuguese family, that of Tony Freitas.

In the later era of the early epoch of settlement, Fenton Wharton lived in the Burnt Ranch area, and later moved west to Donnybrook, to establish his home on the pioneer ranch of John Creegan.

A second era of heavy settlement in northwestern Jefferson County occured in the teens of the 20th century, most of it between 1910 and 1925. In that era practically every foot of Government land in the range country was filed on.

It was in the early teens, as new homesteaders demanded

access to the county seat at Madras, that a county road took shape easterly across Jefferson County into the Horse Heaven country. On township maps this is listed as the Gonser Road.

Early homesteaders in the Horse Heaven mines area were Lester N. Kelsay, Anthony Romo, Ralph and Estella Darling and more or less adjacent areas were filed on by Floyd and Jesse Kilts, Dewey Degner, Charles Lowther, Halbert Hawkins, and Clarence Slobig. Andrew Oller and Charles Noonan homesteaded to the east of the old "Stock Trail". These homesteads were all taken up in the early "twenties". In passing, it should be noted that one of the post offices of the homesteading epoch in Central Oregon was named after the Kilts family. For a number of years, the Kilts Post Office appeared on the map of Oregon, and there were old timers who decried the fact it was not named Donnybrook.

Virtually lost among the new homesteads east of Coyote Mountain was the early-day ranch of Dan (Pegleg) Morrisey. Just to the southwest of Coyote Mountain was another old time ranch, that of Dell Eades, whose children attended the first school in the Axehandle, later Donnybrook, community.

So much for the history of the wide region known as the Donnybrook community, and its adjacent country. Many names, many incidents have been overlooked, for this bit of history has been compiled by a person who has been away from the area for more than 40 years. Plenty of recent history has transpired in these four decades.

Madras

By Howard W. Turner

I

Madras was originally called the "Basin" due to its shape, then "Palmehn", "Palmain", now "Madras". It was located first in the "Oregon Territory", then "Wasco County", meaning in Indian jargon "Little Nation". Wasco County was at one time comprised all of the territory from the Cascade Mountains to the westside of the Rocky Mountains, including all of Washington, Oregon, Idaho, and a part of Montana. This was gradually cut down, and in 1853-54 the Territorial Government actually created Wasco County, though much larger than at the present time.

Madras was in Crook County in 1882, this being named for Major General George Crook; and is now in Jefferson County, since 1914, the latter named from Mount Jefferson located on the western boundary.

There were four homesteads in the beginning, whose lands are a part of the Basin, now Madras—John A. Palmehn, 160 acres, government patent issued April 24, 1893; Frederick J. Waymire, 160 acres, government patent issued May 7, 1888; Mary J. Brown-Weber-Boyce, 160 acres, government patent issued

114

April 10, 1899; and Samuel E. Gray, 160 acres, government patent issued February 4, 1909.

The original Plat and Dedication was filed July 18, 1902, by John A. Palmehn, calling the town "Palmain" (note the difference in spelling). The Madras Townsite Company was incorporated November 14, 1904, by John A. Palmehn, A. E. Hammond, and Don P. Rea. The city of Madras was incorporated March 2, 1910, with Howard W. Turner as the first mayor and John H. Jackson as the first city recorder.

The way that Palmain came to be known as Madras was from the Post Office Department, after a petition was filed for the establishment of a post office here in the fall of 1902. The Post Office Department in Washington, D. C. found there was in the State of Oregon a place by the name of Palmer and thinking the names confusing, they substituted the name of Madras. (A later version endeavors to connect the name Madras with a bolt of cloth, common in the early days and called Madras cloth. This, however, is not correct, as some people are still living who were here at the time the office was established and knew the circumstances.)

The following is an excerpt from a letter received by the writer in April of 1944 from John A. Hoffman:

Jefferson County Reminiscences

RALSTON, WASHINGTON

April 8, 1944

MR. HOWARD W. TURNER

MADRAS, OREGON

DEAR FRIEND HOWARD:

I was not the first postmaster at Madras. That honor belongs to Martin T. Pratt, now living in Portland, now Sheriff of Multnomah County. The mail then, as you state, came to Madras via Culver.

In 1903, Joshua P. Hahn erected the first store building in Madras, on the site where the New Madras Hotel is now located. Hahn was succeeded by John McTaggart, who can tell you the date when he took over the office. I think it was in 1905.

McTaggart was succeeded by Fred Davis, and John will also know when Davis took over. The rest of the history of the Madras Post Office is as well known to you as to any one.

I think the nephew of Joshua Hahn is in error about the naming of Madras. The name that was sent to the Post Office Department was "Palmehn", which was rejected by the Department, which substituted for its present name.

Sincerely yours,

JOHN A. HOFFMAN

The writer received the following letter (in part here) from Martin T. Pratt in August of 1952:

116

HOWARD W. TURNER

MADRAS, OREGON

DEAR SIR:

If my memory serves me right, the application for a P. O. asked to have it named after John Palmain who had homesteaded the basin. It seems to me that the P. O. Dept. advised that a P. O. with a similar name already existed in eastern Oregon so they (the P. O. Dept.) named it Madras.

Sincerely yours,

MARTIN T. PRATT

The following is a letter which appeared in the Madras *Pioneer* March 9, 1955:

EUGENE, OREGON

February 28, 1955

TO THE EDITOR

Madras Pioneer

MADRAS, OREGON

DEAR SIR:

I understand there has been quite a discussion as how Madras got its name. So many different tales being told that are not true. I am one that really knows the truth about it.

My husband Max Wilson and I were living in the Palmain house when the plot of the town was made and he decided to apply for the post office. When he sent in the name Palmain to

117

Post Office Department in Washington they would not accept it. Their excuse was it was too much like Parmen, another Post Office in Oregon. He then sent in the name Madras which was accepted and he was given the Post Office. However, he did not run it as he decided to move away and turned it over to a man that had a store there by the name of Hahn.

My husband helped survey the townsight and Madras was named for Madras, India.

I would like the people of Madras and vicinity to know that the name did not start from dry goods even if the town did start on a shoe string.

Sincerely,
STELLA WILSON
Wife of Max Wilson

The writer has discussed this matter of the naming of Madras, and along with other information that I have been able to assemble, I am sure that the above is the correct circumstance in this connection. I was well acquainted with Mr. Max Wilson and also his wife, the writer of this letter. I have also talked with Mrs. Marie Galloway-Dizney and others. Mrs. Dizney was working for Mr. Hahn very soon after he took over the post office from Mr. Wilson, who did not attempt to operate it.

The name "Palmehn" is of interesting orgin to people of the Basin—Palmain, and now Madras. It seems that two brothers who made their home here in the early 1890's came over here from Benton County. They were born in one of the Scandinavian

118

countries and came to America under the name of Peterson; but they are credited with stating that they found too many Petersons here in Oregon, and applied to the court to have their names changed to "Palmehn". Their reason for changing to this name cannot be learned; however, the name "Palmain" after being applied to the original plat of "Now Madras" seems to have been more agreeable. The change in their name occured before coming to Crook County in the early 1880's.

The town (now City of Madras) was located here in the Basin because of the water in open springs for livestock that was rounded up here—both cattle and horses. There is one man almost 100 years old, James Blakely, who visited Madras in 1950, and who states that 70 years ago, he fed and took care of about 800 head of cattle for several months in this Basin until they could go out on the range. These cattle were not worth as much as they are now, while horses were worth more then than at this time.

Before 1890, quite a number of acres of land in the Basin was placed under irrigation for the raising of wheat, rye, barley, and oats. These were the principal crops at that time. Irrigation water came from dams in Willow Creek (named from the willows growing along the upper reaches of the stream). There were three dams at various times, in the Madras Basin, the first one being about one-half mile above the grade school, the last one at the mouth of the two upper canyons. All were washed out by too much water from water spouts and spring run-offs.

One of the original homestead houses is still standing, but it has been remodeled and built over—the one where Tom Monroe lived, in the east part of town. This was on the Frederick J. Waymire homestead. There was a well on this place that for many years furnished water for the homesteaders of the early days, when they had to haul it for domestic and livestock uses— in some instances twelve miles via team.

2

During the early part of the century the mode of travel through this section was of course via horseback, later on by horses and wagons. Of course they had to come to stopping places for the care of horses as well as people. Rube Jones, one of the early-day homesteaders, just west of the Union Pacific depot, built and operated a livery barn in 1905 and 1906 on the west side of Fifth Street. About the same time Harvey Filey built and operated a livery barn on the east side of Main Street (Fifth) and rented out livery horses and teams. He operated this barn about three years, when he sold out and later on the barn was torn down. This was about the time that the road was opened up to the north by way of Young's Post Office and then on down through the Mud Springs area, coming out through the gap below the Quaale place, Chistensen place, and up over the hill and through the gap.

The mail at that time was coming into Madras from Young's, and Young's was served from the post office at Haycreek. John Lockard carried the mail from Haycreek to Warm Springs. Later on, the mail came to Madras more direct; being across from Haycreek, the junction of the stage lines by way of the U. S.

Crooked River Bridge in 1906, now on U. S. Highway 97.

Oregon King Mine, part of the "gold rush" starting in 1896.

Ashwood Post Office, established in 1898. Other early buildings included the Grater Hotel and the Ashwood Saloon.

Madras wearing quite a frontier look in 1907.
All but one of the buildings are identified on the picture.

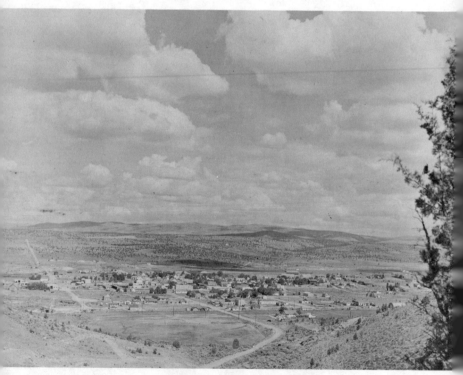

What a difference a half-century can make—the Madras of 1957, with its third name,
first "Basin," second "Palmain."

Cowles Ranch (Morris and Julian Place), where sheep was the principal livestock at the time.

Joseph W. Livingston bought and operated his livery barn on the west side of the same street. He was the one that I hired a team from and drove to Shaniko in 1909 with Mrs. Turner, and when we arrived in Shaniko that evening, we learned that the first carload of construction equipment came into Grass Valley for the start of the Oregon Trunk Railroad up the Deschutes River. There was very little sleeping in the hotel that night as there was a celebration going on in all parts of the town as well as opposition from some people who felt that a railroad up the Deschutes would have detrimental effect on the town of Shaniko.

In 1907, Mr. Dunn also operated a livery barn for a short time on the west side of Fifth Street. This was also about the time that Lou Young had and operated a gallon house on his homestead. He later moved the gallon house down around Sage Brush Springs, being a few miles east of now Gateway. Also people hauled water from these springs, being close to the Christensen Place, on the road going through "Old Maid's Canyon" and on out through the pass to the stage line at Heisler Post Office.

Speaking of "Old Maid's Canyon": While this was still Crook County, William Farrell was acting as road superintendent for this area and was ordered to build the road through the canyon. There was a woman by the name of Beasley who came out and ran the men off, as she did not want any road going past her house. After considerable maneuvering, the road was built and used as a stage road for some time after the writer came to the country in 1903.

3

In the matter of hotels, we had several during the early part of the century and the following is a sketch of these hostelries from about 1902 to the present time.

The first hotel in Madras was built and operated by Joshua P. Hahn and wife Lula, who moved his store from old Culver to Madras in 1903, building on the corner (southwest corner of Fifth and D Streets). He had a store in part and overhead sleeping rooms, and alongside was the dining room and not very far to the west was the livery barn. Tom Maloy and wife also had some accommodations to keep travelers before this time.

The next was the Green Hotel—the large house moved down from one of the mills at Grizzly (the Dee and Compton Mill) to a corner lot south of the Main Street Garage (Fifth and B Streets). The building was painted green, as was the livery barn in connection. Archie Mason moved it down about 1906, later it was greatly enlarged on the back, allowing for many more sleeping rooms and a large dining room. This was a stopping place for travelers because it was in the vicinity of most of the livery barns and horses were the means of travel (stage stops also) during that period. The barn was torn down before the fire destroyed the main buildings, which was in 1922. Our water supply was short and we had a hard time keeping buildings across the street both ways from going up in smoke.

Madras

The next hotel was built in the fall of 1916 and early 1917 by Fred Fisher and Mrs. Fisher. They had been divorced but worked together in this project. Fred had been a farmer out in the Mud Springs district and in 1916 had a good grain crop and made a considerable amount of money which he put into this hotel. They ran it for a number of years, later selling out and going to The Dalles, where they died. (Fred died first). This hotel is still in operation.

Along in the early twenties, Charles Hobson, a character about Madras for many years, who had operated a saloon and several restaurants, bought a large two-story building up by the old Oregon Trunk Depot which he moved down to its present loction mostly by himself and fixed it up for hotel purposes. After he died it was sold to Mr. E. W. Weber, who continued to fix up the building and built a series of cabins on two sides, so that it makes a very nice hotel and motel.

There have been several rooming houses during the early days. The building now owned by Mr. Moore was built by Harry G. Keys and wife, which was later used by Dr. Haile as a hospital, then as the county clerk's office in 1917-18 after the county seat was moved to Madras. Later on it was turned again into a rooming house.

The present Mason House was built by Mr. and Mrs, William Ellis in 1910. They lived in it and operated it as a rooming house until 1943. Then it was sold to Mr. and Mrs. Ed Mason, the latter being a niece of the late Mrs. Ellis. It has been a restaurant and rooming house for many years.

Mr. and Mrs. Samuel E. Gray took up a homestead that

came close into town (west side of Fifth Street). They used their cabin and built on to it and made the Gray Rooming House that operated for many years and is operating at the present time. They lost a daughter, LaVelle; have a son, Wendel Gray. Mr. Gray died several years ago, Mrs. Gray is close to 80 (1954) and has Mrs. Pillette with her, helping her take care of the house and their rooms.

4

As to physicians for the care of the sick and injured, we have had a variety of personalities, mostly good, who ministered to the residents of this section. In the early days this town and section had quite a reputation for increase in population. The principal income of the doctors was from this source.

Early day doctors, say from 1902 on, have not been very scarce. In fact, Dr. W. H. Snook, who came from near Moro, in Sherman County about 1902, settled at old Culver, with his family and started in the practice of medicine, driving a team at that time, it being before the days of the choo-choo wagon. About 1904 he took a homestead just south of Madras, where he resided for some time, proving up on the same, then moved into Madras, living on the tract known as the Lockard & Snook Addition. He started the first drug store in Madras (see some of the old pictures), later on built a concrete building on the property on Main Street which he owned at the time of his death in 1953.

About 1903, Dr. T. A. Long came out from Missouri, having

been a friend of the Ramsey family back there. He took up a homestead on the Agency Plains and also practiced medicine soon after coming to Oregon. He proved up on a homestead and later moved into Madras in a red house near the public school, later built a new house. He also had a drug store in Madras later on, after Dr. Snook had been dispensing drugs for many years.

Dr. Homer B. Haile, a native of Oneida, New York, came to Madras as a physician for the Oregon Trunk Railroad in 1910, later buying some property and putting up a building and remaining here until his death in December, 1919. He was an able physician when not under the influence of liquor. His practice was large at times and he did some very fine work. He did considerable surgery, and like all of the other doctors here, one of his specialties was the bringing of babies into the world. He had several citations from the railroads for his bravery in saving lives during a severe train wreck. He was a genial and deep-thinking man. He was in two world wars, serving the medical corps in both, and came out with a wonderful record. He was his own worst enemy. His remains were taken back to his former home in Herkimer County, New York, December, 1919, for interment.

Some young men came in and stayed for a time getting started, and some have made good; also we had a few of the fly-by-night kind that came and went.

Dr. Harry Blair practiced here and later became a noted bone specialist. He was here about 1914.

Another young man, Dr. Kettle, came in with the Harriman Lines construction work in 1909 and 1910. He was a very en-

125

ergetic person and did good work in his profession, moving to some other place after the railroad construction was finished.

Still another doctor came in to help Dr. Haile—Dr. Gale, who later moved to Coos Bay where he practiced many years, until his death in the early 1950's. He was a very efficient person and did fine work while in this vicinity.

We had one doctor who was a character: Dr. J. W. Cosnaugh, who worked with Dr. Haile a short time. He later became quite noted in and about San Francisco, where his principal work seemed to be rejuvenating some of the human race by transplanting monkey glands into people. However, I understand that this became quite a racket.

5

One of the first places fixed up to deliver water from a well to tanks and barrels for use by the farmers and residents in the country was at the old John Isham well, located in the south and east part of town (now Tom Monroe home). This was along in 1903-04. About this time the water table was up within about 16 to 20 feet of the surface. Several other wells were drilled and dug about this time, furnishing water to farmers.

During the years 1905-06-07, Frank Loveland started drilling wells in this area, putting down several water wells here in the Basin. In several, he went too deep and lost the water. In several other places, due to the atmospheric pressure, these wells would either draw in air or blow out air. The water table at that time was under 20 feet; then it dropped down to better than 60 feet. Since irrigation, it came back and is well up at this time (1954).

Another large well was dug over on the east part of town and water was sold there about this time. And later, the Fred Waymire well operated. It was afterwards acquired by Calvin Fox, who did not operate it long. The J. W. & M. A. Robinson Company also dug a well back of their building, put in a gasoline engine pump, and put a large tank on a tower over the building and also delivered water to the farmers for a time in 1907-08.

This hauling water by the farmers was a strenuous as well as an expensive task, as some farmers had to haul the water for a distance of twelve miles. This was during the early homestead days. Many water tanks, as well as the barrels, sprung leaks, and then many of the barrels were open and because of the rough roads the water would slosh out; consequently before they got home, they would have lost a lot. Then, too, the water standing in these barrels a long time was a disease breeder and much sickness was the outcome, such as typhoid.

Many times when the weather was hot the men would have to wait a long time to get their water, as the wells could not supply it fast enough; or when there was a breakdown in the machinery, I have known of their being at the well all night. Of course in the winter time the barrels and tanks would freeze so that hauling was very much of a handicap at any time.

6

The town was surveyed and platted in 1902, and the town lots commenced to sell and some buildings was started by J. P. Hahn, Dr. W. H. Snook, T. J. Meloy, J. W. Livingston, Harvey Filey, Max Leuddemann, and others. In 1904 many more buildings and dwellings were built, like the Tucker blacksmith shop, 1905, Loucks Saloon and the Stevens and Cramer Saloon.

In 1904, Mr. Meloy built a two-story building and when it burned in 1939, it had housed the George Dee General Store. About 1905 the Madras Milling and Mercantile Company started building a general store. Max Putz, Henry Dietzel, and Simon Peter Conroy were a corporation and the writer was the first secretary of this company. After the store building (which has since been moved over on Main Street and known as the Irving-Turner Building), they started the flour mill. The writer at the time was working in the Charles Durham Mill up on Foley Creek and helped saw out most of the timbers and building material in this mill and store building. Max Putz being a carpenter and millwright, did most of the building work on these two buildings. The mill was run for several years, furnishing various brands of flour, all unbleached, as Mr. Dietzel did not believe that bleached flour was healthy (he was not far off), and of course there was quite a feed business at the time.

At the time that the flouring mill burned it was owned by Douglas Hood and Godfred Drexel. The building and warehouse burned in 1921.

It was not an uncommon thing to wake up in the morning to the jingle of freight bells as many of the freighters sure did get out in the morning. The principal reason for the freight bells was that the roads had many short curves, and the bells served as a warning which could be heard for some distance. All of the freight at that time had to come in that way and it was quite a sight to see some of the freight trains come in and at this time realize the things that were brought in by this method. Due to the conditions, the stores had to ship in quantities of merchandise in order to have sufficient supply. Flour was shipped to other points via freight teams.

A man named W. K. Brewster was the first photographer to set up a studio in Madras, which was in 1906. He built a building with a north light window, being where the lower Union Oil station is now located at Fifth and B Streets. He was here about five years, and was succeeded by O. Hedland who took more scenic pictures, including many of the railroad coming into Madras and many others. He had a post card business and sold thousands of cards all over the West.

Harry Keys and his wife, Myrtle, started the first confectionery store here in Madras on the east side of Fifth Street between C and D Streets. This was later turned into a pool hall in 1906-07. These people also built the square house now occupied by the Moore family as a rooming house. This house also was used as a part of the County Office after the removal of the County Seat from Culver to Madras in 1917. The pool hall mentioned was operated by Austin Culp and at another time by Perry Wible in 1913. Culp was one of the original instigators of the famous Fish Fry on the Deschutes River, was an ardent sportsman as well as a fisherman, and later moved to The Dalles, where he passed away in the late 1940's.

During the years 1902 and 1903, through the efforts of Archie

Mason, who had been in the contracting business, the idea was conceived of an automobile road from the end of the railroad to Bend. It was thought at that time that the Columbia Southern which was built by Mr. Lytle would not extend farther south than Shaniko.

They, with the improved road equipment of the times—horses of course and hand labor—built this road to about five miles south of Madras. A. W. Boyce and wife would not consent for them to go through his place and the road stopped there. The road crossed the Basin (Palmain) in a sort of southeast and northwest direction and on south up the Willow Creek draw, through the Chester E. Roush place and on a water grade towards the C. F. Smith place, or Rim Rock Springs.

Don Rea and Robert Rea, also A. E. Hammond, were interested in the new company; also a Mr. Johnson of Bend. They wanted to have transportation for their towns and they thought this was the complete answer.

The following is an excerpt from the Madras *Pioneer* files of April 20, 1905:

> Coming with a rush down the hill north of town with the roar of a steam engine, and giving a series of warning toots, which roused a general exclamation from dogs and chickens and a stretching of all kinds of necks, the big gasoline automobile belonging to the Central Oregon Transportation Company arrived in Madras last Friday evening, commanded by M. W. Taylor accompanied by W. A. Gill of the Gill Engine and Machine Co. of Port-

land, who built the machine, and Don P. Rea and Frank Lucas, and the monster was immediatly the center of attraction with Madras townspeople.

The big machine, while traveling from Shaniko, averaged a little over eight miles an hour over difficult roads and very much unsuited for this type of vehicle.

This auto is the largest ever constructed in the United States and is truly a monster machine, it weighing 6800 pounds.

It is 40-horse power, equipped with four engines which run in conjunction, but should any one of these engines break, the machine can still be propelled, providing the gearing is intact.

. . . It is difficult to state just when regular trips will be made over the auto route between Cross Keys and Bend, as the big machine will have to pass over the roadbed and locate any defects which may have been overlooked in the construction, and it may take several trips before all these obstructions are located.

A new road had been built a part of the way for the new gas automobile and the driver was a man by the name of Dewey. Something happened on this trip that was typical of the time. Mr. Dewey had asked a hitch hiker this side of Redmond to ride with him, and when they came across Crooked River over the old bridge and up on top Mr. Dewey had to stop for some mechanical trouble. When he was ready to start, he told the fellow to get in; but the fellow hesitated and said, "If it is all the same to you, I believe I will walk," indicating he did not think much of the gas buggy.

On this same trip they had stopped at the Perry Read stopping-place for dinner. Don Rea asked the girls, Lilly and Pearl, if they wanted to take a ride in an automobile, so they got in and rode down the road a couple of miles and then walked back home.

The car mentioned was built in Portland and made only a few trips from Shaniko to Bend. It was too unstable for the roads it had to travel over and too costly to operate at that time. The whole project was quite a pioneering job and probably set the standard, or helped, for future better roads and equipment.

The first time I came to Madras, was in February, 1904. The "White Elephant" was being built by Jerry Cramer and George Stevens, on the corner of Block 19. This became quite a place in after years and I finally became the owner of the property, later sold it, and it now belongs to Walter McCaulou (1954).

8

The first school was established in the Basin (Madras) in 1902, after the urgent need developed, and was located in a building the settlers built by donations, pie socials, etc. The first teacher in this one-room school that started in 1902 was Charles Crowfoot. This room soon became too small, and another room was added and the school term of 1904 was conducted in a two-room building and Mr. Crowfoot and a P. C. Fulton taught there that year. When the two-room building came into being, this was moved and forms a part of the present Catholic Church.

Another room was later added and in 1908 William R. Cook, P. C. Fulton, and Miss Elva J. Smith taught school that year. The larger square building was built in 1908 and many of the early teachers were residents and homesteaders in this vicinity.

The first building, becoming too small to accommodate the growing school population, was sold to H. K. W. Nisson, who moved it down to the west side of Fifth Street where he opened up a saloon and used it until the early railroad days.

The large two-story square building also became too small and about 1938 when irrigation came into being, the present brick building system started taking form. Our schools have expanded and along with the increase in population, the buildings have had to be enlarged and also the corps of teachers have had to be expanded. At this time, 1955, we have one of the best primary and secondary school systems in Central Oregon.

The first telephone came into Madras about 1905, when a line was brought in over the hills from Haycreek, connecting with the first through line from Shaniko to Prineville. The system at that time was operated by Jack Summers of Prineville, and the local station was first established in the John McTaggart and Charles E. Bye store at the corner of Fifth and C Streets. They also had a kind of rooming house and sometimes fed the public.

9

This question of moving the county seat has been written about many times and many of the factual details can be secured by reading both the Madras *Pioneer* and the Culver *Tribune,* both papers being published at that time.

The preliminary work began, of course, when the county division fight developed. This started about three or four years before it was actually placed on the ballot. There was much work and joking prior to that time. The boundary was a sticking point for a long time, but finally early in 1914, a group came to an agreement in Prineville where it should be. J. H. Haner, then interested in timber holdings and also in Crook County, having moved to Bend at a little later date, had much to do with the establishment of the boundary, especially along the southeastern part and along Grizzly Mountain, it being thought that the high points should be the lines and too considerable timber was allowed to remain in Crook County.

After the south boundary was set and the petitions were got out (the securing of names being a simple matter in this part of Crook County), and through an understanding with the part now Deschutes County, we were able to secure the signatures readily. At that time it required 65 percent of the vote in the part cut off and 35 percent in the part remaining, so through an arrangement it was decided that both Deschutes and Jefferson were to cut off from Crook at the same time and each one could give the other the required vote, so the people in Deschutes County filed their petition and both were on the ballot at the same time in November of 1914.

At the election, whether through a better campaign or of the need for the people of this section to have some say in spending their tax dollars, this part received the majority votes in its

134

own part and on the remaining part, so Jefferson County was thereby cut off as of January 1, 1915. At the same election concerning the part of Deschutes County, it was found that they received their 35 percent in the part to be left; but they did not receive the required 65 percent in the part to be cut off, so they lost out. But in another two years they tried again and it was carried.

The matter of a county court and other officers for the county was up to the governor of the state at that time. He was Governor Oswald West, who appointed William Boegli as judge, John M. King and Roscoe Gard as commissioners. They in turn selected the county seat. It developed that Mr. Boegli had Culver in mind, John M. King had Metolius in mind, and Roscoe Gard had Madras in mind. Madras at the time was larger in population than the other two. A meeting was arranged at Metolius by the county court at which there was a large gathering and the voting started. The three members of the court voted many times; the law stated that they had to select the county seat. An adjournment was taken and it was a deadlock until after some 280 ballots had been taken, when John M. King switched to Culver. This was a hard blow to the Metolius community.

Through the efforts of the owners of the Culver Townsite and the people interested there, a building was put up before the next two years and the officers were moved into it. At the election in 1916 the matter was placed on the ballot as to where the permanent county seat should be, and Madras, having the largest population and being nearer the center of the county, received a majority vote and the fight began in the courts.

135

A suit was brought by the Culver people in the circuit court, a temporary injunction was issued (the matter being heard before Crook County Judge Guyon Springer), and it came into the circuit court with Judge T. E. J. Duffy presiding. The hearing was held and he took the matter under advisement, this being in December of that year; and he held it until the Saturday afternoon before Monday, the first day of January, 1915, when he dissolved the injunction and for removal the following Monday, the first day of January, as required by law. No one thought of this before. Most of the officers elected to the office by a vote of the people were favorable to Madras. The other officers, having been appointed by the county court, were in favor of still residing in Culver.

The actual removal came about in this way. On Saturday evening our attorney, W. S. U'Ren of Portland, heard of the injunction being dissolved and called one of our representatives, Orin A. Pearce, and advised him that we were at liberty to appear Monday morning at Culver (it being Monday, January 1st, as required by law) and remove the county seat to Madras. Of course the feeling at Culver was very bitter at the outcome, and they felt they were entitled to hold the county seat after putting up their building. The principals in this were A. C. Young, W. C. Barber, District Attorney W. P. Meyers, and others.

At a meeting of those from Madras, it was decided that we should not go after the records until time for opening of the offices Monday morning. This was on the advice of Mr. U'Ren who came up Sunday to be with us at the time of removal, and it was well that he was, as at his advice probably some incidents

136

were avoided. For instance, some of the boys were rather jubilant, having imbibed a little too much and were in a very belligerent mood—particularly Hap McLauthlin and Alfred Parkey. It took several of us to restrain them from using strong-arm methods after some remarks were passed by Attorney Meyers. As the removal of the records proceeded, he came into the hall and stated that he would have all of those participating in the penitentiary in 24 hours. Attorney U'Ren was standing on the stairs and called out, "Go to it boys. I will defend you."

Many other incidents took place at the time. One was when Mr. Black, the late sheriff, refused to give up his office until a complete audit was made and would not let anyone into his office. One of the boys from Madras engaged him in a heated conversation and while his back was turned, Austin Culp stepped up behind him and took the Sheriff's sign off the door.

Another incident that was rather funny was when Mrs. Meyers, the wife of the district attorney, came into the hallway and began taking down the names of those from Madras participating in the removal and she came up to Uncle Bobbie Barnett, who was looking on rather than working. She came to him and asked, "What might your name be?" Uncle Bobbie with his chin whiskers bobbing up and down looked a little surprised and replied, "I do not know that it is any business of yours!"

Very few of the Culver people appeared while the work was going on. The operation was well organized; cars to carry the books and things from the clerks office, heavier wagons and sleighs to load on the furniture, safes and so on. The boys with the teams left home early in the morning and nothing was touched until the regular opening of the offices. At the proper time the work began and was carried out rapidly, the writer being in a car that made a round trip before any of the Culver people appeared. It was stated there that many of them remained up until midnight, thinking that we would come after midnight, so they were slow in appearing on Monday morning.

Monday being a non-judicial day, no further injunction could be procured so the moving proceeded and after the proper audit and other adjustments, all of the books and equipment were moved to Madras, where they were placed in many buildings on a temporary basis. The county clerk's office was in a building that belonged to Dr. Haile, the sheriff's office was in a building (formerly the White Elephant Saloon) belonging to Howard W. Turner, and the other offices were mostly in the homes of those who were elected the new officers.

In 1918 and 1919 the present court house was built. This was not built by the county, but by the City of Madras and if the county was not to use it, then it was to be for the city. The cost of the building was about $9,500. Improvements have been made to this building from time to time and it has been in continous use by the county to the present time.

Much had been said and written about the stealing of the county seat from Culver, but this was not the case. The people voted for the removal to Madras in a legal election, a hearing was had in the courts, injunction issued, and a hearing on it, and the decision was in favor of Madras as the county seat. The removal was strictly in accordance with the law at the time and no stealing of the county seat was involved.

Madras

10

Along in the early summer of 1910, while I was the mayor of the City of Madras and along with the other troubles incident to the railroad construction and riffraff, and while there were close to 3,500 people in Madras and some 3,000 men outside in various camps along the Deschutes line, there was an incident that was out of the ordinary.

We had hired a day policeman and a night policeman—A. J. Weston and Bogue Harper, both large men and hardboiled, having had considerable experience around saloons with handling of the rough element. They got into a shooting scrape on the main street in the middle of the day. There were several shots fired each and both men were hit, Weston through a flesh wound on the right side (the bullet did not enter the intestines or stomach). Harper was hit in the head and hand and several bones were broken. One man was taken to Dr. Snook and the other to Dr. Long. This created quite a sensation and was in all of the papers.

The real cause of the escapade was over which one would be the night man and who should be the day man. This was settled, and later one of them quit the force and Frank Stangland was hired in his place. Also, later on, the other quit and Frank was the only man on the force for a long time. Frank was the man who was ordered by the city council to clean out the red-light district.

The early peace officers and other county officials filled in, in many different capacities as time went on. The first officer that I

139

recall was Frank Elkins (later sheriff of Crook County) who lived out on the Agency Plains, as deputy sheriff, this being in Crook County. The first sheriff in Crook County was James Blackley who lived at Prineville. This was in 1882.

Then a few years later Vern Stanton became deputy sheriff after Frank Elkins was elected sheriff. Mr. Stanton lived in Madras and officiated in the northern part of Crook County for some ten years or until the county was divided. In Madras we had as the first justice of the peace, M. C. Mason, living at the north edge of town. In 1905 Frank J. Brooks was elected to that office and served several years. About 1912, Howard W. Turner took over the job for Madras precinct and was in that office about 20 years.

The early justice of the peace acted as coroner and by virtue of his office could perform marriage ceremonies; some of course did not stand up. Also, about 1908, the writer was appointed clerk of the U. S. District Court (United States Commissioner) and held that office nearly 20 years. After the town was incorporated, John H. Jackson, having moved into Madras from his ranch, became city recorder, and being ex-officio justice of the peace, was very active in that office.

During the terms of these officials many funny things happened, one of which I will relate. The writer, as stated, was U. S. Commissioner. This was during the first World War when we had several pro-Germans in and around this section. About a half-hour before train time, when the train for Portland was due to depart at 9:00 p. m., the deputy U. S. marshal came in with a pro-German prisoner and wanted to get him on the train that evening. Knowing that I could not get the papers made up in time, I told the deputy if he could not get on the train he would have to wait until the following night. So I suggested that I call the railroad agent, A. F. Shugert, and have him contact the dispatcher and see if the train could be held a short time. This I did, and of course he thought it would not be possible. However, after assuring him of the details about the pro-German prisoner, he did so. The reply soon came for him to hold the train for three hours if necessary, to get the prisoner on the train, and it was done.

There were strenuous times for these officers in picking up the bad men, especially during the railroad days (with 13 saloons operating in town). Most of us were out on patrol when the notorious Kelley was on the loose and came up through Central Oregon. During the dry cycle and local option, which was after 1919, the enforcement of the prohibition laws was a headache, with all of the stills located all over the country. After the county was divided, most of the work devolved on the sheriffs and many interesting things could be told by Ira Black, the first sheriff of Jefferson County, and James Wood, H. C. Topping, J. M. Freeman, Bern Gard, Ira P. Holcomb, and Henry Dussault.

11

Madras experienced several disastrous fires during its existence. Along about 1907 we had several small fires and the only way of fighting them at that time was an organized bucket brigade. In some instances, by getting on the job early, we were able to do quite effective work.

The City of Madras was incorporated in 1910 and we soon commenced to talk and work towards the seeking of a supply of water. Wells were drilled and dug; one well was drilled to a depth of over 400 feet and only a small amount of water was found. Then along about this time a water system was installed and we were able to get some water for domestic and fire prevention purposes. Our first reservoir had a capacity of about 150,000 gallons. In the meantime we bought some chemical engines that we hauled by hand, and were they man killers! In several fires we used them quite effectively. One of these fires was the Christian Church, which caught fire from paint rags. The damage was mostly in the upper part where the flames were contained and the chemicals saved the building. This was in 1910.

About the next large fire was the Hahn Hotel, and the store and the livery barns of Hood and Stantion. Very little insurance was carriied in those days. This was in 1913, soon after the electric juice came into Madras. The writer was on the end of a hose line when a wire broke and dropped into the water, and some fellows received very heavy jolts of electricity, not a very pleasant experience.

The water systems in the beginning were of wood pipe and later on of cement, neither of which were at all satisfactory. Later on, iron pipe was installed. During this period when we were short of water, the fire fighting was handicapped, as was the case when the Green Hotel burned in 1922. This was a very hot fire, being well under way in the middle of the day when discovered, and we had a hard time saving the building across the street as well as the Main Street Garage. Pictures were taken of the old bank building on the east side of the street where the boys, after the mains were emptied, used buckets and finally saved the building.

On July 12, 1923, we had a rather spectacular **fire** in one of the Standard Oil storage tanks that had been moved up on the present site from the Oregon Trunk site in the southwest part of Madras. This tank caught fire from the stick that Glen Stockton was using to measure the gas in the tank (static electricity, because it was a hot and sultry afternoon). Of course by the time we were able to get up there with our chemical engines, the upper part of the tank was very hot. Knowing that cement was good for stopping oil fires, we had some sent up and with the assistance of Lewis H. Irving, the writer was able to stop the fire in a short time. This was due to the fact that the tank was always full and could not accumulate any amount of gas. Had it been partly full, it would have blown up long before.

In 1924 we had another conflagration by a fire starting on the west side of Fifth Street in Block No. 19 and spreading across the street, taking all north of Dr. Snook's drug store on the east side and from the Abstract office on the west. This included McTaggert & Bye picture show, pool hall, confectionery store, and others on the east side. On the west side, Baldy Nisson's Saloon, two rooming houses, S. J. Sellars' Saloon, butcher shop, two restaurants, and the First National Bank. This fire wiped out most of the center part of the town. The fire equipment from Bend was brought down on a flat car, but was too late to do any good; however, many people from Redmond and Prineville came down and were of some assistance in saving other buildings. During this fire, the telephone office was destroyed and Mrs. Julie Hobson-Dussault remained at her post until the wires went down and the fire was on the roof of the building. She received a medal from the telephone company for her act.

Another old landmark was razed in July, 1939—the old Meloy building, better known as the Central Oregon Mercantile building (R. T. Olson), then being operated by George Dee as a general merchandise store. The building had been built by T. J. Meloy in 1906. On the porch in front was where E. H. Harriman, the noted railroad builder, made his statement, "You people will never see a railroad through Central Oregon. There is not enough tonnage to justify one."

The writer was present and heard him make this statement; however, in about two years or less, when James J. Hill started building down on the Deschutes, Mr. Harriman evidently changed his mind.

Along about this time the flouring mill burned. This mill was started by Max Putz, Henry Dietzel, and Simon Peter Conroy in 1905, along with a large store building. The company was called the Madras Milling and Merchantile Company and was operated for around 20 years. The store building was sold and moved over on Fifth Street by A. C. Sanford, who used it for a mercantile establishment. The building was moved by Ed Harbin of Prineville.

Madras

Several small fires of dwellings and other buildings occurred but those above mentioned were the principal ones, and with the limited equipment, it would seem that the volunteer department did very well in holding the fires to a minimum.

Speaking of the flouring mill, two partners in the company, Putz and Dietzel, being of German descent, were very thrifty and very much set in their ways. However, the writer seemed to be well in their favor and acted as a secretary for the Madras Milling Company. During its early operations, beginning in 1907, I did not have anything to do with the store. The company failed and Mr. Putz moved to California. Mr. Conroy moved to Vancouver, B. C., and Mr. Dietzel refinanced the project and later took in Fritz Drexel, and later on Douglas Hood became interested in the mill. Henry Dietzel died and Mr. Hood and Mr. Drexel were the owners at the time of the fire which destroyed the whole property in 1921.

Mr. Dietzel was born in America and was educated in Germany, then came back to the States. His attitude and beliefs were for Germany, of course, according to the time that he was attending school in that country. So when the First World War came on we had quite a time with several pro-Germans. It took some personal restraint in his case, but he did appear at the celebration the evening that the Armistice was signed.

A short time after the mill burned here at Madras, the flouring mill at Metolius, operated by Henry Seethoff, burned about 1924. This was quite a pathetic thing, because there was no hydrant close to the mill. Someone phoned to Madras that the mill at Metolius was on fire and the writer and Glenn Stockton,

145

who was handy, jumped into a car and drove to the fire and loaded in a few sections of hose. When we arrived at the mill at Metolius, we found that the nearest hydrant was some 1500 feet away. Even with the hose they had at their fire hall and with what we had, it was inadequate to reach the blaze. We were up to the second floor but there was nothing we could do to stop the blaze which started in the upper end of the elevators, supposedly, but the writer believes it was a still that exploded.

There were several quite large fires at Metolius and also at Culver where the Madras fire department was called and assisted as much as possible. Now, with the improved systems and added equipment, the fire loss can be reduced very materially.

Another fire that I failed to mention was the livery stable barns that belonged to G. V. Stanton and Douglas Hood, in which several horses were burned. At least one was supposed to have been a very valuable race horse that had been left in the barn overnight. This was in the fall of 1917. This was started from someone sleeping in the barn. They thought it was a transient and that he had been smoking. This was quite a loss, and no insurance those days.

During the early days most of the horse shoeing was done by someone on the ranch; however, in 1905, the first blacksmith shop was established here in Madras by Frank J. Brooks, who homesteaded up the canyon southeast about three miles. Along about this time the people began to require that their horses be shod, especially the horses on freight teams. The going price at that time was $1.50 all around.

The next shop was opened up by Thomas B. Tucker a year or so later. He had been a homesteader down on the Deschutes River above the Dizney place. He and his family moved into town so the children could go to school. He was one of the first councilmen and was active in civil affairs. Tucker took in a a partner, Austin Culp; both were ardent fishermen. Mr. Tucker was drowned near his old homestead while on a fishing trip.

12

Speaking of councilmen and city government, the election to incorporate was held January 31, 1910, and on March 2, 1910, the county court of Crook County confirmed the election for the incorporation and also for the following officers to serve the city until the general election:

Howard W. Turner, mayor

J. H. Jackson, city recorder

J. M. Conklin, city treasurer

Austin W. Culp, city marshal

The following were elected aldermen: W. H. Cook, W. Riley Cook, S. E. Gray, T. A. Long, T. B. Tucker, and Warren Smith.

The first charter was unanimously adopted February 14, 1911. There were many nights of strenuous work in getting the ordinances set up and spread. Lots of mistakes were made, but later corrected, so that for several years things moved along very well under the various administrations with the coming and going of the population. After the water was assured, from 1940 on, the population started to increase so that many changes had to be made in order to keep up with the increase. Many funny things happened in the early days, some of which might be told, but a lot that should not be, as long as the names of the people are common in this area.

In 1922 we had quite a spirited race for the city offices. Mrs. Grace Shugert ran on the ticket for mayor, with a platform, "More Water for Wash Day". Mrs. Millie Morrow ran for councilman. The feeling seemed to be against a woman holding public office, so that neither was elected at this time; however, Mrs. Morrow was later elected and served as one of the city councilmen. She also served for several years as one of the directors of the First National Bank of Madras, the only bank in this section that did not fare in the depression.

Some of the early merchants were T. J. Meloy, J. P. Hahn, Simon Peter Conroy, Henry Dietzel, Max Putz, Alfred C. Sanford, Lena M. Lamb, Chester E. Roush, John Robinson, James Robinson, John McTaggart, Howard W. Turner, E. C. Bye, Lloyd Hunter, James Rice, R. T. Olson, Dizney and Hall, and later on, George Dee.

The first saloon in Madras was established by M. L. Loucks (Tice) in 1904, followed by the Cramer and Stevens. Later on several others came and went until the railroad days, when we had a rash of them, while this was in dry territory. Some of the names most common were Beany Sellers, McCormack Brothers, Baldy Nisson. At the high point, there were thirteen saloons open and doing business in Mardas.

One night in the winter of 1906-07, while the mercury was down below zero, a man by the name of George Rankin pumped

148

water all night to keep from freezing to death. He had imbibed too much, the saloons had closed up, and he was run out of the livery barns. He did not have any home, so that this was the next best thing on such a cold night. The writer happened to be trying to sleep in a room upstairs not far from there and the squeaky pump kept me awake most of the night. I did not know what was happening until the next morning.

<h2 style="text-align:center">13</h2>

At one time we had two banks in Madras—the Madras State Bank and the First National Bank of Madras. Both did well until the depression, when in 1926 the Madras State Bank closed its doors, creating quite a stir among the farmers and business-men of the communtiy. The First National Bank remained open all during the depression of 1933 except when the President and the Federal Reserve Board declared all banks closed.

It might be interesting to relate a few things in this respect. The writer, being in charge of the bank at that time, learned late one Saturday night that the Madras State Bank was not going to open Monday morning. After consultation with the cashier, Jesse J. Gard, we found that we could not get additional funds to take care of our customers until Wednesday morning. Mr. Gard went to Portland Monday, as all of our securities were locked in the time vault until Monday morning. He secured the extra cash necessary after we had paid for guards to come from Seattle and also to have the postmaster at the depot to sign for the money off the train early in the morning. That morning we piled all of the cash behind the cages and called in about ten men from the street and asked them to come in and count the money and then go out after banking hours and tell the people that they could get their money if they desired. This seemed to keep the people well satisfied as far as the First National Bank was concerned and we lost only one account, which came back in a few days.

The Madras State Bank was organized about 1909 and was operated as a state bank with Mr. J. M. Conklin as the first cashier. Banks in those days had to make money some way and the prevailing interest rate was 10% and sometimes I have known it to be 22% per month. It was said that Mr. Conklin charged for cashing his own checks. It was very expensive those days to have money shipped from one place to another. The bank was located on the east side of Fifth Street where the Standard Oil station is now located. Later on it was sold to some interests, headed by Orin A. Pearce, J. C. Corruthers, and R. T. Olson.

A new building was built at the present bank location. The building contractor at that time was Dusty Rhodes. During the vault construction several local people were working on the building and among them was Lester Pummell, an old-time homesteader who had moved into Madras. He was told to take the forms down. He tried to tell the contractor that it was not set enough, but the contractor insisted. When the forms were removed, the whole top of the vault fell and pinned Mr. Pummell under brick and concrete; however some of the forms fell so that he was not badly injured and the writer was the first person there to help him get out.

In 1902 Don P. Rea was appointed the first clerk of the United

Madras

States District Court (United States Commissioner) to take filings on the homesteads and other land filing of the time. Later he was succeeded by Frank Osborn, and in 1908 Howard W. Tu*i*ner was appointed to this position and held it for a little over 20 years.

Many interesting cases came up and were disposed of in the way of land contests and filings, a particular one being the filing made by the Hill Railroad interests on the site where the railroad now crosses Crooked River. Matt Clark, Johnson D. Porter, one of the Hill boys, and a driver came into Madras late one night and routed the writer out of bed and had him complete the filings for this land by which was known as scrip (Northern Pacific Scrip). This was in the winter time and they were in one of the old E. M. & F. cars without a top. They started for The Dalles, the location of the district land office, and arrived there just as the office opened. It was learned that the Union Pacific (Harriman interests) came in about an hour later with a filing for the same tract of land. The first filing was allowed. The bridge was built at that location and it is still under the Hill Lines control.

The mail service into Madras, around 1902 and before, was very limited. The first mail to Prineville, Haycreek, Willow Creek, and the surrounding country came through the Basin (now Madras). One of the early carriers was Edward Campbell, who carried mail from The Dalles by way of Dufur, Wapinitia, Simnasho, and Warm Springs. The roads at that time were not as good as they were later on, because they were merely Indian trails with ferrying across the Deschutes River.

After 1900 when the railroad came into Shaniko, the mail for

151

this area included Warm Springs. It came via stage to Haycreek and was taken out from there to the residents in the Basin and vicinity. The first route, however, was by way of the Youngs—the post office was operated by Lewis A. Young and the carrier was John Lockard, a crippled person but he seemed to get along very well. After the railroad came up the Willow Creek Canyon in 1911 the mail came into Madras and was then distributed from here to Haycreek, Grizzly, Ashwood, Kilts, and Lamonta. In 1954, a new truck service was started directly from Portland over the Warm Springs cut-off, giving this section adequate service.

14

The coming of the railroad into Central Oregon opened up a new epoch in the Central Oregon area, affecting the whole country as far east as Burns and the John Day Valley. The writer had a rather peculiar yet interesting experience.

During the winter of 1906-07, I was a guest at the Hahn Hotel for a few weeks and had the pleasure of becoming acquainted with a man who was ostensibly running all over the country on foot, taking pictures of the beauties he highly extolled, and went under the name of John F. Swanson. We became quite well acquainted, usually eating our meals together and spending several evenings together. I thought little of the experience and did not connect the circumstances until later on. In the fall of 1909 the writer and wife drove a team into Shaniko, on our way to Portland, and when we arrived in Shaniko that evening, we learned that the first carload of construction machinery had ar-

Loading the stage at Madras in 1905 or 1906. Jim Sears is holding the lead horse.
Doug Hood is the man in the overcoat.

Big locomotive No. 702 and all the derbied dignitaries when the coming of the Oregon Trunk
to Madras was celebrated on February 15, 1911. There was a welcoming crowd of 6,000. It had
cost Hill and his Oregon Trunk $10,000,000 to come from the Columbia to Madras. Harriman,
in that railroad contest to tap Central Oregon, had spent $8,000,000.

Main Street of Lamonta. The first post office in 1890 was named Desert. It was soon moved and then was closed in 1892. With its new name of Lamonta, meaning mountain, it was reborn in 1896.

Left—Hotel Lamonta, owned by M. T. Cowan, remembered as a very jolly fellow, who also owned the post office and one of the store buildings. The hotel was burned down in 1914.

Right—The Campbell Stage in 1896. From 1869 to 1902 John E. Campbell carried the mail from Wapinitia through Warm Springs, and Haystack, to Prineville. He also operated the Deschutes River ferry, at Ferry Canyon, from 1895 to 1905.

rived in Grass Valley. It seemed that everyone was either celebrating or immediately became interested in the construction of
the Oregon Trunk Railway, the Hill Lines, and there was no
sleeping in that town that night.

The work was carried on rapidly and very soon after the starting of the Oregon Trunk Railway, the Union Pacific Railroad
tried to beat the Hill Lines to some of the important and contro-
versial points along the right-of-way. Both roads were under
construction at the same time; some of the rights-of-way were
settled in the courts after many fights. Firearms, dynamite, and
black powder were used in trying to keep the other fellow out.

The Hill Lines came up the canyon and had stations at Coleman, Mecca, Vanora, Pelton, and then Madras. The Harriman
Lines started with South Junction, Gateway, Paxton, and then
Madras, coming in around the bend northeast of Madras and onto
the Agency Plains, crossing Willow Creek Canyon, and on south
to Metolius. The Hill Lines from Madras built on south to
Metolius where they expected to have a division point and build
quite a town. It was said that the Madras Townsite Company
asked too much for the right-of-way and the railroad just skirted
the town on the west side of the Basin. Later on, the railroad
operated into Bend, Oregon. However, the road was constructed
by the Hill Lines.

When the Oregon Trunk Line (Hill Lines) came into Madras,
February 15, 1911, we had a big celebration on that day. In the
evening at a dinner meeting, when all of the head men there were
introduced, I learned that John F. Swanson was in reality John
F. Stevens, the engineer that I had spent time with during the

winter of 1906-07 in the hotel. He remarked that he was wondering if I would recognize him which I did. In his remarks he made the statement that the Oregon Trunk Railway cost (from the Columbia River to Madras) $10,000,000, and the Harriman interests also stated that their line cost better than $8,000,000. With the construction of these lines, the hardest fight in the world had taken place at that time.

The construction of these roads imposed many hardships on the people of Madras, as the town mushroomed, with quite a numerous tough element of people. During the time of the work on the incorporation, we estimated that there were at least 5,000 people here, including those in the camps close to town and the several thousand laborers on both roads close to Madras. For all the crowds, we felt that we came through very well. After this element drifted away, we settled down to a gradual growth due to our agriculture area round about.

When the railroad came to Madras (February 15, 1911), something like $1,500 was raised locally. The day was ideal, people were in their shirt sleeves, the parade was nearly as long as the street; and we estimated that there were around 6,000 people here for the pot roast and speaking which included many of the railroad men from St. Louis, Chicago, St. Paul, and other cities. This was the celebration of the Oregon Trunk Line.

The head cook for the pot roast was S. J. (Beany) Sellers, one of the saloon keepers. He did a good job in roasting about two tons of beef in the ground, cooking beans, potatoes and other vegetables in the ground, salad by the barrel; also coffee by the quantity and around 900 loaves of bread. I think this was the largest celebration that Madras had for many years, at least as far as enthusiasm was concerned.

Early in the summer of 1911, the writer was called to Portland by the railroad company and attended a dinner in the Oregon Hotel at which Al G. Barnes was present. After much talk and argument, Mr. Barnes decided to bring his circus into Central Oregon. He was afraid of not making expenses, and asked me if I thought the people would attend if he charged $1. I told him I thought they would. (When the show was over I asked him if he was satisfied and he was).

We had to furnish considerable road construction on the old grade from the depot, several water wagons, and about forty head of horses to help them bring their circus from the depot downtown on the then vacant lot back of the Madras Main Street Garage. We had to strengthen the bridges, cut off some curves, but with the aid of the extra horses, the elephants, water wagons, and the extra price, there were about 4,000 in attendance. It was a sight never to be forgotten for anyone who just watched the crowd. Many had never seen anything like a circus. People came from Burns, Lakeview, and of course nearer places. After the evening show we managed to get them all loaded and on their way before daylight.

The writer had great sport watching some of the youngsters, and also some of the gambling games going on. The short-change artists sure did work plenty so I felt that no one lost any great amount of money. Thus we had the first circus coming into Central Oregon on the Deschutes Railroad on May 11, 1911.

15

Our social activities during the early part of the century were varied of course, mostly man-made, so to speak. We did not have to travel so far to have a good time, unless we made a night of it, as I did the first night I came to Madras for a dance in February, 1904. I came over from Haycreek in a spring wagon and team; there was no open road, just a trail with 13 gates. I know, because I opened them both ways.

We were all night and the dance was held in the second story of the J. P. Hahn Hotel that was not completed. The next morning we wanted breakfast before returning home, so went down to Tom Meloy's Place and Mrs. Meloy fixed us up the following: Coffee that would hold up an egg, sour biscuits that were really sour, cold side pork and cold potatoes, with butter that had seen better days. But I guess we did not complain. I think we paid 35 cents for the experience.

Dances, pie socials, literary societies, spelling bees, as well as church activities were the principal amusements. Later on came the first picture show in 1910. It seemed that the people who could not go too far for their entertainment just made it near at home and I feel that at that time the pleasure of meeting and being with people was of more importance than at the present time.

A few times the entertainment might have seemed a little rough on some people, such as the time a group of ladies had all of their dinner stolen from the Higdon kitchen and taken over in the back room of the bank where the boys sure had a swell feast.

Madras

It happened like this: after a rabbit drive, the rabbits were shipped to Portland and the returns were used for a stag dinner to which the ladies were not invited. They thought they would have a stag dinner of their own, so it was decided to have it at the Charles Higdon House, the house just south of the picture show. The time was evening, being very soon after the electric juice came to Madras. Warren Smith saw to it that all of the lights in town were conveniently out, then there appeared a group of musicians who serenaded the ladies in the front yard. The ladies left the kitchen for outside, and when that happened, the boys dropped into the kitchen and lifted everything available in the way of food, even to the hot water on the stove. There were some stormy times over this among some of the couples, which became rather serious.

Another time, C. P. (Doc) Wilson bought two nice turkeys for Thanksgiving and had them hanging on his back porch, when a couple of ladies saw fit to purloin them, and at the proper time cooked them. A big dinner was held in the hall at which Doc Wilson was invited, as well as his wife. She was in on it, and Doc was called on to make a speech after it soaked in that he was furnishing the turkey for the dinner. His wife whispered to him to get up and make a talk and he replied, loud enough to be heard by several, "Sis, I just cain't do it".

Along about the same time, chickens, roasting pigs, and other things disappeared and usually turned up at some public dinner or the party was invited to some person's house to help eat it. Another source of enjoyment was the sharivari after a couple was married.

157

Of course we always had plenty of fishing those days, and it was quite a chore to get up, say at 3:00 a.m., drive down to the river with that team and wagon and perhaps get back, wet and tired after dark; but it was fun as you could catch plenty of fish and did not have to work so hard for them. Hunting was another sport engaged in by many. Horse racing and bucking contests all came in for their share according to the desires of those who participated.

About 1909 a couple of young women came out here from Seattle to teach school in the Lamonta country and finally took up homesteads. It was a sight to see them coming to town with their old ring-boned and spavined horse, one women using the whip and the other driving with the reins as high as her head. I do not think they will object to my using their names (both are alive at this time) : Miss Matilda McCrudden and Mrs. Emily G. McDougal. The latter married Andrew Morrow, a large livestock man of that time.

16

We had quite a few violent deaths in Madras and the immediate vicinity. The first one I recall hearing about was in 1905. The first fall that I came into the country, Jim Sticona, an Indian, was killed by his companion, Corbett Holt, also an Indian. This happened at the head of an old grade going to the Agency Plains. It seems that they secured a bottle of apple-jack, which was potent as far as alcohol was concerned, and it worked on the Indians to the extent that while riding up the grade on their

158

horses they became embroiled in arguments and Holt hit Sticona over the head with the bottle and the latter never recovered from the blow.

The next was that of the Preston Crissman murder. It seems that he was very much out of his head at times. He had a homestead up on the Plains not far out, and seemed to have a hobby thinking that someone was trying to kill him. He would run around at night with his rifle, going to people's houses and scaring them to the extent that many people carried a gun. This went on for several years until 1904, when, as I understand, he had an argument with George Hurt-Huntington, who just happened to beat him to the draw with the results that Crissman died almost instantly.

James Magness, a nephew of Mrs. Gray and a cousin of Mrs. Effa Pillette, came to Madras soon after the town of Palmain was platted and lived around here for several years. He married a redheaded woman, Myrtle Borden, and they had one child. Their early married life was rather stormy. He did jobs as carpenter and general worker, turned very despondent, and finally committed suicide in a tent located over on the corner south of the Harris building.

It was a hot afternoon, in 1908. J. H. Jackson was the acting coroner for this section in Crook County. The writer took down the testimony in the same tent where the body laid as it had fallen. There were several witnesses examined and I wrote out the testimony of several pages on an old-style closed typewriter. The conditions and the odor were not too pleasant; however, it had to be done at that time where the death happened.

Another suicide was that of a woman who was enamored over a man on the railroad construction in 1910. She hired Vern Stanton to take her out to one of the railroad camps and while she was talking to her man, she pulled a gun and shot him. He was not hurt badly, but on the way back to Madras, under charge of Stanton, who was a deputy sheriff, she took a severe poison and died in the back of the drug store before the doctor could get there.

Another murder happened down below Vanora during the railroad construction. A foreman, I do not know his name, was killed by a foreigner who had been discharged by the foreman. The murderer came into Madras, had his breakfast and then started south. He was trailed and was captured in a wheat field on the Charles Winters place near the German cemetery, west of Metolius.

We had several deaths from smallpox, having had several epidemics of it along in 1909 and 1911. The first epidemic we had was rather severe and quite a number of people caught it.

After one death from smallpox, we attempted to close down things in the nature of gatherings and succeeded very well. One church failed to cooperate and the authorities had to use stringent measures. The church people felt they were being discriminated against, but the State Health Department offered to send up the Militia if we could not handle it. One of the councilmen was appointed to be at the church on Sunday to see that there was no gathering. Some started to rush him and he stood on the porch and said that the first one who stepped up would go sprawling on the ground. He was a big man and meant it. There was no church nor other gatherings for some little time, and the epidemic died down, with loss of only two transients.

17

Speaking of churches, the Methodist Church was built largely through the efforts of Mr. and Mrs. William A. Ellis and their close friends, including the Masons and Shutts , in 1908. Some of the funds were contributed by a patron, Daniel Fraylic of New York City. This church has since been rebuilt and improved and has been quite an influence in the community. It has had its ups and downs; of late years the congregation has grown so that additional rooms have been added, also a basement. Very few of the old original people are now living.

The Christian Church was built in 1909 through the influence of several people, including Mr. and Mrs. Fred Green and family, W. R. Cook and family, Mrs. James Watts and her relatives, the Ramsey family. They had a hard time keeping up for a while due to the poor times and lack of cooperation during the depression; however, this church also was quite an influence in the community. At this time a regular pastor is employed and a large congregation is the rule from all over the county.

The Baptist Church that was located out at Mud Springs was moved into Madras at an early date, about 1912, and has become a large congregation.

The Catholic Church, as I have stated, purchased the two-room school house that became too small and has used the same for church purposes until the new St. Patrick's Church was built in 1956.

Several other denominations have since come in and built churches. The new church buildings are a credit to any community.

During the early part of April, 1906, while driving down at the saw mill on the Deschutes River located at the Cowles Orchard, Charles Durham had passed away and I was trying to close out quite a lot of the lumber and get things in shape to turn over the estate. I was out early one day running the planer. It was a nice warm morning and I was working in my shirt sleeves. I was alone in the mill at the time, facing the rimrock and the saddle on the reservation, when I noticed some dark clouds coming over through that saddle, but soon discovered that it was dust and along with the dust seemed to follow a cold wave of air. Before an hour had passed, I had to get my overcoat and did not go to work in the afternoon as the thermometer was down to about zero. It killed a lot of young livestock and injured a lot of grain that spring.

Another blow that topped them all since I have been in Oregon, was in March, 1931. One Tuesday morning the wind came up and blew harder until the climax that night and Wednesday morning. The dust was so thick that we could hardly see across the street and the dust was so dense in many houses that one could not see across the room. Several families had to go to other places in order to exist. Many cars were stalled and the paint was ruined on lots of cars. This blow damaged millions of feet of

162

timber in this area and closed the roads for several days. On Wednesday afterneen the wind stopped suddenly and there seemed to be a sort of vacuum for about three or four hours, then it started to blow the other way. At first the wind came from the northeast and at last blew from the southwest.

It was found that the yellow dust of the first day came from as far east as Montana. At our house we had company from San Francisco. Though the house was fairly tight, we could not see across the room and the lights were dull. The damage to the crops was heavy, fall grain was blown out, and the fields had been swept clean of the topsoil in many places. In certain areas it was possible to see the effects of the storm for many years. At the time, ships reported the red dust out on the Pacific Ocean. Since 1931 we have had several very hard winds but none as hard as that one.

It was very cold the winter of 1884. Lots of livestock died and at least one person in this vicinity died. In 1919 there was another very cold winter. As nearly as could be found, it was 47° below zero and the snow was nearly four feet deep on the level. Since that time we have had several winters that were very mild, with very little snow, as was the case of the winter of 1954-55.

My first visit to the Cove was in the spring of 1907, when Al Zeigler and I started out one Sunday morning from Cowles-Durham sawmill down near the present Highway Bridge. We had two horses and started up the river, crossed Willow Creek near the mouth and had quite a time getting across because of the rimrocks.

Along about 2:00 p.m. we found a nester (homesteader), Ed

Graham, and we finally persuaded his wife to give us something to eat. Was it good—bacon and eggs! Also we fed our horses. From there we started south and followed that direction until we finally came to a trail leading down from the top. (The Grahams lived on the east side of Round Butte). We did not find the trail off the rimrock and ambled up the canyon until dark caught up with us. We found an overhanging rock with sand under it and tried to sleep there during the night. The sand became very hard before morning and the breeze became cool.

As soon as it was light enough, we started back down the trail and found the trail breaking off the rimrock and finally found Opal Springs, which as far as I can learn, was discovered by Mr. Orla Hale. When we were there, the *opals* were boiling up from the bottom, thousands of them! We took a can on a stick that happened to be there and dipped up quite a number and brought them home. Wonderful springs and water for breakfast.

We stayed down in the canyon until about 11:00 a.m., came up on top before it became too warm, started directly east and came first to Mr. Elon Grout's place, a homesteader. He was not even going to let us feed our horses and was not going to let his wife get us anything to eat, although we were willing to pay for both. We finally prevailed on them for both, and that evening we made it over to the Read Ranch where we put up for the night. The next day we rode back to the mill.

This was my first trip off the roads in what I had been told was a desert country. Soon after, the country filled up with homesteaders, there being someone on nearly ever 160 acres. This of course made business good here in Madras. However, with adverse weather conditions, the lands soon drifted into large holdings.

Opal Springs has been greatly changed in latter years by the use of the water for domestic use, being pumped to the upper levels and piped over the country and also into Madras for domestic use.

19

The Madras *Pioneer,* the only newspaper in Jefferson County for a number of years, was established by Timothy Brownhill August 25, 1904, was first printed on a foot-power press. It was of small size for a time and this type and press were operated in a tent. Later it was moved to the upper floor of the Tom Tucker building. Mr. Brownhill sold his interests to Max Lueddemann in 1905, and Mr. Lueddemann bought the northwest corner of Block 33 and built a building where he added to the equipment and ran the newspaper from there until he sold out to Howard W. Turner in 1908.

Later on, Turner bought all of the property on this corner and later the Library Building was on the corner before being moved to its present location. Vine W. Pearce and Sons bought the paper in 1916 and ran it for several years until William E. Johnson and wife bought it. Mr. Johnson died in 1924 and Mrs. May B. Johnson ran the paper until about 1919 when it was sold to the present owners.

This paper has been very active all its life in helping to develop the whole community, through its columns and its news medium, as well as a business employing several people at all times. It might be interesting to note here that when Turner bought it he did not know anything about the newspaper business and bought it only on the promise that Sydney D. Percival would stay a year. Before a year was up, the news came of the railroad starting work and he stayed much longer. The shop had no mechanical typesetting machinery and it had to be done by hand. In order to do a good job, we had to employ sometimes six to eight people to get the paper out and keep up with the job work.

Turner installed one of the typesetting machines (Unitype) that was shipped around the Horn from New York and also installed a power press that was operated by a gas engine. Later on, of course, after electricity came in 1913, motor power was used and the business has increased as the years have passed.

With the advent of the automobile it became necessary to have a garage to repair cars that had a bad habit of breaking down quite often. The first garage in Madras was built and operated by Charles P. U'Ren about 1912. Later he sold to John Conroy and Clarence Watts, the latter finally selling out to John Conroy who operated the Main Street Garage until his death. Douglas Hood was associated with Conroy for a time; also L. A. Newell.

Colonel William Thompson, also known as Bud Thompson, printer, newspaperman, died at Alturas, California. He had a ranch on the present Ashwood Road along east of Haycreek flat and south of the creek bed, just opposite the big rock point where the road turns sharply around toward the north as we travel east on said Ashwood Road. The large house was on the site in 1903 when the writer came to Haycreek.

George Thompson, a brother of Bud, owned and lived on the

place known as the Dunham place. Dunhams later bought it from Thompson. These places were where the Thompsons lived when the Snake Indians were making their raids driving off horses and cattle. Horses were more valuable than cattle at that time.

Pete Lagursie was the first to run sheep north of the Okelley place; this was close to the James Garrett homestead at the head of the canyon and near the Elkins place. This was along in the 1870's.

The book, *Reminiscenes of a Pioneer,* tells about the Thompsons and several other things in the vicinity of this place.

20

Joel McCollum's father lived at the mouth of Beaver Creek just across from the Jones Ranch or in that vicinity, with his family. Joe tells about riding home one day and thought he spied a bunch of Indians but was fooled—he was young and became scared.

On October 19, 1953, in company with Leslie Priday and wife, Mrs. Turner and I drove over to Haycreek and down to the old Priday Place which is below the Parrish Place and we discovered the old cave in which Felix and Marion Scott lived during the winter of 1862 and 1863.

A. L. Veazie was authority for the information that these people lived there in a cave, which was along the rimrock (not the one that shows from the road above) being about 100 feet above the creek and facing the south. Mr. Veazie said the Scotts kept their horses in a box canyon to the northeast of this cave. He also stated that they had about 70 yoke of oxen (which seems a large number for the time) along with their horses; also that they were on their way to the Baker mining region with supplies.

We drove down to within a few hundred feet of this cave, and unless you know where to look, you would not see it; yet a person could look out from this cave and see anyone approaching. All of the flat at that time was covered with rye grass, very high no doubt, and there was brush along the creek.

There are many names written on some of the rock in the cave with dates back in the early days. I noted one, 1878. It was surprising how these people made out, living in this small cave, with a fire for warmth and cooking and sleeping. At one time the cave was walled up partly in front. Mr. Priday remembers when he was young and his folks lived on the place.

The Indians never found the Scotts before they left; however they were anxious to secure better protection during the summer of 1863 and started on. During the fall of 1862 when they got over the mountains they could not go back on account of the storms and were obliged to stop some place and this was the best they could locate. At the same time, they started what was the first settlement east of the Cascade Mountains in Central Oregon.

At the old Priday Place, located just below the old Parrish Place, and above the old road, we found the old grave of John Pearce, aged 65 years when he died. Date of death on the tombstone was August 14, 1875. There is an iron fence about the grave and someone had visited it recently.

Mr. Pearce was the father of Mrs. Colburn McPherson. The McPherson Place was located about four miles north of this location. Later this place was sold to the Hunters and then to the

Madras

Baldwin Sheep Company. The McPhersons are nearly all dead; one woman still lives in The Dalles.

We also found another grave south of the Brewer place, which Mr. Priday thinks was about 1910 or during the railroad days. The location is close to the railroad and a little north of the road coming into Haycreek from the southwest, or where Purl Lytle's father formerly lived, and not far from the old school house, a little way from a large juniper tree standing in the fence line. There is a faint outline of the grave and also of rock that was around the grave.

It seems that on one trip of the mail stage from Shaniko to Prineville, as the driver passed, he saw a man lying on the ground with his head on a bed roll. Upon returning the following day, he saw that the man was in the same position. The driver went over to him and found that he was dead. Since no one was able to identify the corpse, and in its state, those making the investigation decided to bury the body where it was, and did so. Since that time no one seems to have been able to identify anything that would lead to the name of the person.

There was another death at the box springs just below the above location—old man Osborn's, the father of Dan Osborn. He was killed, it is thought, by falling off his freight wagon. He was buried in the Haycreek Cemetery. The road now runs over the top of this box spring.

The location of the cemetery for the Madras area is on quite a rise from the surrounding territory, nor what you would call a hill, but a slightly location northeast of Madras. This cemetery has served the community since 1902, when a daughter, Miss

Nannie Holt, who died in September, 1904, of Mr. and Mrs. John Mayes, was buried on the Holt homestead. This tract was set apart from her homestead for cemetery purposes. About 1910 the I. O. O. F. Lodge No. 196 took over the cemetery and has improved and operated it since that time.

Many of the early settlers have been interred there. It has been expanded to its present size and is considered a beautiful setting for a cemetery. Although it cannot be kept as green as some, still it is not low, and the ground formation is conductive to the preservation of the underground elements.

21

The elevation of Madras is 2,142 feet above sea level, which allows for the growing of most of the trees. Gardens are not successfully grown in other sections of Central Oregon. There are many things that cannot be grown with any degree of success; but on the whole, trees, flowers, gardens and shrubs do grow very well.

For several years the hands of fate seemed to plague us, but recently the wheels of fortune have turned in our favor. I mean the Portland General Electric Company and the citizens of this community.

This has been an interesting fight. Having been in the railroad situation, county division, irrigation, and now this one which involves the greatest amount of money, I have greatly enjoyed all of them—more, perhaps, because we have won in each case. All have been fought for the upbuilding of this community and have brought about the creation of a better place to live; also making it possible for more people to have homes with all of the modern conveniences.

My fifty years in this locality from the times of the horseback, the stagecoach, train, to the airplane—as the panorama of time passes through my mind—I have enjoyed it. I have enjoyed all of the associations with people come and gone, until now in the eventide of life, this last development I feel will bring to a large number of people the pleasures, the work savings and the largest financial return. Irrigation was the longest and hardest fight of all, but together they make a fine combination for good.

We find new thoughts cropping up in education, farming, rearing of children, and everything that has seemed more or less static for many years. However, there are certain fundamentals that will always prevail.

The following are a few of the early settlers in and around Madras, who contributed to the upbuilding and development of the vicinity:

Walter D. Arney	James Magness
Dave & Robert Barnett	John Mays
Dr. J. A. Bartlett	Archie Mason
Fannie Barton	Ed Mason
Joe Beddingfield	M. C. Mason
M. W. Bennett	Tom & Patrick McCormack
A. W. Boyce	J. F. McGhee
George & William Branstetter	Thomas P. Meloy
W. J. Branstetter	W. C. Moore
W. K. Brewster	Andrew Morrow
J. F. Brooks	James M. Moyes
Timothy Brownhill	H. K. W. "Baldy" Nisson

Dave Burdin
Tom Burdin
John Campbell
Dr. Harold Clark
J. M. Conklin
John Conroy
Simon P. Conroy
Bill Cook
W. R. Cook
Jerry Cramer
Mrs. Ina B. Crosby-Robinson
Austin W. Culp
Henry Deitzel
William Ellis
Harvey Filey
Fred Fisher
Dr. T. Fox
P. C. Fulton
Dr. J. H. Gale
Marie Galloway-Dizney
Bruce Grady
S. E. Gray
J. P. Hahn
Dr. H. B. Haile
William H. Hess
Charles Higdon
M. A. Hobson
Gus Holmes
Douglas Hood
Lloyd Hunter
L. H. Irving
John Isham
John H. Jackson
Harry Jennings
Neil S. Jennings
Ben Jones
Lena M. Lamb

Otto Northy
R. T. Olson
Frank Osborn
John Palmahn
Orin A. Pearce
Sydney D. Percival
A. S. Phillips
Milton G. Pillette
Martin H. Pratt
Max Putz
B. O Randolph
George Rankin
Don P. Rea
Robert Rea
Perry Read
Ora Rhodes
James Rice
Walter Rice
J. W. Robinson
Chester E. Roush
Alfred C. Sanford
S. J. Sellers
A. F. Shugert
I. F. Shutt
Wade Siler
Elva J. Smith
Jennie Smith
Warren Smith
Dr. W. H. Snook
G. V. Stanton
George Stevens
Della Sweeting
Roy Thielman
T. B. Tucker
Howard W. Turner
Charles P. U'Ren
Ore VanTassel

Madras

Ben Larkin
J. W. Livingston
John H. Lockard
Dr. T. A. Long
Kyle Loucks
M. L. Loucks
Tice Loucks
J. E. Loveall
Frank Loveland
Max Lueddemann

Charles Waterhouse
Clarence Watts
James Watts
J. C. Waymire
Mary Webber-Boyce
Mancel Wheeler
Jerry Wible
Charles P. Wilson
Max Wilson
Fred Zell

Lamonta

By Neva McCaffery, Eureta Horney and Martha Thomas

The first mention in history of the site later to be known as Lamonta was in 1843 when a scouting party led by McDowell camped there while on a trip for the Government.

One of the first settlers was Jerry Achey who homesteaded near the Rimrock Springs Ranch in 1883. He later married Mary Russell who had five children—Bill and Arthur who now live at Lone Pine, Earnest at the Cove, and Nora McMeen in Bend.

Colonel Smith homesteaded the Rimrock Spring Ranch in 1887, and there was enough water from the Springs to irrigate 40 acres of alfalfa. Mrs. Bill Morse of Prineville is his daughter. George Ridgeway came in 1884 and located west of Lamonta. He had two sons, Glen now living in Redmond and Charlie in Walla Walla. After his death in 1889, his widow married John Grant who many years later was killed by lightning. Two of their sons, Mason and Jimmie, live near Madras.

The first post office in the Lamonta country was granted in 1890 and Bill Rodgers was appointed postmaster. It was named Desert at that time, but Rodgers didn't qualify and it was moved to the Sanford Pringle place where his daughter Lizzie was its postmaster but it was closed again in 1892.

In 1896 it was granted again with the name Lamonta, which

174

Lamonta

is a French word meaning mountain. It was kept in the Helfrich home with his daughter Katie as postmaster. Later it was moved to the Lee Moore home and was there for several years, then to the John Rush store, but with the change of politics and Presidents it went to the M. T. Cowan store and stayed there until the building burned in 1914. It was moved to the old Walt Rice Drug Store with Charles Freenias as postmaster until rural delivery started. Dwight Roberts was the first rural route carrier, next Ralph Peck, then Lou Nichols, and the last driver was Edgar Barnes.

The first school was held in the old house of T. M. Smith (Ethel Smith of Redmond is his daughter) and then in the homestead house of Walter Lithgow. One of the first teachers was Lillie Read (who was Mrs. Howard Turner). She was followed by Jerry Banks, Warren Brown, Miss Omeg, Eunice Horney (Mont's sister) and Charles Dinwiddle. There were 68 pupils on the roll at that time, whose ages ranged from 6 to 21 years.

A large and better school house was needed so in 1901 a new one was built half a mile from Lamonta. Riley Cook of Madras was the first teacher in this school. The next teacher was Alta Snyder, whom the pupils ran off the first month. Sanford Fields took her place and after a short while left in the night, as the larger boys threatend to rotten egg him if he showed up again.

In desperation the directors hired a man by the name of Andrew Larson, who was a boxer. He carried a harness strap in his pocket and used it freely. After whipping one of the larger boys, who was ringleader in most of the mischief, he had no more trouble and the school settled down, but not before the directors were called to settle a dispute and they got into a fight, knocking the stovepipe down so that school was dismissed for the rest of the day.

Some of the next teachers were Floy McGhee, Della Foster, Olive Mortimore, Irene Barnes, Edith Rideout, Emily G. McDougall (who married Andrew Morrow one of the largest stock raisers in the county), Z. T. Gideon, Mattie Grey, Nellie G. Terrill, Avis Cadanaugh, Mildred Miller, Lucille Morgan, Eva Dodd, Hester O. Siment, Neva Weigang McFaffery, Ada Bullard (Mrs. Francis Clarno), Lila Maddox (Mrs. Edwood Bolter), Bessie Reardon.

The community was growing and a new school district was formed about five miles south of Lamonta called Pine Ridge. Some of the teachers there were Grace Landis, Gladys Breen (Mrs. Chas. Keegan of Ashwood), Agnes Kongrasky, Jean Nesbitt, Helen Pederson, Delia Stewart, Anne Riebhoff.

In 1888 Abraham Dawson homesteaded at the foot of Grizzly Mountain. Some other early settlers were Bill Sann, Squire Cain, John Hauley, Oren Waite, Charles and Ira Paxton.

A sawmill was built on the west slope of the mountain in 1903 by a man named Hawkins, but he soon sold it to William Peck, Guyan Springer and Henry Window who operated it until 1910.

Ernest Weigand settled south of Lamonta in 1895 and was joined by his brother Joseph and his family in 1899. (Two of their boys, Pearl and Jack, live at Terrbonne and the other three children, Norman, Rolla, and Neva settled at Powell Butte.)

Freight was brought from Shaniko to Prineville by wagons pulled by teams of four to ten horses. The Joe Weigand Ranch was one of the stopping places where the freighters stayed overnight.

The stage coaches stopped here for passengers to eat, and to change horses on their way from Prineville to Shaniko.

Joe Taylor and family lived at the foot of Grizzly and had a very nice orchard.

In 1910 an oil boom really put Lamonta on the map. Frank Forest and Frank Loveland started drilling for oil on the Taylor Place. People came from miles around and staked claims all over Grizzly, but after a year of drilling it failed to produce oil and was abandoned.

Oscar Cox and his family lived on this place later and some of his neighbors were Lee Knorr, Boggs, Julius Retzloff (whose granddaughters are Mrs. Melvin Cyrus and Mrs. Russell Gailbraith of Redmond), Luther Melton, George Ragner, Joe and Myrtle Markee, and Simon Negus.

To the south of Lamonta is the Lone Pine District named after a big pine tree growing among the junipers. The Lone Pine Ranch was homesteaded by Doc Sights. There was a big barn with an old-fashioned windmill that ran a feed grinder which was a real landmark. It had the only artesian well in the country. Ferd McCallister and Frank Forest lived there. Also the O'Neil brothers had a general store where the pioneers traded butter and eggs for groceries. Other families who lived between Lone Pine and Lamonta were Jack Ferguson, Delbert and John Jenkins, Charles Freeman, Jim Bettis, Charles Stranahan, Jim Corey, Ed Love, Kimbells, Sam Evans, John and Lucy Hockett, Moses Bryan, Charlie, Bill and Noah Floyd, Hattie and Joe Quinn, and Joe Larson.

Between Lamonta and the Big Divide on the road to Prineville lived the Ed Batesons, Lynn Morford, Flether Wright, Dick and Lillie Frogge, Cal and Jim Curtis, Willis Stacks, Nora Barker, and Irvine Basey.

The Jim McMeen Place on Willow Creek was filed on by his uncle in the early 80's and Jim came in 1892. They had three sons, two of whom are Charlie of Bend and Bruce of Prineville.

In Lamonta and north to Willow Creek lived the families of Lee Moore, Farquharson, Homquist, John Eagon, Joe Breeding, George Hendrick, Lorenzo Thomas (father of Jim Thomas of Redmond), the Franks (parents of Lou and Walter of Redmond, John of Culver, George and Oscar of Bend), Walter and Emery Hurst, Frank Hype, Emery Seales, Irwin Bradon, the Fowlers, Willis Benefield, Asa Mishler, Millard Thompson, Irene and Joe Bales, the Bennetts, the Eads, the McDades, the Pearsons, Mike Bigelow, William Meek (nephew of Joe Meek, the celebrated Oregon pioneer).

The Albert Moores family gave dances in their home, with Mrs. Moore playing the fiddle and some one seconding on the organ. Whole families would go and dance all night. The children were put to sleep on the beds or benches, midnight lunch was served, and every one had a good time.

On July 4, 1905, a celebration, held at Grizzly Lake, just

178

above the mill, it was a great success, as people came from miles around. They built an open-air platform and stage where the program was held in the morning and a basket dinner at noon. They had foot races, sack races, and various other contests during the afternoon and danced all night. I can well remember the thrill of the old merry-go-round where a horse went round and round the post to give us a ride.

Several years later another Fourth of July picnic was in pro gress when a big rainstorm came up and everyone got in his buggy, hack or wagon and started to Lamonta to dance. Some of the gayer young fellows started to race and, before we arrived, all the older people joined in and it was a mud-splattered group by the time they arrived.

Jake Merrill had a homestead near Grey Butte in 1893. With the passing away of his wife, the people found it necessary to have a cemetery; so they started the Grey Butte Cemetery which is still used by the old pioneers.

Other settlers in this section were Julius McCoin (father of Numa, Walter, and Minnie Helfrich), Evick Cyrus (father of Dean, Omar, and George), Bill Rodgers, Jake Strand, Helfrich Brothers Walter, Ben, John, and Jim Windom Brothers Jesse, Lance, and Henry (father of Harry, Pauline King, and Hazel Laird of Redmond and Winifred Harris of Prineville), Neil Milligan, Bob Johnson, Lou Patterson, Johnnie Colman, Walter Adams, Thomas McGhee, Everett, George and Frank Miller, Clay and Dick Butler, Theresa LaNell, Bill Kickler, Guyon Springer, Albert Seals, Jim Robinson (father of Mrs. Glen Ridgeway and Mason Grant), Henry Roba, Toni Leach,

Sam Pierce, W. F. Hammers, Lew Carson, Bob Armstrong, Kelly and Clara Messinger, Joe and Ballard Giles, Charles Lott, Alex Houk, Henry Mitchell, Martha Hash Straight, Ira Black, J. M. King (father of Merle of Redmond and Carl of Culver) and John Dobkins (who had the old-fashioned threshing machine).

A school house known as the Grey Butte School was built on the Bill Rodgers Place. It was also used for church services where we had a preacher once in awhile. The people came for many miles bringing basket lunches and would spend the day. That was the horse-and-buggy era and it was a great pleasure for friends to get together for good visits and for the children to have others to play with.

To the north and west of Lamonta was the Red Rock district and among some of the early settlers there were Sam Brown whose family all settled near him; the Boyce Place where people dug wells and hauled water for many miles; Jeff Healy and O. G. Caslioet who moved to Old Culver and ran a store until the railroad came and then moved to the present town of Culver. The old school house was the scene of many a grange picnic.

Lamonta in its boom days was a very busy place with M. T. Cowan's Hotel, post office, general store, and livery barn, Walter Rice's Drug store, Fred Mingers and Pete Yancer's Blacksmith Shop, Emery Seal's Saloon, the Tom Benefield Dance Hall, and John Rush's general store, dance hall, telephone switch board and grange hall (which boasted over 100 members, as it was the first in Central Oregon). Dr. Clark came from Madras to do dental work once a month. Judge Miller had a home in Lamonta and he held court when necessary.

Lamonta

There was a literary society and debates were very popular—also a football and baseball team and many rabbit drives were held over the hundreds of acres thickly inhabited by the animals.

I asked Martha Thomas, daughter of William H. Short who clerked at the Rush Store what she could remember about Lamonta and she wrote the following:

John Rush's store and dance hall was a large building for that day. He sold shoes, yardage, notions, shirts, ties, underwear, dishes, kettles, and all kinds of smaller hardware, nails, wrenches, hammers, lots of pocket knives, all kinds of groceries, guns, fishing tackle, and the loveliest candy of which he was himself very fond. Many hundred dozens of eggs I've counted and packed in rolled barley or sawdust after the settlers brought them in to trade for needed supplies. In turn, the eggs were loaded in a light wagon to which were hitched two horses, and Mr. Rush traded them in at Madras for more supplies. But most of his supplies were brought from Shaniko by freight wagons.

Automobiles were quite new and I have sold the prettiest crystal clear gasoline from five gallon cans. There were many gallons of kerosene and cases and cases of candles sold, before the least dreams of the wonders of electricity. Of course, when I began clerking I was asked for a left-handed monkey wrench by Lynn Smith, which I tried to find much to his joy.

Floy McGee was the teacher in the fall of 1907, and when my sister Clara attended there were 32 pupils enrolled. The school house was also used for church and Sunday school. The people of Grizzly community always came to the Lamonta church meetings. I well remember when all the young folks of the two communities, while practicing for a Children's Day program in June, got marooned for some hours at the school house by a terrible thunder storm and flash flood.

M. T. Cowan, who owned the hotel, post office, and the other store of Lamonta, was a jolly old man with always something funny to say. He sometimes read our postcards to us and made rhymes of the messages. His son Frank and daughters Hazel and Myrtle were near my age. There were also his grown-up children, Maud (Mrs. Fred Mingers), Robert, and Florence (Mrs. Carl McGhee). Frank married Lillian Frogge and when the hotel burned in 1914 their little son was burned quite seriously. The fire was at night when all were asleep but every one got out safely except for the one mishap.

The country wasn't dry as it is now. There were heavy thunder storms all summer and how the crops and gardens would grow, and such corn, watermelons, blue victor potatoes, squash and red Mexican beans. The soil is the deepest and the best in Central Oregon.

In winter there were heavy snows and very cold weather. I look back on those cold trips to school and that old shell-like building and wonder how we stood it, but what fun when school was out and we started home with those chilled horses that stood all day. The races we had would compare favorably with what we pay to see now.

182

Lamonta

One evening a group of us young folks rode to Lamonta in a new Buick which was really something in those days of 1910. One of the citizens was very drunk and was just in the act of clearing the earth of Cowans, so he had two men lying unconscious and with a line drawn across the street was dancing a jig and sweeping the ground with his hat and in no uncertain terms daring anyone to cross the line. Were we scared? The oldest of the young folks there that evening had some influence with this man and finally got him in the car (Neva wasn't afraid but I was scared most out of my wits) and took him home where the sheriff, coming from Prineville, soon picked him up.

John Rush was a wonderful penman, whose writing and drawing were a joy to everyone. He kept busy writing his interpretation and prophesies of the Bible. He often spoke of people flying like birds and spitting fire from their tails. Of course, we thought he was a little balmy but it has all come to pass. His foresight caused him to buy up all the scrap iron in the country and when the war came along and the scrap iron drive was on he had a corner on the market.

John Rush's great-grandfather was the famous Benjamin Rush who signed the Declaration of Independence and was physician general of the Continental Army.

During the drouth in the middle-twenties many families had to give up their farms and move away. The Government declared it a drouth area and in 1934 purchased the many thousands of acres as marginal land.

183

Gateway And Lyle Gap

By Noah Vibbert, Ward Farrell, and Allie M. Farrell

We will start this story at the northwest boundary because the Vibberts took up their homestead there and they were among the first to settle in this portion of Jefferson County and have stayed the longest.

In the fall of 1903 Peter Vibbert, with his son Noah, arrived on the plains above Weber Wells, now Paxton. It being too dark to follow the faint wagon trail through the sagebrush, they stopped for the night. The horses were unhitched from the wagon, tied up and fed, and they crawled into the wagon-box and went to bed. In the morning, as told by Noah, he awakened to find himself alone. Being very young, he was greatly frightened and it didn't help much when he saw a strange man approaching. The man was John Thomas, father of Grace, Nick and Lulu, who said good morning and went on his way. Noah thought he had lost his dad and that this strange man would get him. However, his dad soon came back; he had taken the horses down the hill to the well to water them. They proceeded down the trail past Frog Springs and on to where their original homestead is on the northwest end of the Gateway boundary.

Until a tent was set up, they lived in Uncle Andrew Vibbert's cabin. Late one afternoon, Dad Vibbert told Noah to stay at

Freight wagons on Shaniko Flats, with the stage at the right.

Deschutes Ferry at Ferry Canyon in 1898 when operated by John E. Campbell.

Metolius. A vast prairie, 80 miles south of The Dalles and on the east side of Deschutes River, was opened under the Homestead Law in 1900. In four years 100,000 acres had been homesteaded.

Holt Caterpillar and Combine in Jefferson County in 1912. T. A. Taylor, two miles north of Metolius, brought in the first of these machines.

A pair of noted hounds owned by T. A. Taylor, notable because of the way they could kill coyotes. This picture was taken just after one of their kills, which lies all abject and done for in front of them. The dogs were much apprecitated for what they did, only they couldn't do enough in much coyoted Jefferson County.

the cabin and prepare the evening meal while he went to Mr. Chriswell's for some hay for the horses. On returning he didn't see a light in the cabin nor Noah. He lit the lantern and was going out to search for the missing boy when he found him asleep in bed. The sleeper awoke to a sound scolding.

All of the lumber for building their own cabin had to be hauled from Grizzly, where two sawmills were in operation, one run by Jack Dee and the other by Mr. Compton. The trip was long and tiring so they stayed overnight during the several trips required for getting the lumber.

After the cabin was built and a homestead residence was established, father and son returned to the old home to make preparation to move the family to a new home. So in the spring of 1904 was started the new life. Peter Vibbert and sons James and Noah came by boat to The Dalles, from there by road, Noah leading the way with two cows and James driving one rig and Dad Vibbert the other. When the road was steep they would put one team onto the other. The trip from The Dalles took about seven days. Toll had to be paid to cross Shears Bridge also through the gate in Cow Canyon.

As we leave the Vibberts and the Plains and look east we see a bowl or basin and it is easy to realize why it was named Gateway. From this viewpoint we see three different natural outlets or gaps. Eastward there is Lyle Gap, named after Al Lyle who ran a large cattle ranch on the other side of the Gap.

This gap is a natural cut through a long range of hills which extend for miles on both sides. This was and is a blessing to travelers. Highway 97 goes through it.

185

Looking south, we see a road winding up the hillside and it goes through a natural gap at the top. This road connects with Highway 97, about four miles south. Then, of course, coming up the hillside towards us is the road onto the Plains. In making this road they ran into good gravel which has been used all over the county. It is, moreover, the gravel pit where they found the bones of prehistoric animals and fish.

A railroad depot was built here at Gateway. Also stockyards and both became important shipping points.

Last but not least is the large gap on the north of the basin. This too is an important opening. In 1910 the Union Pacific built their railroad up through this canyon into Gateway and on through to Madras and points south, with important stock-yards at Gateway. Even before the railroad was built there was a road or trail through this gap. Trout Creek runs into the Deschutes River just below and, there being some good land down there, people took advantage of the water.

In 1898, U. S. Coles took up the first place on the right and in 1892 John Jackle took up what is now known as the Kampher Place. The homestead on the left of the road was taken up by Milt DeHaven about 1904.

Still looking down, we see still another natural gap or canyon. It looks like a handle to the bowl. This was a blessing to the railroad builders, for it winds its way on through it.

2

In this handle is land that was taken up by Willis Brown and his son Ralph. They had the land on the south end and Sydney

Gateway and Lyle Gap

Percival took the land attached to the Gateway end. Sydney was quite active in civic and social life and was well liked. I will copy an outline of his life written by his wife Alice.

Narrative of Alice Percival

Sydney D. Percival was born December 24, 1869, in Polk County, Oregon. He attended school in Monmouth where the family lived and also Monmouth Normal School.

He worked throughout the Willamette Valley doing various things, some being newspaper work in Dallas and Salem. He came to Central Oregon around 1900 and worked on papers in Shaniko and Bend. About this time he filed on a homestead in Gateway and retained this land throughout his life.

While working in Bend he met and married Alice Reynolds. They went to live on the farm at Gateway and remained there until Mr. Percival ran for the office of county clerk, he being in 1916 the first elected clerk after the formation of the county. He retained this office until his death.

Mr. and Mrs. Percival had seven children, three of whom worked for him in the county clerk's office. All seven went through the elementary school and Union High School in Madras. He also was a member of the elementary and high school board of directors and chairman of the high school for many years.

Mr. Percival belonged to the Independant Order of Odd Fellows, the Masonic Lodge, the Knights of Pythias. He was a republican and a member of the Christian Church.

187

Jefferson County Reminiscences

It was also of this handle that Phil Brogan spoke when he wrote the Geologic History of Jefferson County which I will copy:

3

Geologic History

You will find enclosed a sort of geologic sketch of Jefferson County with emphasis on the Gateway area...As an early-day resident of Jefferson County and of Crook before Jefferson was created, I am deeply interested in your undertaking, and I am sure that when all contributions are on file they will be a most valuable addition to the history of Oregon. My family settled in the early 90's in the present Donnybrook community, then generally known as Axehandle, and Ashwood was our post office. I hope your history of Jefferson County will include its beginnings.

Vastly older than the story of its human habitation is the story of ancient Jefferson County interpreted from its river-cut valleys, its tilted hills, and its white peaks ruled by the great glacier mountain that gave the county its name.

Few counties in Oregon hold more points of geologic interest than are found in Jefferson's 1,794 square miles. To the east, the country is anchored in some of the state's oldest formations— sea beds formed in that remote era, the Mesozoic, when giant reptiles ruled the earth. In the south are grotsequely pinnacled Smith Rocks, whose volcanic strata were laid down in the earth's dawn age of mammal life, the Eocene. Along the western skyline where the serrated Cascades are ruled by a giant volcano, Jefferson, are some of the most recent formations in the entire North-west—the lavas that spilled from fissures and flowed from craters only a few hundred years ago.

In the eroded and at times up-ended formations that reach across Jefferson County from Cherry Creek to the western Cascades is a story of the earth that gropes into the dim past more than 100,000,000 years. And not far from the center of Jefferson County, in the Gateway area, are formations that out-line the story of prehistoric Oregon from dawn-age days to the present.

Along Hay Creek where Highway 97 sweeps north toward the early-day Priday Ranch, the dun-colored hills have been found by geologists to be Clarno rocks of the remote Eocene. Above these brownish clays where Highway 97 moves through "The Gap" of the Gateway country over the pass into Haycreek, are a formation of the John Day age which has yielded remains of the abundant Oreodons, creatures of Oligocene days intermediate between the deer and the pig.

Over the John Day formations of long eons spilled the Columbia basalts that blanketed some 200,000 square miles of the Pacific Northwest. Those lavas are exposed to Two Widows Canyon, east of Gatewey.

Geologists say that the massive Columbia lavas blocked ancient drainage and in places sagged into huge basins. These basins in Oregon's mid-Miocene times were occupied by vast lakes, one of which formed in the John Day Valley south of Picture Gorge. In Central Oregon, another of those so-called Mascall lakes formed in the present Gateway country. Brown knolls just east of Gateway are remnants of sediments that eventually filled that old lake basin.

On the shore of Gateway Lake of long millions of years ago were animals that would be strangely out of place in the Oregon of the present. Three-toed horses were present in great numbers and left their stony bones on the lake shore. Also present were the huge giraffe-camels of Miocene times. Various forms of deer-pigs, the Oreodons, were also present.

Bones of all these creatures have been found in the brown hills east of Gateway.

When the Mascall lakes disappeared, probably millions of years ago, a new age, the Pliocene, came to the Gateway country, and it was this age that streams, their westward course to the ocean blocked by the volcanic Cascades, meandered over central Jefferson County to form the gravel cliffs at the top of the grade west of Gateway. In these gravels have been found remains of a giant rhinoceros species, last of the creatures to live in Oregon. The Gateway gravels have also yielded remains of fish, including a large species believed to have been a prehistoric relative of the salmon family.

The Gateway gravels, geologists have determined, were deposited in torrential waters, probably the hot waters from an exploding volcano, or the heavy flow of a stream that broke through a volcanic barrier. Trees were uprooted, and their forms remain in the Gateway gravels to mark their resting place of long ago.

Not the least of Central Jefferson County's geologic marvels are its old formations that hold semi-precious stones, especially in the Trout Creek area. No part of America has provided the wealth of rare agate material, especially of the plume type, found in the aged Jefferson County hills.

The story of Jefferson County's primeval forests is even more interesting than its vanished animals. In the Cherry Creek-John Day region are found remains of semi-tropical forest, including the yew and palm of remote days. Uplands of ancient Jefferson County were mantled with redwoods, dainty needles of which are found in a score of localities, including the Smith Rocks.

Jefferson County's geology is primarily the story of Oregon geology. That story can only be sketched in these brief pages. It is a story that nature has filed away in gaudily-colored strata, hidden in lake sediments, illustrated with mammal and plant fossils, then carefully bound in basalts which now form the sage-covered rimrocks.

4

Now we will linger in Gateway which has become quite a nice little village. Before 1910 no one lived there but when the railroad was built it took on activity.

I believe that a man by the name of George McFarland, a water-pumper for the railroad, gave Gateway its name, a very appropriate one.

In 1912 the saloon was used for a school house. The mirrors were covered with Bon-Ami and the building made presentable. Miss Viola Smith was the first teacher and she had 10 or 12 pupils. There were Charles and Dorothy Daly, Kenneth Hershy, several Larson children, and others. Miss Smith stayed with the John Daly family.

A traveling salesman by the name of Kegler put in the first store and a Mr. Lewis ran it for him. John Daly put one in a little later and had the post office in the back. Before that the mail had been pushed around from place to place.

The first mail was put in a large box by the stage driver who drove between Hay Creek and Warm Springs. This box was set up in about the middle of the Agency Plains and people would come there for miles around and sort their mail from it. Later Louis Young built a store at Sagebrush Springs and had the post office there. Still later William Blair had the post office in his home. After that John Daly had it in the store and John Lochard brought the mail down from Madras. Finally the Kepler store building was used for the post office. Kepler had sold out by that time.

We turn east now and leave Gateway, headed towards The Gap. On both sides of the trail, in those days, were homesteads that had been taken up since 1904. William Blair and his family owned the land on the lefthand side of the road and it extended almost to Sagebrush Springs.

On the righthand side of the road the land was taken up by George McFarland. It is at the east side of his 160 acres that Phil Brogan spoke of geologists finding bones of prehistoric animals, including those of a three-toed horse.

Jack Watson homesteaded the next place. He was the village blacksmith. He cleared most of his land of sagebrush but could not part with all of the juniper trees, having come from Kent, Washington, where there are lots of trees. Or maybe he cherished them because it is said that the trees in Jefferson, Deschutes and

Crook counties make up the largest juniper forest in the world. Jack also dug a hundred-foot well and always had a wonderful garden.

Next was the place taken up by Jim Gott and then the one taken up by Charlie Craig. The latter was very famous in those days, being Sagebrush Springs or should I say the Godsend to farmers.

Farmers came from all directions to haul water from this spring, for there was very little elsewhere. They put in a large hand force-pump with a 2-inch pipe and were able to fill a 600-gallon water tank in 45 minutes. It often took less time to fill the tank than it did for the horses to pull the tank home.

The land across the road was script by J. N. Teal who took that land up thinking the spring was on his land. However, the surplus water ran through his place.

Carl Christian homesteaded the next place on the right and then we go on into Old Maids Canyon, named after an old maid whose name was Miss Beasley. She took up the land there. It was very poor soil but apparently she wanted to live where she could be alone. A road went through her place and it followed along the side of a cliff where nature had made a tall cave-like place in the rock. Here we would often see her. Of this cave she had made a grotto in which she would recite her Rosary.

While making a new road through this canyon the workmen found a skeleton of a man with an empty six-shooter by its side. It had been there so long that it was impossible to identify him. I believe the bones are still in the court house.

As this canyon road connected with the main road or what is now known as Highway 97, it was used a great deal by the people from Trout Creek, Ashwood and Antelope who did their shopping at Gateway. There were no automobiles in those days, so people shopped at the closest store.

5

As we came out onto the main road it wasn't unusual to see a mile-long string of freight wagons, some pulled by as many as 16 horses. The Silver Lake outfit generally had two horses on the wheel and 16 mules.

Some of the drivers took great pride in making their outfit look nice. Their harness was cleaned and the traditional bells hung on a frame on the hames. They too had their rules of the road and if one outfit became stuck in the mud or dust and another pulled it out they would have to forfiet their bells.

All of the material for building the railroad and merchandise for the store was hauled for miles out of Shaniko, where the railroad that ran out of The Dalles unloaded freight into large warehouses.

In this line of freight wagons would often be horses and buggies, hacks, farm wagons, and, of course, the stage which brought in most of the mail as well as passengers.

As we come out of the canyon onto the main road and turn north we find some other homesteads which were taken up by Herman Stollicker and Joe Oswald, and in the canyon at the back of Joe's homestead is the Two Widow's canyon where the

194

lavas are exposed that Phil Brogan spoke of. Now we have told you about The Gap; so we will head south again.

The land in this valley was fairly good and most of it was taken up by homesteaders, some of whom were Morison, Trotter, Mont Ekerson, Spicer Brothers, Mother, Brother and Mrs. Elizabeth Long.

A school was built in about the middle of the valley. They called it Lyle Gap and it was organized in 1907. It was built by donation in 1908 and 1909, and school started March first to June first, 1909, with Miss. Edith Rideout of Maine as teacher (visiting a brother in Prineville when she accepted the position). Some of the first pupils were Marvin Akeson, Monte Akeson, Ester Coburn, Alice Coburn, Mabel Young, Ruth Blair, Nick Thomas and Lulu Thomas.

Rocks and rattlesnakes were plentiful around the school but as far as it is known none of the children was bitten by them. A few years later, in the winter time, some of the boys were exploring a cave not far from the school and found a large ball of snakes—rattlers and blow—rolled up together. The boys had evidently learned by experience to be careful about them and decided to get a man to help get rid of them. They killed about 32 but some got away. The boys said the man was so excited that he threw them out so fast as to fall all over them.

6

Coming up a grade out of the valley, we now come to quite an interesting plateau. The soil was very rich but needed more rainfall to make good crops. This land is all being farmed under

195

irrigation now but by new people. The only oldtimer is Ward Farrell's son Philip and he has part of the old homestead.

In the days when this land was homesteaded there were no running water, electricity, refrigerators, and other conveniences. Wood stoves made a lot of dirty work so did the coal-oil lamps. The chimneys had to be cleaned every day and the lamps filled with coal-oil.

The first ones to take up their 160 acres on this plateau were A. T. Martin, William Farrell, Ben Wanberg, Jim Barton, George White and his mother Mary J. White, George Laughlin and his sister Emma, Arthur Cottenjin, Fritz Wild, and John Thomas. Farther south were the homesteads of James Fleck and Otto Hoefeld.

The latter had the only dug well, where the freighters stopped to water their horses and to get meals. Naturally it was a very important place in those days, for it was a long distance between eats.

Practically all of the farmers grew wheat and rye at first. The rye was used for winter feed for the stock and the wheat was headed and stacked and later a threshing machine would come in and thresh it for them. Ed Kutcher and A. P. Clark traveled around with their threshing machines.

These outfits would bring their own help and cook wagon. It took 19 men to do the work. They brought their own bedrolls and would sleep around the stacks. Quite often they would be serenaded by the coyotes.

Having their own cook wagon with them helped the farmers'

wives tremendously; they were glad to get out of so much cooking. The farmer furnished the wood for the fire, potatoes, and sacks for the wheat—also hay for the 10 or 12 horses required to pull the outfit. Two four-horse teams were kept busy hauling water, one for the cook house and the others for the threshing machine.

Some years the farmers didn't have very much to thresh, between the sheepmen being careless about keeping their sheep off the wheat fields and the rabbits taking at least a quarter of it. The farmers finally got a bunch of people together to hold big rabbit drives when hundreds of the animals would be killed. It was a great sport for the people too. In one drive they killed 1500.

Vanora

By John L. Campbell

1

With the coming of the railroad in 1911 a small town was built and called Vanora, a name derived from its founder, Ora Van Tassel. When the railroad was abandoned through this area in 1923, the little town vanished. Where once there were two stores, a post office (1911-1920), a grade school, a near-beer joint, the Van Tassel residence, and a grain warehouse operated by Van Tassel who bought and shipped wheat which was hauled to his warehouse by the early settlers on the Agency Plains—all that remains today to mark the spot is a small portion of the concrete foundation of the school house and a small concrete underground cistern used for storing water hauled in barrels for the use of the school.

The location of this trading center was mostly in the SE of SE Section 1 T 10S, R12 E. W. M. The school house was just across the line in T 10S, R13E in Section 6, the railroad station in Section 7-10-13. Alex Smith owned the main store, John T. Dizney operated the post office, Miss May Campbell also ran the post office for a short while. This little valley lies between the Agency Plains and the Deschutes River on the Old Wagon Road and Indian Trail between The Dalles and Burns.

Vanora

Domestic water was pumped from the Deschutes River during most of the town's existence and the population boasted of water being piped to their homes. Today this area is a cultivated field.

The first history of this area, now in Jefferson County, that I have been able to find is mention of a ferry boat across the Deschutes River, in the year 1875. It was in bad condition. This ferry is mentioned in early explorations through the Warm Springs Reservation Area by Ralph M. Shane with no reference to its operator. In later years, in the 80's and 90's, it was operated by Chester McCorkle, John Luckey, Isom Cleek; then in later years by John E. Campbell, John T. Dizney, and an Indian, Robert Smith. This ferry was abandoned in 1913 when a bridge was built at Mecca a few miles downstream.

This ferry was located at the mouth of what was known as Ferry Canyon, less than one mile upstream from the present highway bridge. Lee Weigle started a store at this point in 1892, then Mr. Luckey operated it, and last Mr. Isom Cleek, until 1893. The store was moved to Warm Springs and later sold to W. H. See. Mr. Campbell took over the operation of the ferry in 1895 and continued until 1905, first moving it to a site about 400 feet above the present highway bridge, then later about one-half mile south of the bridge where Robert Smith also operated it. Mr. Dizney moved it to a new site at what was known as the Upper Dizney Place directly west of Vanora.

2

During this time the Campbell family lived on the river and operated the ferry there were many exciting moments, some of

199

which might be interesting. For instance, along in the middle 90's a wildcat while prowling near the homesite was discovered by the two farm dogs. Just what happened at the beginning of this fracas, on one knows, but the cat was finally pressed so hard that just any place to hide was welcome, and apparently the first hole it saw was the partly-open kitchen door in which a baby girl was standing. The mother, hearing the commotion, raced to the door to discover the big cat a few feet away headed in her direction, with the two dogs doing their best to stop him but not quite able to do so. The mother pulled the youngster back out of the cat's path and slammed the door just in time to catch his front feet and hold him; The dogs soon ended his prowling days. At another time these same dogs got an unsuspecting coyote in a similiar predicament and he headed for the front door, also open, but with no youngster in the way. So in he came, and squeezed in behind an old-fashioned organ that sat out just far enough from the wall for his body but not far enough for the dogs to squeeze in. The father was called to the house and after quieting the dogs and getting them out of the house, he got the coyote by the rear legs, pulled him out of his hiding place, out the door, swung the animal over his shoulder and broke the coyote's neck over the porch railing.

Antelope and sage hens were plentiful in these days, as were ducks, geese, and fish; but quail, partridge or pheasants were not to be found. Quail migrated to this area in about 1903; partridge came later, and pheasants were planted much later.

In 1901 the Campbell family filed on a homestead at the mouth of Negro Brown Canyon where a large spring was located, and moved there in 1902. From this watering place cattle were grazed over the breaks to the Deschutes and horses were pastured on the Agency Plains until crowded out by the homesteaders. Excellent gardens and fruit could be raised on the lower elevation and was the only source of fruits and vegtables in these days.

During the time between 1890 and 1903 there were no schools in this vicinity for white children. So the Campbell family built and furnished their own schoolroom, and hired, boarded, and paid their own teacher. This arrangement made the teacher practically one of the family except that she was paid from $25 to $35 per month. One of the teachers, Miss Daisy Hays, and the oldest Campbell girl, Ruby, attempted during the father's absence to ferry a four-horse team and wagon with its owner across the river during high water. At about the center of the stream the cable gave way at one end, turning everything loose with a jerk which threw the horses down and the wagon piled on top of the struggling horses causing that corner of the ferry to sink below the water. At this point of the rather exciting situation, the teacher decided to jump overboard, but was stopped in the act of doing so by the owner of the wagon, who was also busy trying to keep his horses' heads above water. But before long the boat righted itself and drifted downstream and came to rest on an island in mid-stream where the occupants were marooned for several hours until help was notified by an Indian who happened to see the accident from the Indian side of the river. A row boat was secured, the two girls and their passenger were taken ashore, the horses swam to shore; and in time the wagon and ferry were restored to their right places.

In 1903 this ferry was moved upstream about one-half mile to a point now obliterated by highway construction where a small one-room cabin was built. The Campbell kids took turns baching here and operating the toll ferry. The charges were 25 cents for a man on horseback, 50 cents for a two-horse, 75 cents for a four-horse wagon, and 10 cents each for loose horses or cattle. Indians were charged 10 cents for each horse loose or otherwise, 10 cents for a man without stock.

At the old ferry site, where the highway now crosses the Deschutes River, is a tunnel through a point of the hill that was made and used by the Oregon Trunk Railroad. After the road was abandoned, Lewis Irving, known as "Turk", purchased the land in which the tunnel was located with the intention of raising mushrooms in the damp interior for commercial purposes, but "Turk" never quite got his project started and finally abondoned the idea. Some day this scheme may be carried out, but at this writing (1953-54), the tunnel is being used for potato storage.

Along about 1910 the Rod and Gun Club of Madras started the idea of an annual fish-fry in June at this same old ferry site, then known as Cowles Orchard. The club members would catch the fish, fry them in deep fat, and serve them to all who came along. With the fish were served hot chili beans and coffee; each family would furnish its own dishes and cups. Fish in the Deschutes River in those days were plentiful and it was not uncommon for a good fisherman to bring in a catch of from 50 to 100 trout, with the majority of them 12 inches or longer. Those above 14 inches were split down the back and served in halves; below that size they were served whole. This fish-fry got to be so well advertised that most of Central Oregon made it an annual picnic day, with people coming from Portland, The Dalles, and almost any other place you might name. But it outgrew the ability of the club to catch enough trout to feed the fish-hungry crowds, and salmon had to be shipped in from the Columbia River. So what started out to be a local picnic day grew so large that it had to be discontinued.

3

In 1906 a sawmill was moved from Foley Creek to the Deschutes River and located at the present highway crossing and operated there for a number of years. Most of the homestead cabins on the Agency Plains and surrounding country were built from lumber cut at this mill, owned by Charles Durham and U. S. Cowles. The logs were floated down the Metolius and Deschutes Rivers; logs were also floated down these streams to a mill close to the mouth of Tygh Creek near Tygh Valley.

A still for the manufacture of whiskey was built by Mr. Cowles near the sawmill, but a U. S. license was never issued and the still never opened for business.

Some exciting happenings took place in and around the old mill which was powered by a steam engine fueled with slabs from the logs. Howard Turner was bookkeeper, salesman, sawyer, engineer, and all-around helper. He tells of two of the loggers whose task it was to work the logs down through the log pond to the mill. They settled a long-standing argument by a man-to-man encounter on the floating logs in the pond. These logs are hard to ride without interference, and with someone ruffling you up, it is almost impossible to stay on top. These river men were too eager to show the other who was the best man to take time to get out on firm ground. So they threw each other off the floating logs and settled their differences by holding each other under water until there was no fight in the one who ran out of air first.

Sol Masterson was king of the river drivers and could not be surpassed in riding a log down the many rapids of the Metolius and Deschutes rivers or rowing a small boat with provisions, bedding, and camp outfit when following the log drivers which numbered six to eight men.

A boom was built across the Deschutes to divert the logs from the river to the mill pond. This boom was built from large sawed timbers and was about 150 feet long. It was tied to the west bank of the river and extended down and across the stream to the entrance to the mill pond. Fins were bolted to the downstream side of this boom, with hinges and operated with cables and windlasses to cause it to bow up against the current with the curve upstream. After the mill was abandoned this boom was pulled loose by high water, floated down the river, and was broken into many pieces as one would hit the bank and buckle. Later, driftwood fires burned it and no trace is left.

4

In the winter of 1884-1885, the snow fell to a depth of over four feet and remained on the ground for a period of five weeks. During the time of this snow an old cowhand known through

Vanora

Central Oregon by the name of Whistling Smith was staying at a sheep camp where Alonzo Boyce, the owner, was tending some 2,000 sheep. It appears that he got lonesome and started for the Negro Brown Ranch on foot, as he had hobbled his horses and turned them loose. He returned to the camp that night to find that Mr. Boyce had left for his home on the upper Willow Creek, as he could do nothing for the sheep in four feet of snow with no available feed. The Whistler wrote a note on the cabin wall saying that the snow was too deep to break all the trail in one day, about two and one-half miles, so he was forced to return but would try again in the morning. The next evening he wrote a similar note on the wall also saying that he would try the next morning. There were no more notes on the wall but he never reached the Negro's home.

His body was found the next spring by Mr. Boyce about one-half mile up the canyon from the Negro's place under a large juniper tree where he had apparently frozen to death. Some cowboys dug a shallow grave and buried him there with his boots on. Along about 1903, after John E. Campbell had filed on a homestead where the body was buried in an unmarked grave, the skeleton was plowed up, boots and all. These bones and boots were put in a small wooden box and placed on top of a large rock where they remained until destroyed by a range fire in the summer of 1941. The 2,000 sheep were also found the next spring, huddled in a small place and all dead. The bones and wool remained there in sight until this particular spot was plowed for a wheat-field about 1904 on the homestead of Frank M. Heath on the NE¼ of Section 21, Township 10 South of

Range 13, E. W. M. The three horses were also found dead. Not until December 8, 1919, did another snow of this depth occur in this area, with the temperture dropping to 40 below zero. By Christmas this snow was about all gone.

The Negro Brown Ranch that Mr. Smith tried to reach is located at the center of Section 7 at the mouth of what was known for years as Nigger Brown Canyon. The Negro's wife was Mexican and Indian. He homesteaded there in 1881. In these days the neighbors were few and far between and the cowboys were forced to stay with far-away neighbors when gathering their cattle. This happened to a young cattleman, Perry Read, from near Grizzly Butte, a distance of some 30 miles. He arrived at the Negro's home late in the day to find the husband was on his way to Prineville to get a doctor, as his wife was expecting an increase in the family. Being good neighbors, the cowman made the best of the situation and stayed for the night. The next day when the husband and doctor arrived, all was well, the mother was taken care of, the baby was fed, and the cowman was preparing to go on his way.

The first account of U. S. Mail through this area was in about 1879 from The Dalles to Warm Springs, Hay Creek, and Prineville. From 1869 to 1902 it was carried from Wapinitia through Warm Springs, Haystack, and on to Prineville by John E. Campbell. Then a Mr. Criswell carried the mail on horseback from Warm Springs to Hay Creek and would get his breakfast at the ferry cabin: coffee, hotcakes, bacon and eggs for 15 cents; this was not a public boarding place.

About one-half mile south and west from the town of Vanora,

Vanora

Tom Tucker filed on a homestead in 1903. After living there a number of years he drowned while fishing from a small boat which overturned. His two companions, A. W. Culp and son reached shore.

During this time Vanora was a busy little town, a baseball diamond was grubbed from the sage flat, and at one of the hotly-contested games between the Warm Springs Indians and their white brothers, a bolt of lightning hit a juniper tree to which a team of horses was tied. The result was a pair of dead horses hitched to a perfectly good wagon. Some of the occupants of the wagon were out for a while but were soon revived and the game went on.

5

Pelton Dam Site

In the early 1920's a group of power-minded men from Portland joined in a company including some Eastern cities for the purpose of building a dam across the Deschutes about two miles upstream from the then abandoned townsite of Vanora. R. F. Schanck of Portland was in charge and Levi Smith was foreman and engineer on the job. Buildings were erected to accommodate 15 to 20 men with sleeping quarters, and for a shack, dining room, an office, blacksmith shop, and a horse barn. All material was lowered to the building site on the river bank, by a windlass operated by hand power, directly down the steep mountain side from the Old Oregon Trunk Railroad right-of-way, a descent of about 700 feet. A wooden track was built down this steep bank and a small car was used for lowering each article too large for a man to carry. It took about two hours for two men to let the car down and bring it back to the starting point, the revolution of the cable drum being only a small fraction of that of the windlass handles. Later a brake was devised on the drum to let the car down, but the pull-out was real reducing exercise, and down in that canyon of sheer rock walls the temperature has gone up to 117 degrees during the working hours.

The work of testing by core drills, with black diamonds set in steel for cutting edges, went on for about three years, although part of this work was at another site some seven miles upstream.

During this time a tunnel through solid rock was made some 700 feet long, to be used as a diversion tunnel while the dam was being built.

The project was abandoned from the belief that the public dam then being proposed on the Columbia River at Bonneville would more than supply the Pacific Northwest with needed power. When this theory proved to be false, another company was organized to build a larger dam at this same site, for which a permit has not been issued at the time of this writing.

Metolius

By Clara H. Hoffman

1

A wide prairie, as large as the state of Ohio, 80 miles south of The Dalles on the east side of the Deschutes River was the domain of the stockmen, who used the dry land for grazing, and grew alfalfa on the lowlands where the creeks were.

About 1900 this region was surveyed by the National Government and settlers rushed in. The Agency Plains, comprising 100,000 acres, were taken up within four years, under the Homestead Law.

The first important dry-land farming to be undertaken here, was done by a colony of German Methodists whose migration to this country was inspired by an article which appeared in the *Christliche Apologete* in the Spring of 1902 from the pen of a German Methodist minister of Portland, Oregon.

They came with various degrees of wealth; some had very little while others had much more. There were a number of carpenters among these settlers. Those who could afford it built very nice homes, some using siding and painting their houses. The lumber for all building was hauled from Dee's Mill at Grizzly. Usually the windows and doors were hauled from Shaniko.

Until fences were built of juniper posts and barb-wire the range cattle took over. Where there was hay for the family cow and the horses, strong corrals were made to protect the feed. By winter the family stock was sheltered in sheds of straw walls and roofs. Often the chickens had partly-frozen combs and toes by spring.

Water was one of the greatest problems. At first it was hauled in barrels but very soon long boxes were made, called tanks. Later cisterns were dug and kept filled with water, hauled several times a week. A few hauled from Old Culver but the most of the farmers hauled from what was known as Palmain. I believe the well was owned by a man named Isham.

There were howling coyotes but the jackrabbits and sage-rats did the most damage to the grain fields and gardens. Eventually the rabbits were controlled with poisoned wheat and neighborhood rabbit drives. A few sage-rats died eating the poisoned grain. Many traps were used, set if possible several times a day. This was a big chore for the sage-rats were only out in the spring and early summer which was the farmers' busy season. Later a liquid gas was used. A small rag was placed in the hole and liquid poured on and the hole stomped shut. With this treatment they began to diminish.

As the rodents became less and less, and more and more grain was grown, there was need for a threshing machine. Conrad Strasser, with several others, bought the first one. The "header" for cutting grain came on the market. A group consisting of Charles Wawrinofsky, John Hoffman Sr. and his son John A., and Emil Zemke bought one with which they cut their own crops and the crops of others.

Metolius

Many of the housewives raised very good gardens. Mrs. Hoffman Sr. always had muskmelons and watermelons to eat when many of the rest of us failed.

The children had great fun with the large tumbleweeds as these began to roll after the first freezes. One game was to play that the roly-poly weeds were horses, and the boys in that make-believe would tie them to the fence posts, which at least ended the traveling. During the winter months the men would go away to earn extra money so that they could continue farming the next season. But life was not dull for the young people, as they met together at one home and then another on Sunday afternoons.

Some who came in 1902 and later were able to buy relinquishments from earlier settlers who had become discouraged because of the hardships of pioneering. Amongst them was Albert Hennenan and his two sisters, Clara and Kate. Al's homestead joined William Gomer's to the north, where he built a cabin that fall and kept a bed and some canned food there. Clara was married in September, 1903, to John A. Hoffman from Spokane, Washington and they settled in the community right after the wedding. Until they had their house built they lived in her brother's house located in the midst of the German settlement. The second evening, after arriving, a rattling of pans and cans was heard at the door. John opened it to welcome a few of our new neighbors. Among them were Henry Gomer, Herman Degner, Edwin Wawrinofsky, and perhaps another one or two. Not having had time to set up housekeeping, we treated them to canned Bing cherries and crackers. This was a special treat to these midwestern boys who had never tasted sweet cherries before.

John drove to Dee's Sawmill for lumber for his house and on the last trip he lost his roll of two new blankets.

The insides of the dwellings were lined with a variety of materials to keep the cold wind and dust out. John and his bride decided on figured-red oil-cloth over building-felt paper. And a double floor with paper between.

Across the property line about 100 feet, John built a cabin for his sister-in-law, Kate Henneman.

In the summer of 1905, Louis Arensmuir took sick with typhoid fever. Theo. Hartnagel had been an orderly and cared for male patients in a Portland hospital but that didn't qualify him to nurse a typhoid fever case. However, Clara Hoffman had taken nurses' training at the Deaconess Hospital in Spokane and had experience in nursing typhoid cases. Even though she had a small baby, she consented to care for Louis by putting his bed in her sister Kate's cabin. Although he needed to be in bed several weeks, the case was a mild one and by the generous use of formaldehyde no one else in the community took the fever.

"Casting your bread upon the water" was the prevailing spirit among these pioneers. They were always willing and ready to go the limit when the need arose in any emergency. These were labors of love and given freely.

On December 16 and 17, 1912, the church was moved from Methodist Hill, about two miles, to new town Metolius. This was the railroad division point and the round house was located here. The townsite presented the church with the lot to induce it to move there.

Metolius

Very soon after building his house, Albert F. Zemke, father of Gustaf and Emil, offered it to the colony for a meeting place. It was well located on the only hill in this settlement. On October 26, 1902, they organized a Sunday school. The officers were Charles Winters, superintendent; Elizabeth Degner, secretary; William Gomer, vice superintendent; Gustaf Zemke, treasurer. Mrs. Julius Degner taught the children and B. Dombrowe the adults. Reinhard Strasser was librarian.

As time went on others served as superintendent, among them Theo Hartnagel, Frederich Henske, John Hoffman Sr., and John A. Hoffman. As secretary Conrad Strasser served very efficiently, as did Louis H. Arensmeier. It is from the Sunday school records of these two men, I am indebted for most of the report on the progress of the organized German church.

The outstanding event of this colony was the organizing of the first church in the northern part of Crook County, in the summer of 1903. It was located near the house where they had been meeting. A. F. Zemke gave the land on which the church was built. Those who had, gave generously. Others gave many days of volunteer labor. Gifts of money came in large and smaller sums from nearby and also from farther away. By February, 1904 a minister, J. E. Traglis, was sent by the German Methodist Church. He also took up a homestead, where he lived.

On July 10, 1904, the church was dedicated. The need of a bell was proposed and on that day an offering of $16.20 started the fund. And in 1905 a tower was added to the front of the church, in which to hang the bell.

Among the early members of the church, with their families,

213

were the following: Charles Winters and family, William Gomer, Albert Zemke and son, Gustaf, B. Dombrowe, Conrad Strasser, Theo. Hartnagel, Julius Degner, Chas. Wawrinfosky, Frederich Henske, Joe Marnach, Joe Rich, Mr. Huchenaur, Louis Arensmeier and brother Daniel, John Hoffman, John Reichen. I humbly apologize to all whose names I have not remembered; I am sorry.

A number of others came during 1905, among them Rev. Jacob Moerhing and his wife and family. They added much to the spiritual and social life of the community.

Early among the trials and joys of the German homemakers came the first sorrow. A younger child of William Gomer accidentally shot his baby brother. No time was lost in finding a burial place. Charles Winters and Bill Grittan, whose land joined across the road from where the church was meeting, gave an acre each, to be used "forever" as a cemetery. It is one of the most beautiful locations of fertile land in the county. The snow-capped mountains are to the west.

The children had a very long distance to go to school. In 1905 a small school was built to the north of the church, on a lower level. The first term was taught by Marie Moerhing, an eight grade graduate. She was followed by Anna Branstetter who was living on her homestead. She became the wife of Cecil Porter. Mrs. Porter was an outstanding and loved teacher in the community, until she retired.

The church having been built on the hill and the cemetery located there, with the school house a half-mile to the north, some one writing the news items for the school district, got the

214

happy idea of calling it "Methodist Hill." News and to this day the cemetery is still known by that name.

About 1909 or a little later, two homesteads were purchased, one belonging to O. Donbrowe and the other joining him to the East, which belonged to Kate Henneman Ritterspacher. It later developed it was for railroad purposes and a residential town-site, Volney Williamson being the hidden investor. He named the town "Metolius." He had streets graded and put down cement sidewalks etc.

This is a little of what happened in the German Colony from 1902 to 1908. There are three epochs— 1st, dry land farming; 2nd, coming of the railroad, founding of the town of Metolius, and getting water from Opal Springs; and 3rd, the irrigation on the land and a new generation.

2

ADDITIONAL METOLIUS TERRITORY
By Mary Brown

Several years before the railroad reached this community many people came here and took homesteads around what is now the town of Metolius.

Among those was T. A. Taylor who came from Kansas in 1902 and took a homestead about two miles north of Metolius A year later came his father and mother, Mr. and Mrs. Henry K. Taylor and two sisters and one brother. They homesteaded about a mile east. Mr. Taylor later married Maud Durham, who also had a homestead on the Agency Plains. Until the farm was on a paying basis Mr. Taylor and his father-in-law Mr. William Durham freighted from Shaniko. Mr. Taylor had the first Holt caterpillar and one of the first big combines in this community. There were pests in those days too. During harvest time the flying ants were so bad that he would put up high white flags on the combine for them to light on, as they always went to the highest spots. The ants would sometimes light on the chimneys and stovepipes and get into the houses.

In 1908, Mr. and Mrs. L. T. Julseth and their family came from Shaniko in a freight wagon and took a homestead on Round Butte where they farmed for several years.

In 1909, Mr. and Mrs. Sam Rowan and family also came to Round Butte. Although there was plenty of work on the farm, Mr. Rowan always found time to raise a good garden from which many people enjoyed vegetables.

Mr. and Mrs. J. L. Mitchell and family were others who came to this community along about that time and they are still running the old homesteads.

People came here from foreign countries as well as from other states. Among these were Mr. and Mrs. D. McLennon from Scotland; Mr. and Mrs. Jerry Sothman from Germany; Pete Larson from Norway; and N. C. B. Kaas from Denmark. Mrs. Glen Graham, who came here with her husband and settled on Round Butte, was from England. Mr. and Mrs. Endre Droblitz were natives of Austria. They had a homestead on the Little Plains which was sort of an oasis in the desert. They had the most beautiful flower garden in this community, even though they hauled water several miles to keep it nice.

There were Mr. and Mrs. Delbert McNemar, Mr. and Mrs. Lewis Wilson, Mr. and Mrs. Franks, Mr. and Mrs. Ringo, Mr. and Mrs. W. A. Ellis and many, many others to whom I apologize for not being able to remember, but to whom we owe a big debt for making possible the present Metolius and surrounding era.

Log school house at Camp Sherman, built in the 80s of hewed 14-by-18-foot logs, of which there were plenty roundabout.

Left—First train over Crooked River bridge, length 340 feet, height 320 feet. Opal City was a busy tent town while the bridge was being built.

Right—Bob Neu (left) and Nick Lambert, first a partner in a land company owning the Allingham Ranch, later owned the River Ranch of 4,500 acres.

J. W. Mendenhall's homestead was the site of Opal City. In 1912 he built there and operated a large feed barn, a very busy center.

Clark Brothers hauling wheat on Agency Plains. They were the biggest wheat growers in the country. Their outfit was quite a sight to see as it came into the warehouse—a string of seven wagons, each one piled high with sacks of wheat, and all pulled by a tractor.

Grandview, Camp Sherman And Metolius River

By Harry Heising

1

I have been asked to write a few stories of our pioneer days in this part of Oregon back to the days of the stage coach, and big freight wagons with four to twelve-horse teams, the leaders carrying a set of arched bells on their hames and guided with a jerkline.

My mother, Mrs. Dan Heising, my brother Dorsey and myself landed in Shaniko some time in September, 1902, coming from Northern Minnesota. My father, Dan Heising, had preceded us. We had supper at the hotel and then climbed into the old four-horse stage and we were off for Prineville. The stage line was owned and operated by Cornett. I was eight years old at the time.

We changed horses at Heisler's and had a midnight supper. Heisler's was on Hay Creek, close to where the small highway bridge is at present time. Our next stop was at the Willow Creek station on the Morrow & Keegan Ranch, and then over the saddle on Grizzly Mountain, on past the Circle Ranch and into Prineville. After we dropped over the divide on the Prineville side we could see Prineville in the distance. I heard a school bell and thought it was the train but my mother said, "No, it will be a long time before you see a train again," and it was.

When we arrived at Prineville we stayed at the Prineville Hotel, run by Mrs. McDowell. My father came that evening and the next morning we started for Bend, our new home.

After many hours of riding across the desert in the burning sun we finally came in view of the beautiful Deschutes River right at the Bend Park picnic grounds. We built a house just above where the railroad track crosses the street and lived there about three years. My mother and father ran the cook house when they first started the big ditch that goes through Redmond. Stidle & Reed had a water power saw mill on the river, just below where the picnic grounds are now. That part of Bend was called Lytle then. My father and a big fat man by the name of Pope cut the timber off of the townsite for this mill. They worked ten hours a day for one dollar and seventy five cents and a bacon rind to grease the saw with.

Pope was so fat that sometimes the saw would get too close and graze the skin on his belly.

My mother got some milk cows and I peddled milk around town, carrying it in two one-gallon pails and a quart measure. In the winter time I also carried a lantern made of a gallon pail turned on the side, with a candle stuck through, called a palouse.

An old man every one knew as Dad West had a butcher shop across the street from where the Pilot Butte Inn now stands. On each side of the big door was a big hook to hang quarters of beef on. Bill Brock and Bill Vandervert each killed a big cougar that winter and they hung them on those hooks for about a month. When it was dark I was afraid to go past them, so would go around the block, about where the Deschutes County courthouse now stands. I had to pick my way through sagebrush which covered the entire section.

In 1904 we got our mail at Deschutes, the Billy Stats place, now occupied by the Brooks Scanlon Mill. My father ran the engine at the old A. M. Drake Mill when it stood where the Shevlin-Hickson Mill now stands.

My father filed on a homestead on Tumalo Creek, a few miles above where Captain John Fremont crossed in early days to blaze a trail through to California. On this trip he carried the brass cannon that he had brought out from Missouri.

On the 28th of March, 1905, we started for the homestead to begin our residence there. My mother and I hooked the team to the old buckboard, loaded a few things in it, and set off in two feet of old winter snow. We made it alright and in the fall we went to Eugene and got a wagonload of groceries and fruit, a year's supply.

Homesteading was a hard rugged life but we didn't know any better in those days; so we liked it. In June 1908 we went fishing on the Metolius River and my father saw a place he liked and he found out that he could buy it for $3000. So when we got home he sold the homestead to Jim Overturf for $2700. So we said good-by to the homestead and went back to the Metolius River on June 8, 1908. We thought it was the most beautiful place in the world, with wild flowers of every description and cold springs on all sides. On the place my father bought there was said to be 108 springs.

219

The first owner of the property was a man by the name of Bamforce. He settled on it in the late 80's or early 90's. The second owner was J. C. Riggs who lived near or in The Dalles for many years. Lee Cover was the third owner, purchasing it in 1905 or 06. My father owned it from 1908 to 1930, when he sold it to H. L. Mack. Then it went to John Zehntbauer, and Leonard Lundgren who now lives there.

In those days the river was full of fish, big dolly trout and white fish. The first salmon I saw was in the fall of 1913. There were lots of bear and all kinds of fur-bearing animals but very few deer. The deer didn't show much sign of increasing until about 1920 or 1925; then by 1930 they really had a good start.

We really pioneered on that ranch, with two neighbors on the river side. Perry South lived at the Allingham Ranger Station and old man Updike had a place on Spring Creek, later known as the Barny Madsen place. Part of this place was at one time owned by a man by the name of Hover and the other part was owned by a Mr. Brown.

The ranch on Lake Creek was known as the Carry place, owned by Jess Harter and Billy Brown of Laidlow, now Tumalo. The ranch at the head of the Metolius was owned by the Black Butte & Livestock Company. The Bruns place at that time was government land and was covered with a pine thicket that a horse couldn't penetrate. Cowboys moving cattle along the road would often lose a cow in the thicket. The name Prune Orchard was given to the place.

The next place of interest along the road was the old log school house built in the 80's of hewed 14 by 18 feet logs. Wells

Bell, a lawyer of Prineville, told me that he taught school there 40 years ago. Daisy Allingham also taught there many years ago.

In the fall of 1917 we built a new log school house, Earl Updike, Ed Parks, and myself doing the work, not far from the old one near First Creek. This has been abandoned and a third one built near Camp Sherman.

This is how Camp Sherman got it's name: Back about 1912 wheat farmers from Sherman County started to come on their vacations, to camp, fish and rest after the summer fallow was ploughed. Some would drive their teams, and a few had cars. Their guidepost for their friends and neighbors was two old license plates crossed and nailed to fence posts and trees. Once in a while I still run onto these old markers.

The old Al Schwartz place was owned by the B.B.L.L.S. Company for many years. Then it was bought by Harry Corbett of Portland and used as a summer home.

The next place on the river was taken by one of the Riggs boys; I think it was Alvin. In about 1900 Alison, or Elison, had this place. He was a trapper who trapped for mink, beaver, and otter along the river, and he ran a high-line for martin and fox. He had one camp in the head of Bear Valley and another at Wasco Lake, a third on the south side of Marion Lake, a fourth at the Hunt Cabins and another at the head of Suttle Lake. He also caught lots of bear by using steel and log traps.

Then the land went back to the government and later was homesteaded by C. W. Allen. Then it was bought by Erskine Woods and is known as the Woods Ranch. Another one of the Riggs boys settled on a place a few miles up Canyon Creek or

221

a branch of Canyon Creek. This was known as the old Riggs place; I think the owner was Perl Riggs.

A man by the name of Phillipee settled on a place on Jack Creek a short distance abve the bridge. Then there was an old man McCloy who settled on Eagle Creek who later went insane. After many years the place was bought by a man by the name of Asher who later sold it to Curtis Baily to get the name of the Baily Place. Dr. Cline settled on Jefferson or Cabit Creek, and his daughter rode horseback to the old log school, a distance of 12 miles.

The Cline Place was taken during the 1880's and no doubt many of the oldtimers will remember Dr. Cline, as he was a dentist in both Prineville and Redmond. Many years ago a nephew of Dr. Cline told us the doctor used to have a blacksmith shop in Lebanon across the street from a dentist. When he wasn't busy making a horse shoe or setting a tire on a wagon wheel he would be over watching the dentist fix teeth. The result was that he moved to Prineville and hung out his shingle as a dentist.

The next place down the river was Arthur King's which he held for a short time and then let it go back to the government. Harry Stout kept his place until 1950 when he sold it to a timber outfit. The Walker Flat Ranch became ownerless when this man was drowned in the Deschutes River and his land went back to the government.

Dad and Grandmother Smith and their daughter Elva had land that joined. They lived there for many years, at first carrying everything in on their backs and later using a packhorse. They sold in 1950.

222

Grandview, Camp Sherman and Metolius River

When Williams was drowned, the same time as Walker, part of his land went back to the government and Carl Hubbard got a part of it in his homestead. The Carter Allingham claim was next after Smith's, then Williams. Carter Allingham's claim was just above what is known as the "Shutin", the point of the mountain that extends into the river so that you must ride your horse in the river to get around it. The Williams cabin is just a short distance below.

The Carl Hubbard Place was a resort for several years. About a mile below the place the road is very steep over a rocky point hardly more than a trail and not a good one at that. The first time Carl took his wife to the ranch he introduced her to pioneer life by tipping the wagon over on this hill and spilling everything down the hillside.

The next place was known as the White Cabin, it was a short distance above Bar Hill and back off the river. It was settled by a man by the name of McCormic. Then we come to the Bean Place, later known as the Adams Place, owned by Laaurie Bean at the present time. Bean Canyon was named after Jim Bean, who cut a lot of saw logs and tried to drive them down the Metolius and Deschutes to the Columbia but failed. Lou Allingham did drive logs down the Metolius and Deschuts and sold them to the Durham Sawmill close to the highway bridge near Warm Springs Indian Reservation. Most of the above-named places were settled between 1900 and 1905. Street was another settler. Adams did not settle on the Bean Place until 1913. E. A. Montgomery became owner of the Street Place on November 1, 1915. It is now owned by Leonard Lungren but is still known as the Montgomery Place. Street was riding a horse along the river bank when some powder exploded and blew him and his horse into the river. The horse and saddle were found but Street never was. Street Creek was named after him.

Another early settler was Dave Riggs, who lived on his place for many years and set out a nice orchard and raised a large garden and lots of flowers. He and his wife peddled fruit and vegetables all summer and fall, driving to Madras, Redmond, Bend, Prineville, and Sisters. Riggs sold the ranch to a Mrs. Graham and then it went to Isaac New and to the Veterans' State Aid Commission. Jess Kane of Prineville had it next, then Guy Lance, then the State got it again, and I was the next owner.

The Allingham Ranch, known as the River Ranch, was settled over 70 years ago by Marsh Auberry. He raised horses and took a lot of them to The Dalles but brought them back when he couldn't get his price. He turned them out on the range and that winter, known as the double winter, lost them all. But he wasn't the only one to lose his stock. Lou Allingham improved his place, setting out a large orchard, built two miles of ditch, and took water from the river to irrigate his land. In 1905 the B.B.L.L.S. Co. bought the place. The company consisted of Bill Wurtzweiler, Thompson and N. J. Lambert. Later Lambert sold out his interest to the company and took this place and some other land, including the Hardy Allen place at the head of Allen Canyon. By adding on to the land Lambert acquired about 4500 acres and turned to raising cattle. I bought the River Ranch from him in the Spring of 1930. Later I bought the rest of his holdings and added to it until I owned 6000 acres. This land was on the point between the Metolius and Deschutes rivers, with Crooked River on the south. This is known as the Three River Ranch.

Captain John Fremont crossed the river here on his way to California and was supposed to have stopped two nights. The ford was later known as the Pitt Ford. Fremont camped several days at Fly Lake and he either left or lost several cannon balls for the brass cannon which he brought from St. Louis, Missouri. His next stop was at Camp Polk, near Sisters on Squaw Creek. From there his trail went to Bull Creek Springs and then crossed Tumalo Creek, about two miles above where the road crosses now. When he left Tumalo Creek he hit the Deschutes River at the tules and then up the river and that is all I know about his trail. Years later his trail from The Dalles across and through the Grandview country was made into a road and many pioneers traveled it. I think the records in Salem shows this trail as a county road and the last rig to go across here was an old man with a team and hack in September 1925.

Camp Polk is an historic spot, as it was an old army post in the 70's and was named after Captain Polk, and Hinkle Butte got its name after a man serving under Polk. Hinkle and four or five soldiers were up on top of the Butte looking around and Hinkle took off his overcoat and laid it on a rock. His horse was feeding down the hillside when one of the soldiers said, "Here come some Indians." Hinkle heeled it for his horse, which ran a considerable distance before being caught, so he didn't go back for his coat and some time later an Indian was seen wearing it. Hinkle Butte is about two miles below Camp Polk on the Squaw Creek Rim.

After the soldiers abandoned Camp Polk it was settled by Hindman and was used as a stopping place for travelers who came over the McKenzie and Santiam roads. Hindman had a store and the first post office in the country. John Craig carried the mail from Eugene. In the winter he made a trip over the McKenzie on snowshoes. He had a cabin on the west side of the lava beds near the highway. One time he didn't come through on time and when he was found he was on his knees in front of his fireplace frozen. He was buried near his cabin, now marked by a marker.

The old Alfred Cobbs Place, about three miles out of Sisters on the Bend Highway, was also a noted place for travelers. The Cobbs family was well known in the early days as were their children, Otto, John, Newton, and Fanny who married George Stevans. After Alfred Cobbs died, his wife Martha married Charles Hindman and made her home at Camp Polk until her death.

The Graham Place was another well-known stopping place for travelers on the old Santiam Road. The road forked, the one on the right going through Sisters and towards Bend, the left one going around the foot of Black Butte and Camp Polk and Lower Bridge. This old road came by the Long Hollow Ranch, now owned by Priday Holmes. The road continued on by the foot of Lafollet Butte. Cash Creek was also a welcome sight to weary travelers, as it was a feed station and a toll gate station where toll was collected from those traveling the road.

Here is a pioneer story as it was told to me by Mrs. Walter Fullerton:

Grandview, Camp Sherman and Metolius River

"In June 1886 Walter Fullerton, with his wife and two daughters, Inez and Augusta, left Salem with four horses and a covered wagon and about 12 head of cattle, headed for Central Oregon. The trip was fine past the Mountain House, up Seven Mile Hill and Fish Lake, I think this was the most dreaded pull on the whole road, but when we reached Big Lake, at the foot of Mount Washington, the weather turned cold and when we got to Cash Creek it was dark and snowing and we went to bed without any supper. The next morning, June 4, 1886, it was still snowing and the wind was blowing and Walt had to shovel snow before a fire could be built. I was trying to get breakfast and the two girls were standing by the fire each with a quilt around her to keep warm, and crying that they wanted to go back home. The smoke was in my eyes and the coffee pot tipped over and I started to cry myself and wanted Walt to turn around and go back home but he said, "No, we are going to stay in this country."

"When we got off the mountain, we stopped with old man Krug who lived at the foot of Black Butte on the south side. We stayed there that summer and all of the following winter. The next summer Walt took up land adjoining Krug's. We built a log house and lived there for many years."

Robert H. Krug settled there in the early 80's and lived there for many years until he was murdered and burned in his cabin, in the winter of 1917 or 1918. He was a fine old man and never bothered anyone and had lots of good friends. I knew him very well.

In 1879 Bamford settled on land joining Krug on the north,

227

later known as the Bob Booth land, then Calbath, and then Ben Fone.

Johnny Steavens settled on Stevens Flat in Stevens Canyon but this land was road land or Eastern Oregon Land Grant.

Part of Squaw Flat was settled on in the 70's by Henry Stricklin, then by John V. Todd, a very well-known man in pioneer days, then by Jerry Young. Each of these people let this land go back to the government. The Fullerton family sold their land at Black Butte to Frank Booth and they moved to Squaw Flat. In 1904 Augusta Fullerton filed on the land and made it her home until about 1935 when she sold it back to the government. Elden Herst also had land on Squaw Flat, as did Lige Sparks who was at the time a partner in the B. B. L. L. S. Company.

Hill Philipi and Tony Trahansham were also oldtimers near Squaw Flat on the Grandview-Sisters Road. Their land all joined the old Potter Place which was a well-known place on the desert. This Grandview country was known as the Lower Desert in the early days.

Potters first settled at the head of the Metolius River. T. M. Post owned the land where the head of the river is, and the Potters' claim joined it. They settled there in the early 80's and later their claim was known as the John Riggs Race Track. In the 1930's the government built a big CCC camp there. The two Potter boys were well known in early days. Their names were George and Pearl.

The Three Pine Ranch was owned by the Buskerks. Others on the Desert were the Nie Ranch, the Joe Kesner Place, the Dan

Grandview, Camp Sherman and Metolius River

Counsel Place, the Athey Allingham Place later known as the Dave Miller Place, the old Davis Place on Juniper Creek, and the old John Buchanan Place. All these places, when I settled here in 1910, were already old places then.

Old John Buchanan with a pick and shovel built the first road down to the Deschutes River. It came down the hill about a mile below where the Grandview grade now is and crossed the Deschutes Bridge and up the grade to the hairpin turn where, by looking straight up, the old Buchanan Place can be seen.

Walter Fullerton died about 1924 and Mrs. Fullerton told me in 1925 that it would be the happiest day of her life if she could go back and see the green hills of Salem again. In 1926 or 1927 a friend came along and took her to Salem where she became sick and died the third day after arriving there. I am glad she got her wish, for she had lived here 51 years.

The Edmonsons were also early-day settlers on the lower desert. They came in the 80's. Bill Edmonson had the first threshing machine in the Grandview country and I think in this part of Oregon. It was a horse-power outfit and was brought from Salem by wagon over the old Santiam Toll Road. Their place was near what is known as the Tate Place now a part of Three Rivers Ranch, which is owned by Heising and is named Three Rivers because the Crooked, Deschutes, and the Metolius rivers join to flow north as the Deschutes. The awe inspiring rush as the three rivers join from three deep canyons is a never-to-be-forgotten picture and may be viewed from Round Butte.

Edmonson raised horses and cattle and his wife helped and always raised a big garden. She also raised a garden down on the

229

Metolius River. There is a government trail down there now, known as Mother's Garden Trail. The garden, on a level spot, contained about one-fourth of an acre which she faithfully watered from the river. Edmonson took a plow down on a pack horse and that plow is still there. No doubt many later-day fishermen have seen the plow and wondered how it got there. Aunt Matty's trail came through the rim near the Tate Place and dropped down onto Juniper Creek and then around the steep hillside above Juniper Creek. The trail is so steep I am almost afraid to ride down it. The trail continues through the Metolius Rim, which is the present trail.

These early settlers went to the Willamette Valley or The Dalles for their needs. Bill Edmonson told me that once when he was coming back from The Dalles he stopped about where Culver now is and he could see his ranch. He should have reached it in three hours but it took him three long days to get there. Because there were no roads or bridges, he had to go to Lower Bridge on the Deschutes River and cross Squaw Creek. He drove over Squaw Flat and down through the desert and home.

About 1905 the next settlers, the Glovers, settled near the Edmonsons. Henry Glover was blind and Frank and Bob now live at Sisters, and Buzz and Luis live at White Bird, Idaho. These boys raised horses and cattle and were great riders. Other settlers were the News, Jordans, Selmans, and Walter Hendrick. In about 1912 the flood of homesteaders came and the whole desert was taken up. Nick Lambert put up a store, Mrs. Wears had the post office, Ransom a blacksmith shop, and someone else

a barber shop. Then a school was built and that was Grandview.
D. R. Ramsey settled at the other end of the desert, a school and
a post office followed, and that was Geneva. A family settled on
every 160 acres. They fenced the land, cleared the sagebrush,
ploughed the ground that could be ploughed after the rocks
were picked off, and then starved out and left.

The water was a great drawback, for the few springs and wells
did not supply the demand. Some of the people hauled from the
Deschutes River and Fly Lake on the head of Fly Creek. It was
a common sight to see some woman going up the road driving
an old poor team of ponies and an old wagon with the tires
wired on with hay wire, three or four barrels and several old
tin wash tubs, and the same amount of children going after a
load of water—a full day's trip.

This is a small picture of what the homesteading days meant.
Today if a woman wants a drink of water she simply turns the
tap.

This is a true story. Fred Loose's wife said she wouldn't eat a
sour-dough biscuit. Later Frank Selman was rubbering on the
phone and he heard Mrs. Loose say, "Fred found an old dead
rat in the Chenewith well today so he must haul water from the
Potter Springs." Frank said, "By gosh, I put a stop to that. I
threw a sour-dough biscuit in Potter Springs."

The Grandview country was a busy community at one time,
but the people finally all left one at a time. They thought once
they were going to have water from Suttle Lake to water the
desert but when that hope faded they all left with the exception
of Velotis, Mrs. Montgomery, and myself.

2

ADDITIONAL NOTES ON METOLUIS RIVER AND CAMP SHERMAN

By Rod Foster and Ruth Bruns

1

(Rod Foster gives the following account of the area on the slopes of the high Cascades): Albert Arnold homesteaded the head of the Metolius River, and David Allingham homesteaded the place now known as the Allingham Guard Station. The latter had a family of five children, three boys and two girls. Al Swartz homesteaded the present H. L. Corbett Place adjoining the Riggs' homestead.

George W. Updike homesteaded the place on Spring Creek which later became the property of Barney Madsen. He greatly improved the place and made a nice house there. He also operated a dairy and supplied the summer campers and the Camp Sherman area with milk and cream and other farm products during the season. He passed away in 1952. Mrs. Madsen still lives on a portion of the ranch but the main part of it is now operated as a salmon hatchery.

Ed Carney of Prineville settled on the place on Lake Creek now operated as a resort by Bud McMullin. Martin Hansen bought the place in 1919 and started a resort which became quite popular for genial hospitality and especially for Mrs. Hansen's marvelous home-cooked meals.

Hansen sold the resort and farm property to Mrs. P. L. Renalds in 1935 and she later transfered it to Haver McMullin in 1937. The farm portion has changed hands several times since. The present owner is Ralph Cake of Portland.

Additional Notes on Metolius River and Camp Sherman

A man by the name of McCoy took up the Eagle Creek Place. I think it is now called Abbot Creek. There is a story that the old man lost his mind and was sent to the State Institution at Salem. It was rumored that he left a considerable amount of money hidden on the ranch at Eagle Creek. I lived there a couple of years and cleared the land of hundreds of stumps and boulders but found nary a trace of the hidden treasure.

My father, C. H. Foster, kept a road house on the South Santiam at Upper Soda Springs. He moved in there with his family in 1882. He had three children at the time and later three more were born at the place. He built several camp cabins and a large hotel and extensive barns. All travel was by wagon and teams. This was a stopover accomodation on the route from the area east of the mountains to the Willamette Valley. Many people stayed most of the summer to take advantage of the curative properities of the Soda Springs.

These people rented the cabins but Mrs. Foster served meals and provided beds for the transients. Mr. Foster kept a small store of necessary supplies, such as tobacco, kerosene, and a few canned goods. The boys fed and took care of the horses. They were 56 miles from Albany, their trading center, and in the fall Mr. Foster would take a wagon and go to Albany for their winter supplies. The roads were impassable after the rains began and what they didn't have they did without.

The children were taught at home. The oldest ones had practically no schooling. However, Mr. Foster was a very intellectual man and gave the children a very good education.

During the winter the boys and their father fished and hunted to provide meat for the table. There were no game laws then and hunting was not restricted. Dad Foster made bacon out of fat bear meat and they made lots of the deer meat into jerky which they sold to the trade the next summer. The deer hides were tanned and carefully made into gloves. Mrs. Foster would make as many as 150 pairs during a winter and they would all be sold to the folks from the east of the mountains. Every possible source of income had to be used.

The buildings at Upper Soda were of interest as being all constructed of logs and boards split out of cedar, made by hand, and there was many of them. This leads up to how we got our first information about the Metolius settlement. Those people would come across the mountains to Albany to get their supplies and would stop over at The Springs.

In those days the fishing in the river was wonderful and sometimes Mr. Foster would go over to spend a few days fishing. Many people from around Albany would go to Belknap Springs on the McKenzie River, thence to the Metolius, and back by way of the Santiam. The road across the mountains via the Santiam was called the Willamette Valley Cascade Wagon Road.

In 1887 the Corvallis and Eastern Railroad was started. They established a camp north of Big Lake, worked one summer and abandoned the project. Most of the laborers were Chinamen, about 250 or 300 of them who walked over from Albany.

Those who built the first homes at Camp Sherman were Martin Hansen, C. L. Belshe, Judge Henrich, Bill Jackson, Bill Ragsdale, George Hannagin, and Lou Peetz. Their cottages were all located on the west side of the river directly opposite the store. These were built in 1918 on land which is still leased from the U. S. Forest Service.

A man by the name of Dick Fuller started the first store. He had a tent stretched over a platform and carried a small stock of staple goods. Then Frank Leithauser, who was the first postmaster of Camp Sherman, took it over and operated it for perhaps two summers. In about 1922 Ross C. Ornduff of Moro wrecked the old building and built the present store. He made almost daily trips to Sisters or Bend for his more perishable supplies and carried the mail from Sisters. At first it was an accommodation then later he was appointed postmaster to act from April to September, and he partitioned off a small corner of his store for an office.

In March 1925, Mr. and Mrs. R. C. Foster bought the store and on April first opened for business. The first customer was Mr. Owen Thompson and the first sale was 50 cents.

Mr. Thompson was a very colorful character, loved by everyone who knew him. He had a pair of Shetland ponies which he used to drive from Moro to Camp Sherman and back in the fall. His ponies were trained and at one time he drove them from coast to coast, giving little shows. The children loved to ride them and sometimes Owen would give the pony a signal and he would buck the youngster off. The ponies loved to drink soda pop out of the bottle.

Mr. Thompson built many of the houses in the Camp Sherman settlement which grew steadily from the first six houses in 1919 to over sixty in 1945.

In June 1925, Evelyn M. Foster was officially appointed postmaster and served in that capacity for 20 years. The office was made an all-year office in about 1928, with winter service three times weekly.

The Camp Sherman residents put in the first bridge there and the Forest Service later replaced it with a more substantial one. Later still, in the winter of 1943, they built the present bridge.

Most of the roads were built by the boys in the CCC camp, which was established near the head of the river in 1933. They put in many fire roads and improved all the main roads in the area.

The Metolius was a wonderful fishing stream for Redsides and Dolly Vardens. The Dollies used to go up into Canyon and Jack Creeks to spawn and it was a favorite sport to catch them. The largest one we ever saw was 38 inches long and weighed 19½ pounds, taken in Eagle Creek. Another taken from Canyon Creek was 35½ inches long and weighed 18 pounds.

Hunting was good in those days and many deer and bear were killed. The beavers were numerous in the river but it was unlawful to trap them. Later, the U. S. Forest Service sent in a Government trapper to thin them out.

Harry Heising used to do a good deal of fur trapping in the high country around some of the lakes, and Paul Striebel had a high trap line.

The first closure of the river was from the mouth of Lake Creek to the head of the river and several years later it was closed from the head of the gorge above the Heising Place.

Benton Burdick has the distinction of killing an Albino bear. He discovered it in his yard and shot it.

The big windstorm that did so much damage was in April 1931. Thousands of trees were uprooted and many homes were badly damaged. The big Corbett home was totally destroyed by fire, caused by the storm and Mrs. Foster suffered a broken leg when a tree fell across the roof of the store and she was pinned in the wreckage.

Dr. Clarence True Wilson, the great Temperance Crusader, had a home on the river below Allingham, and the author Harold Bell Wright spent part of one summer there.

(Ruth Bruns,Mrs., John Bruns—has provided still more history as follows of the mountain community) :

Camp Sherman, Oregon, is situated in the southeast corner of Jefferson County. It lies in a mountain valley guarded over by beautiful symmetrical Black Butte at the south, Green Ridge to the east, the Cascades to the west, and the Warm Springs Indian Reservation to the north. Through the length of the valley runs the Metolius River.

The first tourists came by wagon and camped on the Updike Place, present site of a state fish hatchery.

In the summer of 1915 the Belshe, Hansen and Henrich families motored to the San Francisco World's Fair and on the way home the men kept telling the women about the paradise in the tall pines that they had discovered and decided to show it to them. The women approved of Camp Sherman and thus it was that the first three lots for summer homes on the Metolius were obtained from the U. S. Forest Service on a special-use 99-year lease. Most of the Camp Sherman area is in the Deschutes National Forest. Judge Henrichs, then assessor of Sherman County, gathered up all the old automobile license plates he could find to mark the road that led from The Dalles-California Highway through the Crooked River and Deschutes River gorges, over Grandview Desert and Green Ridge to Camp Sherman. More of his neighbors followed this route and built summer homes until by 1920 there was quite a colony of Sherman County folks. They usually fished, hunted and picked huckleberries as one big family, which included the natives.

Fourth of July was celebrated with a huge picnic at noon, followed by fireworks and ice cream at the Corbett's summer home. And then a swim in Suttle Lake with 3 p. m. the fashionable swimming hour, the ladies sharing one unpartitioned dressing room and the men another.

As early as 1881 when land was originally surveyed by the U. S. Government there were already cabins and cattle trails in this locality. Clearings were made in the forest, and fields were irrigated from adjacent streams by 1888. Some of the ranches were homesteaded and some were school sections purchased from the state.

Most of the early-day ranches are now resorts or summer homes. The Dan Heisings started the first fishing resort on the Metolius in 1908. Today this is the Circle M Dude Ranch. Other resorts are Lake Creek Lodge, House on the Metolius, Rodgers, Band B Resort, Suttle Lake and Blue Lake. There are also the old Allingham Guard Station and the United States Forest Service.

The headwaters of the Metolius are a spectacular sight to view as the spring at the base of Black Butte flows to form a full-grown stream.

Around the turn of the century there was a race track just below these headwaters. The Glaze outfit who had a cattle and horse ranch near Sisters, used it to train their race horses. It also was a favorite picnic and camping spot for many of the Culver pioneers. Wizard Falls (formerly called Allen Springs) Trout Hatchery is a showplace farther down the river.

Until 1950 Camp Sherman's school children attended school in one of the few remaining log schoolhouses in Oregon. A modern school has since replaced the log structure. Several years ago the Camp Sherman Community Hall was built by the united efforts of its citizens. Here dances, movies, dinners, and the usual community activities took place.

In the years since 1915 many summer homes have been built on the banks of the Metolius. The number of permanent residents of Camp Sherman is around one hundred, the summer population varying with the weather and seasons.

Few Sherman County people now have homes here. The addresses of the present summer colony cover several states and many localities. The name "Camp Sherman" is permanent. Probably the oldest homestead settled before the formation of the Deschutes National Forest in 1908 was the Allingham Ranch, a mile downstream from Camp Sherman. Mrs. Frank Zumwalt, lifelong resident of Sisters, remembers David Warren Allingham, a short whiskery man everyone called "grandpa".

Three settlers who later wove much of the destiny of the Metolius River and Camp Sherman country, came into the area in 1919. They were Barnhart Madsen, John Bruns, and Martin Hansen. Bruns came into Central Oregon in 1911 as a time-keeper for a construction firm building water tanks on the new James J. Hill Railroad Line and moved to the Metolius area in 1919 to build the Henry Corbett Ranch. His wife Ruth was one of the first teachers at the old Black Butte School, with a log building reminiscent of frontier days.

Bruns credits the railroad with the change in spelling from Matoles to Metolius. Matoles is an Indian term meaning "white fish" or "spawning salmon". He asks, whoever heard of an Indian word ending in *ius*. That's Latin.

Opal City

By Wilma E. Ramsey

A brisk wind pushes soft clouds across the azure sky. Stately mountain peaks stare across a broad flat plain at tall buttes. Jagged rock formations dot the high horizon like weird teeth on a giant jawbone.

The plain sprawls out—a prone form clothed with broad fields and crested wheat grass. A narrow ribbon stretches from northern butte to southern canyon—carrying the commerce of a state on it's asphalt surface.

A few houses dot the scene. Desert tumbleweed and lush clover grow here with equal abundance.

This is Opal City Flats, Jefferson County, Oregon. It is bounded on northern and eastern sides by tall hills—Juniper Butte, Haystack Butte, Gray Butte, and Smith Rocks. It is enclosed on the south and west by the deep chasm of Crooked River. Standing there as a sentinel, is stately Mt. Jefferson—overlooking the whole region.

Behind every inhabited section of the world lies the dreams and heartbreaks of hardy pioneers. Let us see who built the Opal City community and learn of it's early citizens.

Picture, if you can, a young man coming into this new territory in search of a homestead. Practically none of the land had been taken, and the choicest of locations were available. As far as he could see there were waves of bunch-grass, mottled with sagebrush and an occasional juniper tree. Think of the challenge which lay before him—the decision of where to file for his homestead.

In his hands lay the future welfare and happiness of his family and of their families to come. This bit of land seemed fine, but over across the next little hill, the bunch-grass seemed taller, the sagebrush ranker. Still further on there seemed to be fewer rocks showing on the surface—something to be considered in preparing the ground for tillage.

The young man, faced with choosing his land, decided that the most important factor was water. His homestead must have water on it. So it was that in October 1894 Abe Merchant filed on the very first homestead in the Opal City country; but not until after he had dug a fine, deep well on the property, to prove there would always be a generous water supply. The homestead lay at the south side of Haystack Butte.

As other settlers moved in, the Merchant Well proved to be a blessing to the whole countryside. Everyone hauled his water supply from the generous well, filling his tank or barrels with the aid of an old hand-pump. Some claimed the water had wonderful medicinal qualities to relieve various ailments.

After the Merchant family had settled, the Lamson families, Henry, Charles, Claud, Jim, and Ward took up their homesteads in 1896. Later, the families of Tom Alderdyce, John Harrington, and the Spinks and Clingin families settled. These homesteads were all located close to Haystack Butte. The settlers felt there was a better chance of striking water in that location.

First to settle down in the Opal City Valley were the Mendenhall families, Michael, Walter and Joe. Soon afterwards, the William Ralston family and William Barber came to make their homes close to the foot of Juniper Butte. This portion was called Yamhill Flats, because most of it's residents came from Yamhill County in the Willamette Valley.

The Mendenhalls and Ralstons had originally lived in the same neighborhood in the State of Tennessee. They all moved to Yamhill County, and finally were to be neighbors once more during the homestead days here in Central Oregon. The Ralston family moved to their new home in the hopes that this climate would be of benefit to their son Clifford, who suffered from asthma. The change proved indeed to be very beneficial for him.

A year or so later the Merril Van Tassel, Gus Speaker, George and John Saxton families, and John Henderson settled in the same area. Also there were the families of Jay and Oscar Wilson, and the Lovelace families.

As soon as the settlers had decided on the location of their homesteads, the next important step was to start building their houses. Some lived in tents while their homes were being con-structed—others lived with their more fortunate relatives and neighbors.

Lumber was hauled by team and wagon from the Jack Dee Mill at Grizzly. Rough lumber was purchased for three dollars per thousand feet. With the help of neighbors, the little cabin was soon completed, and the homesteader and his family moved in.

To some of the settlers the cabin was only a temporary one, until there was time and money to build a better one. Others had no intention of really making a home. They were only complying with the homestead law of living on their place for a few years, then selling the land and moving on.

Many chose their building sites in the shade of a grove of ancient juniper trees. Some set out shade trees, but the old-fashioned poplar was about the only kind to survive.

Crude shelters were built for their animals—usually a cow and a team of horses. Some of the settlers made a type of a dugout for their chickens.

A cistern was usually dug close to the house, to store the water supply. And almost everyone dug a cellar, in which to store vegetables and canned fruits.

As soon as possible the settler started clearing and seeding his land, quite a task with the meager equipment available at that time. Often he found it necessary to take time out from his land clearing to engage in hauling freight from Shaniko to Prineville. In this manner he earned money for groceries and supplies and for more lumber. Most of the freighters received sixty cents per hundred weight. William Ralston was one of the freighters.

It usually took about two weeks to make the trip, and the pioneer wife and children spent many anxious moments while the freighter was gone. The four-or six-horse teams pulled two wagons and usually in the teams there was a wild horse in the process of being "broken". The Cow Canyon Grade was a dangerous road for the best of outfits, very narrow and steep. Most of the freighters had sets of bells on their lead teams to warn the other outfits of their approach.

Opal City

Finally the days of waiting would be up and the family would listen every evening for the sound of the returning bells. When these were heard, all would dash out to meet the father, climb aboard the wagon and finish the ride home. An extra good supper was prepared to celebrate another safe journey for the freighter. On the morrow the mother started cooking and baking to fill the grub box on the freight wagon, so he could start on another trip. Often he would have a passenger who traveled with him to Shaniko, the nearest railroad station.

Charles Lamson was hauling freight from Shaniko to O'Neil's Store at Lone Pine. He was driving four horses with two wagons heavily loaded. Just as he started down the north side of Trail Crossing, the brake block broke. As soon as the horses felt the wagons crowding them, they started running. Lamson, seeing the danger, and knowing he could not hold the horses back, jumped from the wagon. He landed against a bank, and the wagon passed over his right foot, cutting off the big toe. Luckily, a fellow-freighter came along to his rescue—caught the runaway horses, delivered the freight to Lone Pine, and took Mr. Lamson to Dr. Belknap in Prineville.

The first post office was established at Haystack in the Elijah Barnett home. The exact location was at what is now the Fred Lyons farm, and the building still stands.

Around 1900 the post office was located at Old Culver. Several business establishments started there at about the same time— a general store, blacksmith shop, and barber shop. Dr. W. H. Snook, noted pioneer doctor, had his first office at Old Culver. Many of the homesteaders did their "trading" at Old Culver, but a good deal of it was still done in Prineville, since Prineville was the county seat. The community was still a part of Crook County.

Later on, the community had the benefit of a rural free delivery route, with Dwight Roberts as the first mail carrier. A post office was eventually located at the town of Opal City.

Children of the community attended school at Old Culver. This was quite a distance and created a hardship for the smaller children, since many of them walked to and from school.

In 1907 the parents decided they should have a school in their own community. A portion of land was donated by J. W. Mendenhall, and a tiny one-room cabin was built on the plot. School records tell us that Merrill Van Tassel and Claud Lamson were the first board members of Opal City School District No. 62.

On April 16, 1907, Miss Ethel Smith said a cheery good morning to the following students: Vern and Nina Merchant, Abijah and Ruth Mendenhall, Paul Lamson, Grace Van Tassel, Roy Saxton, Ruby, Nettie, Ethel, and Nellie Wilson, Elmer Harrington, Harold Richards, Clifford, Earl and Wannie Ralston. Records show that the teacher received $55 a month and the entire term lasted only eight weeks.

In August, school was in session again, with Miss Smith at the helm once more. This time the boys and girls carried their tin lunch pails down the trail to the tiny school house for 16 more weeks. Miss Smith's salary was increased to $60 a month.

School was held in this little cabin and in the abandoned Lovelace residence for several years.

Opal City

A new school house was built about a mile west of the old site, on land also donated by J. W. Mendenhall. This is located on the new Dalles-California Highway, and is still standing. This was a good-sized school building—adequate for as long as it was in use. There are those who recall that one year over 40 pupils attended the Opal City school, with Simon Peter Burgess as the teacher.

As was the case in most pioneer communities, the school house was the general meeting place and served a real need. Sunday school and church services were held there regularly, and several times a month the "Literary Society" held forth with their vigorous debates.

These were all important occasions to both parents and children—a chance to visit with their neighbors. Basket socials were notable social functions. Both mother and daughter put forth their best in culinary art—and hoped that a certain young man would have the money to buy the gaily-decorated basket, which they had spent the day filling with goodies.

Occasionally, in the winter months, dances were held at one of the homes, many of these at Hubert Blair's and Carl Schriber's, being apparently favored with a large "sitting rooms" and a willingness to be hosts. The music was generally furnished by Joe Mendenhall and his "fiddle", by Bill Barber on the "bones", and by Clifford Ralston among the many who "seconded" on the organ.

There was a bountiful basket supper at midnight, and dancing continued on into the wee hours of the morning. The little ones started nodding early in the evening and soon the "bedding down" space was at a premium for the "small fry". They slept while their elders danced their cares away for at least one evening. Whoever heard of a "baby sitter?"

Without benefit of telephone and with perhaps only a wagon to travel in, these affairs were the only occasions at which neighbors would have a chance to visit for weeks at a time. How hungry they must have been for this opportunity to share their joys and heartaches with someone. To exchange ideas on farming with their meagre equipment, and to seek the advice of some of the older, more experienced settlers.

Dr. W. H. Snook of Old Culver was the one who administered to the sick and was usually on hand when the stork arrived. Sickness and death were also met with the helping hands of faithful neighbors.

In time, almost all of the land had been taken in the Opal City community, except along the Crooked River rim. One young man located his homestead in that region. He made a series of crude but substantial ladders down the steep cliffs, and carried his water supply up the ladders from Crooked River. He later erected a windlass apparatus and was able to bring up the water with less effort.

He apparently was a very enterprising young man. The story goes that he "took in" washing, with customers as far away as Redmond. He carried the laundry down the ladders—did the washing by the river and laboriously climbed back up with the laundry on his back. The enterprise came to an abrupt end when his means of delivery was cut off. His neighbor became weary of loaning his team and wagon for the "laundry".

Opal City

Dick Johnson's homestead was along the rim also. He was more interested in wildlife and nature than he was in making a farm out of his rough, rocky land. He had been raised by Indians in the Black Hills of the Dakotas and was a real trapper and hunter. No one ever tired of listening to his tales of earlier days with the Indians.

The families of Frank Bacon and Frank Reynolds and Billie Mitchell were also homesteaders in the rim area, and were among those who spent many weary hours clearing their land of the endless rocks, sagebrush, and junipers. Tom Thornburgh, Myrtle Cochrane, L. L. Hobbs and son Harry, Edward White, Fred Rott, and the Corliss family were also pioneers in the Opal City community.

As has been stated, all of the homesteaders had to haul their water from the Merchant well or from the Osborn well at Old Culver—a distance of several miles. Most of the farmers kept their water supply in a cistern from which the water was drawn out with a bucket or a pitcher-pump.

Volumes could be written on the importance of water in those days, and on the lack of it. It seemed that water colored the lives of the pioneers, so much depended on having it. And to have it meant an endless procession of tired horses and men down the dusty road to the well. It meant waiting their turn at the old hand-pump, and sometimes it meant making the trip at night, after the homesteader and his horses had worked in the field all day. The more livestock he owned, the oftener water had to be hauled. Did you ever try watering several head of stock by drawing water out of a cistern with a rope and bucket? Needless to say, no one ever wasted water.

247

Jefferson County Reminiscences

When Saturday night arrived, lucky was the first youngster to jump into the old round tin tub. Although there were additions of water from the big iron tea kettle, the water was a little on the amber side by the time the last fellow took his turn.

It is very hard to realize now how far a bucket of water can go, or how many different things it can do. It's last duty was to water a few flowers or a tree. It was never just thrown away.

Shortly after the railroad arrived in Opal City the company drilled a 1600-foot well, and erected a huge storage tank. Farmers were allowed to haul water from this well for a nominal sum. Everyone was certainly grateful for having the water supply so close at hand.

However, after the water had been used for nearly a decade, a very disturbing fact was revealed. While being pure in every respect, it was discovered to contain a large amount of fluoride. This mineral, when found in great quantities in drinking water, causes a mottling or spotting of the enamel of the teeth. The teeth look normal at first, then soon become dark-brown in color —almost as if they had no enamel. Without exception this condition was apparent in all of the children who were born after the railroad well water was used. Dentists are not able to remove the dark stains on the teeth. A proper amount of fluoride in drinking water has proved a very great aid in tooth care, but there was too much of the mineral in the Opal City well.

There was wonderful fishing on Crooked River for those who cared to make the trip down the steep canyon trails. Tom Alderdyce and Claud Lamson built a rock monument to mark the start of the trail—thus the name Monument Trail was given to this path.

Wheat harvested by a header on South Agency Plains. Harry Gard at the header box and Cle VanMeter driving the header.

Gathered for a rabbit drive in Mud Springs Valley. Townspeople and Indians joined the ranchers in driving the animals into corrals and slaughtering them with clubs.

Mt. View Schoolhouse on Agency Plains, built in 1903 of lumber hauled from Shaniko by the settlers.

Ranchers hauling water from a railroad reservoir. At South Agency Plains station was a 65,000 gallon tank, filled from a well under the hill. The farmers hauled away as much water as the railroad itself used, being allowed all they wanted free so that blessed were called the names of Hill and Harriman.

Opal City

Rattlesnakes were plentiful along these steep, narrow trails, but in spite of all the dangers, the fishing trips were made as often as possible. At that time no fishing license was required, and the catch limit was as many as one cared to pack out.

A more accessible path was the Stock or Osborn Trail. This was on an old deer trail used by animals to get to the river. Indians had no doubt used it, as there is a large cave a short distance from it, up the river. Excavators have found a wealth of Indian relics in the dusty floor of the cave—bits of baskets, arrowheads, and even the grave of a youngster. Also in the vicinity there are some very fine Indian pictographs.

During the winter months some of the homesteaders added to their income by trapping along Crooked River and in the canyons. There were mink, muskrat, otter, and beaver. Later on, there was considerable trapping of coyotes, as the county paid a bounty for each hide.

Jackrabbits were so numerous that they were a menace to crops and gardens. The homesteaders organized rabbit drives. They built a woven corral, about 40 feet square with long wings made of the same material. The men drove hundreds of rabbits into this enclosure, and either clubbed or shot them to death. Some of the rabbits were dressed and shipped to a market in Portland for $2 a dozen. This helped pay for the ammunition, which could be purchased at the Alfred Munz Hardware Store in Redmond for nine cents for a box of twenty-two cartridges. These drives were not without their dangers. Though each man tried to be very cautious, a tragic shooting marred one Sunday's rabbit drive. A Mr. Mead, who lived at the west end of Juniper Butte, was accidentally shot and killed.

It is always interesting to know how a town or community received its name. It is generallly assumed that Opal City was named after Opal Springs, a place on Crooked River where small "opal-like" stones seemed to boil and bubble up out of the water. This was one of the show places of Central Oregon and the visitor never tired of dipping down into the spring with an improvised, long-poled dipper, and bringing up the jewel-like stones. Many people had them made into ring sets, and every home had several jars of "opal"—souvenirs of many trips to Opal Springs. It is regrettable that the springs were ruined by blasting many years later.

The first mention of the name "Opal City" is found on record when the Opal City Land Company was incorporated on November 2, 1909, by Joseph Houston, Clarence Gilbert, William Morfiett, and Wilfred Jones. Capital stock was $25,000 divided into 250 shares at $100 each. The site of 160 acres had been bought from J. W. Mendenhall, and was his original homestead.

The promoters expressed hopes both verbally and through the press that the prospective town would become the outstanding one in Central Oregon.

A plat and dedication of Opal City was filed soon after the corporation was formed. It is interesting to note on the map of the little town that the avenues were all named after precious stones, such as Topaz, Garnet, Ruby. Also, on close examination of the map, we find that the "Opal City-Prineville Electric Line" went directly through the center of town, on its way eastward to the City of Prineville. So go the dreams of men.

Opal City

In 1912, about two years after the town was platted, the long-anticipated railroad made its appearance. It was generally known that the end of the railroad would be at Opal City for a good while, as a bridge had to be constructed across Crooked River before the railroad could continue on south. So the site of Opal City soon became a thriving tent town.

Mr. and Mrs. Charles Wilson, his brother Frank and her sister Francis, claim to have operated the first business establishment —a restaurant. This consisted of a tent which covered a huge platform. A long table with benches was built and put in the tent. The Wilsons bought a large range which had been used in a railroad construction camp and were ready for business. Mrs. Wilson recalls that the first night they had two customers —Matt Clark, who was surveying the town, and a helper. The next night they had over 50 customers to take care of, and were very busy from then on.

Immediately, other business establishments were started—the inevitable saloon and tents with beds for rent.

There were the usual happenings of a rugged, frontier railroad town. A man was caught stealing a ham from a railroad car. The deputy sheriff arrested him, and on their way to jail in Prineville, the prisoner tried to escape. The deputy shot and killed him.

Mrs. Wilson recalls that they had their restaurant about two months, and then decided the town was getting a little too rough. They sold their business to two young men.

After the bridge was completed, the railroad moved on south and most of the tent houses disappeared. A depot and several section houses had been built by the W. R. & N. and O. T. Railroad. A homesteader, Merrill Van Tassel, constructed a good-sized building near the depot. Here, in 1914, Mr. Van Tassel had the first postoffice in Opal City, and also a general merchandise store. The upstairs was used as a dance hall.

The next 20 years saw many of the homesteaders sell their land and move away. Some of the land was claimed by Jefferson County for delinquent taxes. There were several years of drouth, with almost complete crop failures.

Finally, in 1934, the land was declared marginal by the Federal Government. The farms were appraised by the Land Policy Section of Agricultural Adjustment Administration—later known as the Soil Conservation Service. Many of the landowners used the money paid them by the government to buy farms in other parts of the country.

The marginal land was sowed to crested wheat grass; good fences were built; and springs were developed. Every summer hundreds of cattle graze in the pastures, for a nominal sum per head. One can drive for miles along these fields. All of the homestead cabins have been torn down—but often you can see an occasional clearing of land where you know a cabin must have stood. Then you think of the hardy pioneer, his wife and family, and what high hopes and dreams they must have had. And you think of all the hardships and heartaches they must have endured.

The Opal City townsite reverted to the county for delinquent taxes and was purchased by John Henderson, whose own homestead joined it. Mr. Henderson and Joseph Mendenhall, both now deceased, were the last original homesteaders in the Opal City community. Their sons are now farming their lands.

In the spring of 1946, the mammoth North Unit Irrigation Canal coursed its way through the northeast edge of the original Opal City townsite, leaving only the northern side of Opal City Flats without irrigation—the Mendenhall farm and many acres of marginal land.

Many years have passed since the first settlers came to the Opal City community in 1894. The North Unit Irrigation District gives water to a dry, arid land and has brought new people, new hopes, new dreams.

Not one of the original homesteaders remain. But to the west stands the old sentinel, Mt. Jefferson—looking just the same to these new farmers as to those rugged, hardy pioneers, who first settled the community. Only that beauty and grandeur remain the same; all else has changed.

Pony Butte

By Lucille A. Thornton

There were only a few real oldtimers living at Pony Butte when my father moved his family to our homestead in the year 1913. Pony Butte at that time was a part of Crook County, as Jefferson County did not come into being until late in 1914.

The homesteaders were people from all parts of the 48 states. Idaho had the largest representation; however, such European countries as England, Sweden, and Germany were represented.

Henry W. Thornton and David Johnson still have the land they homesteaded. David Johnson, now in his late seventies, still farms his quarter section. There are but two yet farming the land homesteaded by their fathers, J. Willis Nartz and Lavoy Swanson.

The homesteaders were a Christian folk which probably accounts for the fact that a Sunday school was organized long before we had a school. The old Johnson Place and the homestead of Ward Farrell on Pony Creek were our picnic grounds.

Water was a real problem to the homesteader. In many instances he had to haul water in barrels for household use as well as for his livestock. Ward Farrell built the first dam on Pony Creek, and so had an abundance of water for cattle and irrigation on a garden scale. This watered garden was the loveliest in that part of the country.

Pony Butte

As there was no school, we children enjoyed a whole year's vacation. How we did enjoy that year. We had come from the small town of Dixie, Washington, which is surrounded by rolling hills. The canyon and bluffs held a new and intense interest for us. The beauty of the hills in spring is astonishing. If you have never seen this miracle of springtime when rock roses and cactus blossoms cover the hillsides, then you have missed one of God's most beautiful gifts to Oregon.

We never tired of looking for pretty rocks, of which there are many kinds in this part of Oregon—agates (polka-dot and plume), together with the Indian arrowheads found in sand-banks, a reminder of yet earlier days when there were no home-steaders. Today the Priday agate beds and polka-dot mines have attracted many rock-minded people from not only our United States but from Europe as well. One has to see to really believe the way these people have dug holes in the ground looking for the plume agates found only in the Priday-Fulton plume beds.

When the homesteader came to the Pony Butte area he found only a vast amount of rangeland. He had to clear his acreage of sage and juniper and of what rocks he could haul away. His plow was of the old foot-burner type, totally different from the modern plow. Many times he brought with him his livestock, prepared to stay the rest of his life. A few times he came only with the intention of "proving up" on his homestead in compliance with Government regulations and then selling to the cattlemen. The large-scale cattlemen of that day were H. L. Priday and Bidwell Cram.

255

Thomas Hamilton was a big sheepman as well as cattleman in the Ashwood area who gave the financial aid which so often spelled the difference between success and defeat for many homesteaders. He was known throughout the community as "Uncle Tom" and he and Mother Hamilton became endeared to the hearts of all through their goodness and kindness. Two daughters are now living in Ashwood, Mrs. Beth McDonald, who still owns the original land and lived at the ranch until it burned in 1953 and who with her sons Thomas and Ronald has several large bands of sheep; and Mrs. Joea Johnson who also ran several bands of sheep for many years.

Much has been said both for and against the mining in the Ashwood area. During the depression years of the early 1930's many farmers worked in the mines to provide food and clothing for their families who otherwise would have gone without.

The homesteaders' lives were, on the whole, happy, though this happiness was marred by a few tragedies. One of these was impressed vividly on my memory—the tragic burning of the Frank Morris home. Two of his children lost their lives in the consuming flames. Two others lived although left badly scarred by severe burns.

There was at one time a post office at Pony Butte. The station was called Maud. Mail was carried horseback from Ashwood twice a week. The post office was at Sam Sandvig's homestead and named for his wife Maude.

This same man, Sam Sandvig, was first to bring a threshing machine to the area. All of the farmers worked on the machine and each one, in turn, would have his grain threshed. Some had

256

to wait as late as October or November for the threshing machine to be moved to their places and their grain to be threshed. Each farmer would cut and stack his grain, then wait his turn.

No passable road appeared in the community until 1919 when the county, with Henry W. Thornton as foreman, constructed through the Pony Creek Canyon a road which came out at the foot of Pony Butte and then joined the Ashwood-Gateway market road. The owner of the land through which the road ran disapproved of the construction and obtained a stoppage order when it was but a few miles from completion. The road crew ignored this order and finished the road which is still in slight use.

Very few deer were in the country when we first moved there. In later years it has become a hunter's paradise, in reversal of usual wildlife situations.

The Sunday school of which I spoke earlier was organized at Pony Butte and later moved to Ashwood. Mrs. Sadie Harbison and Mrs. John Billips, Sr. were instrumental in the organization. Each family would take a turn at having Sunday school at their home. Occasionally a preacher would come to hold church services. I recall one incident that happened after my marriage and when we were attending church at the home of my parents. My son Joe was just at the age when difficulties arise from having to sit quietly through Sunday school and church. He finally became so noisy his father had to take him outside to the woodshed where he was soundly paddled. A visiting lady laughingly remarked to me that she wondered what kind of church this was when people inside were praying and a little fellow outside was being spanked. However, the lesson was learned, as the spanking never had to be repeated.

The Sunday school was moved to Ashwood when Mrs. Sadie Harbinson, her son James and Mrs. John Billips, Sr. bought and remodeled an old saloon building to use as a church. This building is still in use, now known as a Baptist mission. Sophia Lierman and Ward Thornton drive the 28 miles between Madras and Ashwood each Sunday afternoon to hold Sunday school classes. Frequently a minister holds church services there as well.

Mud Springs Valley

By Mrs. W. J. Stebbins

Mud Springs Valley derived its name from springs up in the hills where in the early days livestock were watered.

As you travel north from Madras you enter the beautiful Mud Springs Valley via The Dalles California Highway. This paved road is a far cry from the roads the first settlers traveled when they came in to take up homesteads in early 1900. Some came in by train to Shaniko on the Columbia Southern Railroad which wound its way from Biggs Junction, near The Dalles, up through Wasco and Sherman counties every afternoon. Others came in lumber wagons, riding high on the California rack-seats. Some rode horses and a few walked in.

Previous to the arrival of the homesteaders this part of Central Oregon was almost entirely given over to the sheepmen and cattlemen. These did not take kindly to the thought of losing their grazing land. Tales are still told of how some of the pioneers were told to move on or else.

Incidently, at one time during the early days, more wool was shipped out of Shaniko than out of any other shipping point in the world.

It was not an uncommon sight to see large bands of wild horses being driven out of Shaniko to be shipped to a Portland refinery.

Large sheep corrals dotted the valley and bands of sheep fed on the bunch-grass, always attended by the sheepherder and his ever faithful dogs.

Coyotes and jackrabbits roamed at will over the entire area. The rabbits were so thick it became necessary to have rabbit drives. Townspeople and Indians joined the ranchers in driving them into corrals and slaughtering them with clubs.

Prior to the coming of the homesteader and, even after the land was settled up, the most joyous note sounding through in the valley was day after day the freighters' bells. A recent magazine article spoke of them as Conestoga bells and stated they were used on Conestoga wagon horses to cheer up the long trek west. We admit the sound of the bells was cheery but, more important, they were a safety device. Drivers listened for the bells before entering steep and narrow mountain passes and, on hearing them, would find a place to pull out and wait.

Long ago, when Shaniko was the end of the rails and the jump-off point to the Central Oregon frontier, sets of these tingling bells were on the hames of the lead horses of all freight outfits on the winding trail, out over Shaniko Flats, down Cow Canyon, through the Mud Springs Valley, and over on into the town of Madras where they sometimes spent the nights before continuing their journey to Bend and Silver Lake. Not only did the bells help in gaining the right of way but the old-time freighters of the mid-Oregon roads use to say that the bells were placed on the harness of the lead teams primarily to provide the rhythm needed for the horses to step in unison on long pulls up steep grades. One freighter, who once drove eight-horse

260

outfits which were a familiar sight on the Shaniko-Silver Lake route long ago, tells of a time when his string had difficulty in pulling the wagons up a steep hill. In searching for the reason he discovered he had forgotten to attach the bells. He put the bells in place, spoke to his horses, and at the tingling of the bells they all stepped out in unison and continued on up the grade.

It was a great thrill for an easterner who had never seen anything like it before, to watch these men handle their eight horse teams by riding their right wheel horse and controlling the whole string by means of a single jerk-line attached to the left lead horse, the bells tingling softly at every move.

The homesteaders began coming into the valley as early as 1902 and by 1905 most of the area had been filed on at the land office in The Dalles.

The pioneers were a hardy people willing to put up with many hardships they had to endure in order to make a home on this land entirely covered with sagebrush, bunch-grass, and juniper trees.

Many of them had large families. To name a few, there were Mr. and Mrs. C. V. Duling and eight children, Mr. and Mrs. L. A. Young with nine children, Mr. and Mrs. W. C. Darrar with six, Mr. and Mrs. B. F. Preston who had four daughters and two sons, Mr. and Mrs. T. P. Monroe and six children, Mr. and Mrs. Criswell and a family of eleven children, Mr. and Mrs. James Lee with six, Mr. and Mrs. Ollie VanMeter with two sons and a daughter, Mr. and Mrs. Frank Oliver with six children, Mr. and Mrs. S. E. Binder with a daughter and a son, Mr. and Mrs. Snowden White with three daughters and a son, Mr. and Mrs.

261

Bob Cunningham with two children, and Mr. and Mrs. S. P. Loving and three daughters.

With so many children in the community the need of a school was very apparent. At this time we were a part of Crook County and all business had to be transacted at the county seat in Prineville. Men serving on the jury had to make the trip to Prineville and often had to remain there for several days.

In the spring of 1903 a meeting was held at Young's store to discuss plans for a school district. There were nine men present. Otto Hohefel was elected temporary clerk. N. S. Criswell, L. A. Moung, and W. H. Stonehocker were chosen as directors to serve until the annual school meeting on the third Monday in June. A motion was made that the clerk be instructed to get subscriptions of money and labor from the settlers for a school building.

One of the first steps taken was to obtain the land to build on. This matter was taken care of when Mr. and Mrs. W. H. Stonehocker, whose homestead bordered the county road, deeded one and one-half acres to the directors of the School District No. 16 of Crook County, to have and to hold forever, so long as used for school purposes.

At the annual meeting held on June 20, 1903, A. D. Anderson was elected clerk and L. P. Paxton, L. A. Young, and W. H. Stonehocker were chosen as directors. A suggestion was made and was approved by those present that the directors hire a young woman as teacher at as low a price as possible so that the term of school would be longer. An ice cream social was held in the school on the evening of July 3 to raise funds to apply on the debt on the building and purchase needed equipment. The school had been built by the volunteer labor and by donations of time and money from the settlers.

The first school term was held in the fall of 1904 with Mrs. Edith Brown as teacher. She was followed by Miss Effie T. Taylor from Hutchinson, Kansas, who had a homestead a few miles from the school and rode her pony back and forth. She taught in the old school house for a couple of years. By that time so many children were attending that there weren't seats for all of them. At one time there were 47 children in school. So it was decided to float bonds for a new building. The old school house was sold to Russell Lonney to be used as a dwelling on his homestead.

The new school house was finished and ready for occupancy in 1907. Miss Taylor was still the teacher. The bell for the school house was freighted in from Shaniko by T. P. Monroe. Other teachers during this period were: Mina Magness of Madras, Miss Joyce and Blanche Hershner of Corvallis both graduates of Oregon State College, Oliver Mortimore, daughter of an early day preacher in the Opal Prairie community, which is now Culver, Nella VanHorn, Edna Gard from the Willamette Valley, a sister of H. W. Gard, Agency Plains pioneer, Mrs. Josephine Hill; Carl Watts, son of Mrs. Lillian Watts, Jefferson County school superintendent; Ethel Ramsey, daughter of Mr. and Mrs. W. H. Ramsey, early-day pioneers; Helen VanNoy, daughter of Mr. and Mrs. Clark VanNoy, who were also pioneers; Mrs. Ada Brownhill of Madras; Mrs. Selma Trolan of Ashwood; and Myrthena Martin, whose parents, Mr. and Mrs. A. T. Martin, were homesteaders in the Lyle Gap community.

263

It must be remembered that at this time there was very little money in the country. The homesteaders lived in shacks or cabins, as they were sometimes called, built of rough lumber they had hauled from the Grizzly Lumber Mill. Many of the homes had only one room with maybe a lean-to bedroom. They were usually built by the homesteader himself, often with the help of his neighbors or friends.

Water at first was hauled in barrels covered with a piece of canvas. It was a very common sight in those days to see a load of water pulled up to the north side of a homestead shack to keep it as cool as possible. Later, many dug cisterns and hauled in water tanks. At first the water was brought from Sage Brush Springs, a distance of about 10 miles. Some hauled from the Perry Henderson Place. Later, when the railroad came in and put down a well one mile northeast of Madras, the valley farmers took water from there for a time.

About 1912, C. V. Duling put down a well on his place, got water at about 340 feet, and installed a pump. After that the neighbors bought water from him and pumped it themselves. By this time everyone had more stock and it took a great deal of time to keep a supply of water on hand. In harvest time it was not uncommon to see them hauling before breakfast and after supper. This meant starting the day about four and working until after nine in the evening.

The homesteaders were a hardy, good-natured lot in spite of not having much money and of the hard work of clearing the land and putting in a crop with inadequate machinery.

At this time horse-drawn vehicles were the only mode of

transportation. Indeed most of the families had only a lumber wagon to get around in. Then, too, most of the horses were cayuses, or fuzz-tails, as the men called them—untrained, balky, and sometimes downright vicious. It was a frequent experience for a man to lose an hour or two of work in the morning because one or more of his horses refused to pull.

I may have given the impression that all the men coming into the valley were married. This is not quite correct; there were a number of bachelors. Among these were Perry Henderson, Martin Tellefson, W. J. Stebbins and John and Bill Lee, twin brothers from Oregon City, later joined by their parents, Mr. and Mrs. Isaac Lee. A little later were Mr. and Mrs. Marion Hayes, coming from Yakima, Washington to visit their son Charlie who was homesteading on Agency Plains. While here they bought a relinquishment on a claim in the Mud Springs Valley and stayed to prove up on it.

To finish my story, I might say all of these single men married and made homes here. Perry Henderson, besides farming a considerable acreage, was county road supervisor and viewer for a number of years. He married Blanche Hershner. Martin Tellefson, early-day Jefferson County commissioner, married sister Joyce. Both girls had come into the valley to teach school while proving up on their land. A. D. Anderson, school clerk for a number of years and an Agency Plains farmer, married another one of the teachers, Effie Taylor. John Lee married Etta Richardson, daughter of Mr. and Mrs. G. W. Richardson. His twin brother married Adie Barlow who had come into visit her sister, Mrs. T. P. Monroe. Winsted J. Stebbins, who had graduated from an eastern college a short time before migrating west, came in from Gillam County where he had been teaching school. He arrived with a friend who talked him into taking a homestead. He married Eva F. Holdship, who had come west from Toronto, Canada, during the Lewis and Clark Exposition.

Despite a number of handicaps and plenty of hard work, the homesteaders were a sociable, happy group of people. They had plenty of good times together. They also comforted each other in times of distress. They were never too busy to go to the aid of a neighbor who needed assistance. When sickness or death came to the valley the neighbors were right there taking turns spending the night at the sick bed or offering help and comfort to those who had lost a loved one.

Mr. and Mrs. L. A. Young were early-day postmasters at the Youngs Post Office located in the grocery store at Sage Brush Springs. They also handled dry goods and men's furnishings. After the road was changed they and their family moved back to their homestead close to the Mud Springs school house. C. V. Duling used to tell this story of their days on the homestead in 1905. They had four children at this time and were living in a 14-by-16 cabin. The first winter they were there, Mrs. Duling's brother and sister-in-law, Mr. and Mrs. Snowden White and their three daughters, arrived too late in the fall to get their cabin built on their homestead before winter set in. So in spite of the fact that their house was pretty well filled up with their own family, they shared their home with the Whites until spring.

He also tells of grubbing sagebrush ten hours a day for ten cents an hour. A hard way, sure enough, to earn money to feed a family of six. So, like some of the other oldtimers, they sometimes had to live on water biscuits made with lard, water, and flour, and grease gravy called poverty sop, and black coffee. Furniture was scarce; when company came for a meal, empty apple boxes were often used for chairs. Milk was almost a luxury for the first few years; the tale is told of one family so hungry for milk that when they bought their first cow they milked her three times a day.

But life was not all worry and work; they shared each others joys and sorrows and had a good time while doing it. As the years rolled on, prosperity came to Mud Springs Valley. New homes were built, old homes were modernized, every family had a car, sometimes two cars. In fact, they were blessed with almost everything they needed or wanted.

At the extreme southwest end of the valley lived Mr. and Mrs. George Richardson and their family. Richardson was a carpenter and helped construct many of the first buildings put up in Madras, including the Sanford Building which still stands. He and his son Vance, and his son-in-law Bob Cunningham, built several of the new homes in the Mud Springs community.

When Mr. and Mrs. Richardson returned to Salem to live they sold out to their neighbor, H. P. Andrus, who was living on a school section he had bought about 1904.

Mr. and Mrs. Andrus moved to the Richardson house and this is where their son, the Reverend Jacob J. DeShazer of Doolittle fame, grew to young manhood. Jake was a bombardier with the raiders on that historic mission; his bomber was shot down and the crew was forced to bail out. He was taken prisoner and spent several years in a Japanese prison. In spite of the many hardships he endured and the cruel treatment he received at the hands of his jailers, he purposed in his heart that when he was free he would return to Japan as a missionary. He married and he and his wife and their children are home on furlough but he will return to Japan to take up their missionary work once again.

Living in the early days a few miles north of the school house were Mr. and Mrs. Fred Fisher, formerly of The Dalles. The school children used to get a real thrill watching Mrs. Fisher drive by to town in her new buggy drawn by her pure-bred trotting horse Baby Roy. Her close friend and neighbor, Mrs. George White, often accompanied her. In the childrens' eyes they seemed to be almost flying. It was rumored that on a certain night in 1913 electric lights would be turned on in Madras for the fist time. Mrs. Fisher and Mrs. White drove in but to their dissappointment, the light did not go on. They visited for a time on the dark streets with others who had come out to see the display and then turned Baby Roy homeward. The Fishers later built and operated what is now the Madras Hotel.

All through the early years in Mud Springs Valley the real life of the community was centered in the school, and seldom if ever would you find a community with everyone standing so soldidly behind the school activities. Whenever there was a program being prepared, all the teacher had to do was to send word home with that Susie or Johnny needed a certain costume for taking a part in a play or dialogue and, presto, mother would have it ready when the big day rolled around.

Mud Springs Valley

The outstanding event of the year was, of course, the annual Christmas program. There was always a big juniper Christmas tree, which, incidently, took up a whole corner of the room. It simply glittered with decorations made of tinfoil and tinsel, cranberry and popcorn strings, and at the very top a silvery star. When the candles were lighted the pleasure of the children knew no bounds.

Several weeks before Christmas a collection was taken up and a committee appointed to buy a treat of candy and nuts for all the children and everyone else attending. The committee was instructed to shop around and buy from a merchant who made them the best offer. After the purchase, they would spend an evening at one of their homes to fill the sacks.

When the great night arrived the school house was always filled. After the program was over and the children caught the sound of sleigh bells heralding the approach of Santa Claus, their cup of joy was full to overflowing.

There were other programs during the school year and always a picnic on the last day of school. Each child had a part in these programs and other activities which made them especially interesting to all the parents.

The first organization to hold regular meetings at the school house was the Literary Society which met every Saturday night and was always well attended. The homesteaders came from near and far by lumber wagon, in hacks and buggies, and on horseback.

Many a hot debate and good old-fashioned literary program

was given inside the walls of the old school house and later on in the new one.

The Mountain View Debating Society on Agency Plains and the Mud Springs Society used to challenge each other to debate. There was also a number of debators in Gateway who use to attend and take part in the discussions.

A few of the subjects debated were "Resolved that a good-natured, slovenly wife is preferable to a neat cranky one;" "Resolved that Woman's Suffrage is desirable"; "Resolved that there should be Government ownership of railroads".

Sometimes judges were chosen; at other times it was left to a vote of the house. While the debates were lively, even somewhat heated at times, they were always friendly and the decisions handed down were accepted cheerfully, no matter which way it went. Following the debate there was always a good literary program, consisting of readings, dialogues, singing, and instrumental music. To this day it is not a surprise to hear someone remark how he used to enjoy hearing Jim Fleck and his sister Emma sing a duet. "The Church in the Wildwood" was a special favorite which they often sang by request. Their neighbor, Dave Travis, will be remembered for the active part he took in one of the debates and the long poems he use to recite during the literary programs.

The Literary Society did much for the children of the community. They were always in attendance and were encouraged to take part in the programs.

During these early days, any organizations, religious, fraternal or social was free to use the school building without cost. At first the building was lighted by coal-oil lamps set in brackets on the wall. The heating system was a large wood-and-coal heater with a bracket around.

After a time gas-burning lamps were installed and this called for a new set of rules and regulations. The school board requested each group using the school building to fill the lamps during daylight hours or use a flashlight.

As time went on a basketball court was set up on the playground. Later a giant stride and swings and rings were added.

The school water supply was hauled at the rate of 50 cents a barrel and stored in a concrete cistern which was kept locked. A number of the children rode ponies to school, and a shed was built to shelter them in the winter weather.

There were a number of activities carried on at the Mud Springs school which were really unique.

In 1933 the children, aided and abetted by their teacher, published a one-sheet newspaper called *Junior News Paper of Dist.* 6. The staff consisted of the teacher, who was the Publisher, A Managing Editor, and a Society and Local News Editor. The paper covered everything. There was a page of art; a section was set aside for poems and jokes, all original; there was a list of local happenings and announcements. It was typed each week and sold for two cents per copy. A number of copies are still in existence.

Another rather unusual procedure was the serving of a hot dish at noon. Sometimes it was only a cup of hot cocoa, a bowl of soup, or perhaps a meat dish. The children brought the ingredients from home, sometimes pre-cooked, and it was warmed up on the stove and served at noon under the supervision of the teacher. These were the days when a hot lunch at noon for school children had scarcely ever been heard of.

For a number of years after the valley was settled up it was necessary for the farmers to drive into Madras for their mail. After a time a Star Route was established with Mr. Lockard as carrier. The mail was delivered in canvas sacks. Delivery was made every day except Sunday. Long to be remembered is the day that Mr. Lockard was giving a number of the children a ride home from school. In the group were Myrtle and Flossie Monroe, Clara Duling, Ray Cunningham, and LeRoy Duling. Shortly after picking up the group the team of spirited blacks he was driving that day, became frightened and bolted. In spite of the united efforts of the driver and Myrtle, who was sitting in the seat with him, the horses upset the hack, finally broke loose from it, and took off for home on the gallop. Fortunately no one was injured. So they picked themselves up and started to walk home. They hadn't got very far till they met a number of worried parents who had seen the horses racing by their homes, minus a driver. Some of those young people who were in on that ride, still laugh about the excitement it caused.

The Star Route eventually gave way to Rural Free Delivery. J. W. Warren was carrier and he continued for nearly 30 years, to serve the residents in the valley and also those on Agency Plains. Mr. and Mrs. Warren and son Willis lived for a time on their homestead east of the school. When he took over as mailman the family moved to Madras.

A church and Sunday school was started in the valley in the

early days. At first it was a community affair and preachers from different denominations came in from time to time to hold services there. Two of them we remember quite well, the Reverend Hysum, who lived in the community, and Mrs. Hattie Teegarden, who was a teacher in the Madras grade school.

A little later, Elder I. D. Brown of the Baptist church came with his wife to visit Mrs. Brown's sister, Mrs. Nancy White and her daughter Mrs. C. V. Duling. He held a series of meetings at the school house, a number joined the church, and a Baptist church was established. They contiued to meet in the schoolhouse until 1944 when the school district consolidated and school was discontinued in Mud Springs Valley. The Baptist people bought the old school building and moved it into Madras where it become a part of their church. Recently they built a new church at a different location and sold the old building to the Madras Christian Church for a recreational center. The old Mud Springs Valley school bell still hangs in the belfrey of the old building.

The church and the grange owned a piano in partnership a number of years ago when both organizations were meeting in the school house.

About 1915 the Mud Springs Farmers Union was organized at the school house. The organization proved to be popular with the farmers. Locals were organized in several other communities, including Agency Plains and Culver. A county organization was set up and quarterly meetings were held in Madras and Culver. These were the days when wheat was sold in sacks and during this time the members would pool their orders for

273

sacks and twine and with this larger order would be able to buy them at a reduced price.

The warehouse in southwest Madras, now being used as a storage room, was built by the members of the County Farmers Union. This location was chosen because at that time it was adjacent to the Oregon Trunk depot, which has long since vanished. However, the undertaking did not prove to be a success financially and the warehouse was sold. Those who had invested in shares were paid off and the project was abandoned.

The next farm organization to come into the valley was the grange. Thirty-three years ago, on March 23, 1923, State Grange deputy, Frank Gill of Dufur, and county deputy, the late H. E. Keeney of Culver, met with a group of farmers and their wives to organize the Mud Springs Grange. Eighteen members signed up that evening after hearing a talk by Mr. Gill. W. J. Stebbins was chosen temporary secretary and proceeded to collect a membership fee of one dollar from each signer. It was decided to hold another meeting on the next Saturday evening, March 30. Brothers Gill and Keeney were both present for the second meeting and reported that during the week they had obtained an additional 19 signers. Brother Gill ruled that these also would be accepted as charter members. So a grange was organized with a membership of 37 members. Officers elected— J. C. Sothman, master; S. E. Binder, overseer; Perry Henderson, lecturer; and W. J. Stebbins, secretary. Eight of the charter members still belong to the Mud Springs Grange—Mr. and Mrs. Perry Henderson, Mr. and Mrs. W. J. Stebbins, Mr. and Mrs. John Lee, Mrs. Leita Richardson, and Mrs. J. E. Evick. Strange to relate, six of them, the Hendersons, the Stebbins, Mrs. Richardson, and Mrs. Evick were among the officers elected in 1923. Mrs. Stebbins served as secretary for about 14 or 15 consecutive years.

The grange grew and flourished. Meetings were held every first and third Saturday evening and were well attended. Over the years most of the men—and one woman, Mrs. Perry Henderson—were elected to the master's station. We would like to pause for a moment to pay tribute to the masters who served us so well and so faithfully and have since passed away. They are Brothers Sam Mitchell, C. F. Klann, W. R. Cook, and J. C. Sothman.

The literary program which followed the business session was always put on by the lecturer. They were three-point programs—educational, inspirational, and recreational.

A lunch was served after the meeting when the grangers would spend a social hour together.

There was the thrill of having the late Hon. Walter M. Pierce visit our grange meeting one evening while he was governor of the state, and while meetings were still held in the school house. The governor, a long-time granger, made an interesting talk during the evening and seemed to enjoy very much the sociability and also the refreshments served by the grange ladies on the school desks and also the coffee brewed on top of the pot-bellied stove. Mr. Pierce, a wheat raiser himself, was wearing his ten-gallon hat and seemed to be right at home with the group.

About this time the grangers began to plan for a hall of their own. As first step in that direction, they bought four lots in

275

Madras and later they bought an old bank building at Metolius which was moved onto their lots in Madras on November 25, 1938, by William Edwards. However, it was not until June of the following year that they held the first meeting in their own building. Dedication ceremonies were held on March 16, 1940, with state master Ray Gill and other grange dignitaries present.

Much of the credit for the succees of this project is due to the hard work and hearty cooperation of the members of the Home Economics Club. The club was organized in June 1929 at a meeting held for that purpose at the home of Mrs. Perry Henderson. Mrs. Henderson was elected chairman and Mrs. Selma Trolan secretary-treasurer. They met at the different homes on the fourth Saturday of each month to work out plans for making money to buy the many things that would be needed in their new hall. They also made sashes for the grange officers.

In 1928 the subordinate granges of Jefferson County—Mud Springs, Haystack, Ashwood, and Grizzly—met at a joint meeting to organize a Pomona Grange. The movement was started by Mud Springs Grange who appointed a committee to contact the other granges in the county and get their reaction to the idea. Because the Mud Springs Grange was still meeting in the school house, Haystack offered the use of their hall. The meeting was held in March 1928. It was a big meeting. H. E. Keeney was elected master, W. J. Stebbins overseer, Jim Thomas secretary, and Mrs. W. J. Stebbins lecturer. It was decided to meet once a quarter at the different grange halls. Mud Springs was to have the March meeting, Grizzly the June meeting, Ashwood the September meeting, and Haystack the December meetings. Mud

276

Mud Springs Valley

Springs Grange members who have served as master of the Pomona are Perry Henderson, W. J. Stebbins, and Floyd Glass.

Until the Mud Springs Grange had their hall finished they rented the Odd Fellows Hall in Madras when it came their turn to entertain. Governor Pierce was again a guest on one of these occasions.

H. E. Keeney, Pomona master, organized a drill team, choosing the members from the different subordinates. Haystack and Mud Springs put on the floor work, Ashwood and Grizzly were in charge of the tableaux.

Mud Springs Valley was right in the middle of the activities when the Hill and Harriman railroad lines made their historic race up the Deschutes Canyon in 1910. Harriman came right up through the valley, passing through many of the homesteads. Many of the settlers worked on the road with their teams. The neighbors thought they had a good joke on Duling when word got around he had been fired off his own place because he did not trot his team when ordered. The same thing would have happened to Stebbins who also had a team on but he saw it coming and beat them to it.

Those were busy days for the late Mrs. Duling, as she boarded 16 of the men. One day she cooked for 32 men and still they kept coming until her supplies were exhausted and she had to turn them away.

The two big railroad day celebrations were highlights in the lives of the children, many of whom had never seen a train before. The Oregon Trunk won the race and held their celebration in Madras on February 15, 1911. Harriman's line arrived a few months later and celebrated the occasion by bringing in a big circus train to their depot on Agency Plains. It was a very exciting time; the long-awaited railroad had finally arrived in Central Oregon and arrived in duplicate. Many had almost given up hope and had expressed the opinion that they would believe them when they saw it. Well, in 1911 they saw double.

In April 1909, Mr. and Mrs. S. E. Binder, early-day homesteaders, and their two children made a trip to California in hopes that a change of climate would benefit Mrs. Binder's health. To their great disappointment the change did not help and she passed away in June of that year. Mr. Binder, Leita, and Kenneth returned to Oregon just in time to ride in on the first regular Oregon Trunk passenger train. There was no bus to meet the train and they, along with the other passengers, had to make their way into town over rocks and through sagebrush by lantern light, but like a lot of things in those days, it was rough going but lots of fun.

The coming of the railroad up though the valley made many changes. It passed right through the land of G. A. Paxton who was familiarly known to all the pioneers as General Paxton. A depot was built on his place and was called Paxton. Later a large warehouse was built beside the tracks and during the harvest time the warehouse was filled to overflowing with wheat hauled in by the farmers. Here is where the Clark Brothers, Dolph and Roth, the largest wheat growers in the country at that time hauled their grain. Their outfit was quite a sight to see as it came into the warehouse—a string of seven wagons, each one piled high with sacks of wheat hauled by a tractor.

Mud Springs Valley

Right now I would like to complete the story of the old Mud Springs school house. You remember that after the new schoolhouse was built the old one was sold and moved to the Paxton community. After the arrival of the railroad more people moved in and they needed a schoolhouse. So once again the old building was put into service.

There were about 15 children in the district. To name a few of them, there were the three children of Mr. and Mrs. Hull Paxton; George White Jr., the son of Mr. and Mrs George White, the four children of Mr. and Mrs. Miles Fox; Fern and Orpa Tellefson, daughters of Mr. and Mrs. Andrew Tellefson; and Helen Martin, daughter of Mrs. Glen Martin who taught the school for two terms. Other teachers were Mrs. Ava Carter, Jeanette Leach, Mrs. Hans Rammin, Mrs. Ben Kaufman, Alice Olson, and Mrs. Bonnie Thompson, now Mrs. A. F. Lierman. Mrs. Hull Paxton was district clerk.

The great tragedy which overtook the W. C. Darrar family in March 1946 upset the whole community and the county as nothing else ever has done. Mr. and Mrs. Darrar, his sister, Mrs. Martha Thompson, here on a visit from Wisconsin, and the Darrars' son-in-law and daughter and their six-months-old son, Harold, had driven to Willamette to visit with another daughter and son-in-law, Mr. and Mrs. Wm. Green.   Enroute home, while passing through a very busy intersection, they were struck broadside by an oncoming car. Mrs. Darrar was fatally injured at the scene of the accident. Mrs. Johnson and the baby died the next day. Mr. Darrar passed away in a hospital a few days after

279

the accident. Mr. and Mrs. Darrar were pioneers and had lived in Mud Springs Valley many years.

Many and varied were the experiences of the early-day homesteaders. We are remembering the epidemic of scarlet fever which struck the valley in 1906. The children were all exposed to the disease by a little girl who was visiting here. Every child came down with it except Arthur Summer, son of Mr. and Mrs. Wesley Summer. Leita Binder was a very ill little girl and was in bed for several weeks and was unable to return to school for over two months.

In 1912, representatives of 10 of the school districts in Jefferson County met to organize a union high school district.

A room on the second floor of the old grade school building in Madras was obtained and school commenced that fall with Charles E. Cilgore, as the only teacher. There were 13 students enrolled.

That same fall the high school students put on a program and box social to raise money to start a library. It was a financial success, proceeds of the evening being $125. There are only three members of the original student body still living in the country. Roscoe Links, his wife Aural Moore Links, and Leita Binder Richardson.

I might go on and tell many other stories of life in the valley. I might bring to mind the big snow of 1921, when snow continued to fall for several days and lay four feet deep on the level and the thermometer plunged to 45 below zero. I might even speak of the farmers who joined the Home Guards during

Mud Springs Valley

World War One and rode into Madras every evening to stand guard all night over the water supply and the warehouses. But for fear I might weary you I will bring my story to a close, as of now.

South Agency Plains

By Lela Gard Ramsey

1

The pioneers who came to Central Oregon to establish homes were a patient and hard working lot and of such were those who settled the southern part of Big Agency Plains.

Agency Plains, consisting of 28,000 acres and named for the Warm Springs Indian Agency on account of its proximity to the small town of The Agency, was a land of sage and bunch grass, with sparsely-scattered juniper trees at the advent of the homesteaders. The juniper was excellent for firewoood and posts, and was much in demand for ornaments and jewelry as early as 1907, as the wood took a very high polish.

The settlers stood in awe and feasted their eyes upon the grandeur of the panorama that burst upon them when they ascended to the plateau of Agency Plains.

To the northwest they saw the imposing peak of Mt. Hood, to the west was sturdy Mt. Jefferson, and to the southwest the graceful Three Sisters. On the east were the Blue Mountains. On the North stood the Mutton Mountains.

To view a sunrise coloring Mt. Hood and Jefferson in rosy tints, touched their emotions at the beauty and majesty of God's creation. The sunsets were as beautiful. A visitor to this part of the country often exclaimed over the privilege of living where one can enjoy such beauty of nature.

When a settler moved away he was heard to remark, "I am lonely for the mountains."

The land had been thrown open for homesteading in the 1880's but not until the railroads advertised extensively with posters and informative circulars, right after the turn of the century, was interest awakened in this virgin land. The railroad preached the gospel of mild climate and told of many advantages awaiting the homeseeker. They offered colonists rates to those desiring to investigate. The price of a ticket was $30 from Omaha, Kansas City, Duluth, St. Paul, and other points.

Settlers came flocking to Oregon but lack of transportation facilities presented such a problem, and the distance from the railroad was so great, that it prevented all but the hardest and most determined to settle in this new land. Most of the men bached while they built the homestead shacks and hurriedly got things in readiness to bring their families to the "Promised Land" as soon as possible. There were a number of homesteaders who came on account of ill-health of some member of their family, who needed the high dry climate of this region.

Each entryman was allowed 160 acres or a quarter-section. To homestead, the entryman had to be 21 years of age and a citizen of the United States or have submitted his application for citizenship.

Seven years were allowed to submit final homestead proof, after date of allowance of application, but final proof could be made in five years if the homesteader had complied with the

283

cultivation and residence requirements. The entrymen were required to reside on their homesteads seven months out of the year.

Some of the settlers did not wait the required five years to make final proof but made commutation proof—often referred to as "commute"—by a residence of 14 consecutive months and a payment of $1.25 per acre. In all cases, six months were allowed after absence of application for the entryman to establish residence. If a settler did not live up to the requirements of the law, it was possible for a person to contest his right, and, if successful, thereby acquire the land for himself by the usual homestead procedure.

At times relinquishments were purchased from the entrymen who for financial reasons or otherwise were unable to meet the demands of the homestead law. They preferred selling their equity and renouncing all rights to the claim to having it contested and lose the place without compensation. The purchaser filed on the land and became a homesteader subject to all homestead laws.

There are two Agency Plains, which is approximately fifteen mile long and eight miles wide, and Little Agency Plains with a length of twelve miles and a breadth of three. They were situated in Crook County in pioneer days but in 1914 Crook County was divided and the new county of Jefferson was born. It was named for the towering peak of Mt. Jefferson.

To separate, the law required a favorable vote of 65 percent of the population in the new county to be formed, and 35 percent of the remainder of the mother county.

South Agency Plains

Crook County had previously separated from Wasco County in 1882.

Agency Plains had been a pastureland for sheep, cattle, and mostly wild horses at the time of the first emigrants. Once a year, usually in April, hundreds of these horses were driven to a corral in The Basin, where the colts were branded and the horses traded and sold. The coming of the settlers drove the horses from the Plains. There also were herds of antelope on the plateau and occasionally a bear was killed crossing The Plains.

The Basin later was called "Palmain" for a short period; but when the post office was established, the name of the little town was changed to Madras.

Into this land of howling coyotes, sage and rattlesnakes, men brought their families in wagons, and with them most, if not all, of their worldly goods. A few women and children came on a railroad spur-line to Shaniko, where they were met by their husbands and fathers, comprising a round trip of 80 miles for the men in wagons.

There were badgers, porcupines, and lynx cats in this primitive country. As coyotes preyed on sheep and lambs, a bounty of $1.50 a head was given for them. A $2 bounty was passed on wildcats, the state and county each paying half of the bounty.

The land was level and fertile but first had to be cleared of sagebrush before it could be put into production.

To the first settlers The Plains appeared as a sea of sage.

Children earned 25 cents a day piling the brush, but always the highlight of the day's work was the big crackling bonfires lighting up the darkness with the pungent odor of sage on the night air. While the adults solemnly talked of their hopes and fears of carving homes out of the wilderness, the youngsters laughed and made merry. Pioneer children must of necessity invent and improvise their own sources of pleasure. Every day was an adventure and never were there more fun-loving and contented children, They explored the canyons, they gathered the fragrant yellow-bells in the spring and the purple lilies in July.

They also shared the responsibilities of this great enterprise of taming a new land. As soon as a boy was old enough to drive a team of horses he hauled water —always the everlasting water hauling—and helped in every way possible with the general work. The Plains were barren of water and farmers hauled in barrels at first. Even wives took their babies and hauled during the busy season, from the Isham well in Madras, the Deschutes River, and the Campbell Well.

The farmers had the long steep Elkins Grade, later called the Campbell Grade, to contend with when hauling from Campbell's Well or from the river. Men spoke reverently of their brakes and wondered if they would hold. They often arose in the wee hours and hauled before breakfast or late at night after the day's work and chores were done.

What courage and fortitude these intrepid pioneers displayed. They truly were of dauntless pioneer stock.

Some settlers on the way to their homesteads paid as high as 25 cents a bucket to water their horses. Every drop was precious. In the summer the water was too warm to drink from the barrels and in the winter it froze. During the summer it was necessary to haul every day. As soon as possible they purchased or had built large tanks to haul the water in.

South Agency Plains

By 1905 most of the settlers had cisterns. Some stored snow in them instead of the usual method of hauling water and filling them. These cisterns were a blessing and life-savers.

One farmer later drilled a well and found water at 400 feet. N. H. Pinkerton contracted to have a 2000-foot well drilled, if necessary to obtain water, at $2 per foot if water was reached, but if no water was found he was not to reimburse the contractor at all. He never did get sufficient water to supply the needs of his farm.

Some winters when the roads became impassable, it was necessary to melt snow for the stock.

A sheet-iron heater would be kept red hot by one of the family feeding it steadily with sagebrush—what an insatiable appetite it possessed—while others kept the snow piled high in the big kettles and dish-pans. This continued day in and day out but, as a rule there was time for heaping pans of pop-corn—popped in a big covered skillet, and sometimes they pulled taffy.

In the early days the snow was from one to two feet deep, often more, almost every winter. As soon as there was plenty of snow, much of the traveling was done by sleigh. What fun! The sound of tinkling bells, the nippy air, the singing and the thrill of gliding over the sparkling snow, are unforgettable.

In the early days a blizzard struck fear into the hearts of men. The settlers' homes had been hastily thrown together, and were therefore drafty. When the howling wind carrying a load of swirling snow-flakes, beat against the homestead shack, the family plied the stove with an abundance of fuel and sat as near the heat as possible, becoming a well-knit unit pitted against the elements. They feared also for their stock which had little protection against the storm. It would get as low as 26 below zero and, at one time, the thermometer dropped to 34 below. In those long ago days the settlers did not at least have plumbing worries, regardless of how low the thermometer dipped. If one should be so unlucky as to get his toes, ears or fingers frosted, they were rubbed vigorously with snow until the blood would start circulating again. How they would sting!

The settlers liked the month of October best of all. The grain was harvested, the vegetables stored, and life in general became easier. These were relaxing days, lazy days, happy days, so warm and quiet and still that it seemed that all nature was hushed and listening for the first onslaught of winter.

In those first winters there were weeks of dense fog. Many a story was told of some settler getting lost in the wide expanse of The Plains, and wandering in circles for hours until finally locating a line fence and following it until he could get his bearings.

Some years during the summer season thunder and lightning storms were prevalent.

One warm Sunday afternoon a ball game was in progress with much excitement at Vanora near the Deschutes River, when an electrical and rain storm suddenly appeared and interrupted the game. Everyone scurried for shelter, including three girls, daughters of Agency Plains ranchers, Bernice Ramsey, Zelma Cummins and Lela Gard, also a Mr. Frank Ringo who was employed on the Plains, All four ran under the same juniper tree where a team of horses were hitched to a buggy and tied to the tree. A bolt of lightening struck the tree, knocking the un-lucky people to the ground. The horses were killed instantly; they fell to their knees and remained in that position until the harness was removed. Dr. Snook of Madras was hastily summoned for the unconscious victims. All survived and suffered no ill effects. The doctor seemed to think their lives were saved by the horses receiving the majority of the jolt.

The settlers eagerly took up their labors again when the chinook wind thawed the ground sufficiently for tilling the fields. In the spring a bitter wind tormented the farmers as they went about their various duties. There were roads around almost every section of land. These roads were named for the first signer on a petition.

Dust plagued the housewives from the very beginning. The continual hauling of water kept the roads rutted and deep with dust in the summer. One could see whirlwinds or dust-devils continuously during th heat of the day.

Everything had to be done the hard way. There was no easy way. The tub-and-board was the mode of laundry and the tub served a dual purpose as bath tub. The ironing was done with flat irons. A housewife felt that she had walked miles in carrying the irons from the stove to the ironing board and back again to the stove. Not so convenient but these women were sturdy speci-mens and took life as they found it, in their stride.

The women of this drab country yearned for beauty and color to enrich their lives. They had dreams of multi-colored flower gardens. Their efforts were frustrated to a great extent by in-sufficient rainfall, but they never gave up and paintsakingly persevered in their endeavors from year to year.

They were extremely kind and helpful whenever sickness or death struck one of their neighbors, giving unstintingly of their time and sharing any luxury that they might happen to possess. They were bound together by mutual necessity. Those were the good old days when the entire family piled into a wagon and went for a good old-fashioned visit.

The only method of lighting the homes of the pioneers was by means of kerosene lamps. These were very tempermental and needed constant attention. Unless the wicks were kept trimmed they would smoke and blacken the chimneys, or a gust of air from an open door would extinguish the flame. One often found himself groping in the darkness. The filling and cleaning of the lamps were endless chores.

Wheat was the product raised for the market. If there was moisture enough and at the proper time, especially in the late spring, to insure well-filled heads, a good yield of 15 to 20 bushels an acre could be expected.

The farmer received 80 cents per bushel but it cost him 24 cents to have it freighted to Shaniko and 11 cents more a bushel to have it shipped by rail from Shaniko to Portland. In 1908 a million bushels of wheat was raised on Agency Plains.

The railroads carried on a crusade to get the settlers to accept the better methods of dryland farming, such as summer-fallowing-for the wavering faith of the farmers in dryland farming was becoming noticeable. The farmers who accepted the better method, raised much larger crops than those who continued to Squaw farm.

All of the farming was carried on with horses. The men spent many tedious hours breaking wild horses. They were forced by necessity to break the horses to harness and to ride, and most of the farmers preferred taming their own horses. They thought that some "bronco-busters" permanently ruined the horses.

A group of young men would congregate at the home of a settler to assist in domesticating the wild horses. It was tiresome and hazardous work for amateurs but they were venturesome and enjoyed the perils that accompanied the sport.

Sometimes the younger generation would become so enthused that they would venture too near and have to scamper for safety when a wild horse seemed to have got out of control.

One young fellow was breaking colts in the spring-time, working each colt half a day at a time. When he stopped to adjust the plow, one of the colts laid down and refused to get up and no persuasion would avail until finally in desperation the man unhitched the horses and started for the barn. The colt thinking that the day's work was finished jumped up neighing and ran after the horses. Much to his dismay he was returned to the plow.

They generally used what was called "breaking horses" when subjecting untamed horses to harness. In fact a good breaking horse was almost indispensable. The wild horse was snubbed to the breaking horse to help hold him while he was plunging and rearing about.

When breaking them to wagons the men would let the horses run until they mastered their fear or had the bucking and running fever out of their systems. It was a tense and thrilling moment when the driver ascended to his position in the wagon before the start of the wild ride.

In the course of a week, with proper handling, the horses usually would become part of the team, drawing their share of the load like seasoned work horses.

Mules were also used by some farmers. One instance of a farmer breaking a mule team was of a young man who ran into many difficulties during the entire ordeal. After getting the mules harnessed and attempting to get them hitched to a spring wagon, he discover that both mules insisted on getting on the same side of the wagon tongue. After many endeavors the farmer finally got them hitched to the wagon. They took off in a dead run up the lane for several hundred yards. All of a sudden they seemed to sense that they were getting away from home. So, acting as of one mind, they whirled around so abruptly that the wagon made the turn on two wheels.

When they reached the barn lot they seemed deliberately to run between two pieces of machinery standing a short distance apart, to rid themselves of the vehicle and the driver. In the process the doubletree was broken and the mule skinner plunged headlong over the dashboard but still holding the lines. After dragging the farmer to the barndoor they stopped, acting very docile and looking innocently around at him, but the farmer was provoked, to put it mildly.

After repairing the wagon and obtaining a rawhide whip, the man made another attempt to subdue the fractious mules. He started for Madras but the obstinate animals insisted on turning off at every sideroad.

When they finally arrived in town the mules began to bray loudly, much to the chagrin of the farmer. They crossed over the wooden sidewalks, scaring pedestrians, no matter how hard the driver tried to manage them.

A friend whom he told of his difficulties with the cantankerous mules volunteered to assist him in getting out of town.

After arriving home he told his family that they were the first and last mules he would break. When asked why, he answered, "I have no intention of trying to break animals that can think faster than I can".

The mode of travel for men and women in this long-ago era was often by horseback. Some of the women rode side-saddle.

The sulky plow was the one most commonly used. At first the grain was harvested with mower and rake and a binder, but later the header became the standard method of harvesting.

One farmer even cut with a scythe the first 10 acres that he raised.

Each farmer kept out a surplus of wheat to take to the mill at Prineville to be ground into flour. Some families got as high as 40 sacks a year. In 1909 a mill was installed in Madras which eliminated the long haul to Prineville.

After wheat came into production every farmer raised hogs. Butchering time was a big event, what with smoking the meat, grinding and mixing the sausage, rendering the lard, and making a year's supply of soap.

Women baked all their own bread. Some had to bake every day, and fed their families without the aid of deep-freezers, refrigerators, and all the easy methods known today. It was even necessary to grind their own coffee in little coffee mills.

It was a difficult task to purchase food anywhere, at any price.

Some farmers walked to The Agency and carried groceries home in sacks on their backs, often including a 50-pound sack of flour. They bought groceries from a small store east of The Plains operated by Lou Young and later from the J. T. Malloy Store, the first store to be established in Madras.

The farmers raised fine vegetables and watermelons. Fresh fruit was practically an unknown luxury but dried fruit was a part of almost every menu. The vegetables were stored in rock or dirt cellars.

Sage hens and cottontails graced many settler's table and necessity camouflaged them into a delectable dish.

A few families journeyed to the Willamette Valley and canned and jammed their winter's supply of fruit. They crossed the mountains by wagon, taking at least four days over the Barlow Route. The children played and dozed in the back of the wagon. Sometimes they all sang as they traveled along. Oh, treasured memories.

All produce, groceries, and other supplies were brought from Shaniko by freight wagons, which were a spectacular sight. These horses were kept in good condition.

It was the year 1903 when the big hail-storm struck with all its force. Some of the hail was as large as goose eggs, so oldtimers say. It killed hundreds of jackrabbits and sage hens, and pounded all crops into the ground, so that not a stalk was left standing.

Feature, if you will, the poor settlers who had worked so laboriously to clear the land of sage and get it to producing, only to have their first crops destroyed. One farmer was breaking a horse to a wagon when the hail began to fall. Before he could get his horses unhitched and get under the wagon, he was practically scalped for in the meantime his hat had blown away.

A young settler, Harry Gard, who had been visiting at the Ed Campbell home started up the Nigger Brown Canyon after the storm. When he came around a bend of the canyon there was a high wall of water roaring toward him. He had to scramble madly up the hillside to save his life.

In his rush he had climbed the opposite side of the canyon from the one where his home was situated. Consequently it was necessary to make a long circuit around the heads of branching canyons to find a place where the water was shallow enough to wade.

Several hours later he reached home weary and drenched to the skin.

Every child and many adults collected what they called "pretty rocks" as a hobby. They were found almost everywhere. Many relics of the Indians were also found.

There were five Branstetters who homesteaded on The Plains in December of 1901. Four of them homesteaded on adjoining quarter-sections, thus forming a square section of land. They built their homes on the inside corners of their places, thereby enabling them to live near each other.

The first Agency Plains schoolhouse was built in 1903 by donation. The lumber was hauled from Shaniko by the settlers. The first directors of the new district which comprised the entire plateau were Ed Campbell, Milo Gard and William Ramsey, with Harry Gard as clerk. Each father made his children's school desk and bench, and the youngsters were proud of their father's handiwork. Children carried their drinking water in bottles or syrup buckets. Woe unto the child who spilled his water! He would have to borrow a drink if he could be lucky enough to find a schoolmate with a little extra water.

George Branstetter was the first teacher. His salary was raised by subscription and was sufficient for only a three-month's term. The second teacher was Andrew Larson, a young single man, who was quite an athlete. He later purchased a meat market in Madras. Miss Grace Smith, one of the first homesteaders, was the third teacher in the new district. She later taught in Madras and married a business man there. Some children walked or rode horses a distance of four or five miles to attend school. In November 1907 a new room was added to the schoolhouse, as the attendance was increasing rapidly. Miss Marie Galloway was the first teacher in the new addition and was followed by John Campbell, as the second teacher, when Miss Galloway resigned.

The original Mt. View Schoolhouse still stands and is an old landmark.

By 1903 Sunday school was being held at the Henry Branstetter home. Children walked a great distance to attend. Mrs. George Branstetter was the teacher. They enjoyed hearing Miss Edith Branstetter play the organ and sing the hymns in her fine voice. The Agency Plains Pioneer Union Sunday School met in the new schoolhouse on October 23, 1904, with William Branstetter as superintendent. The pioneers, as a whole, were a wholesome and God-fearing lot. The Reverends H. L. Bell, G. R. Moorehead and W. E. Fulgham, all of whom had homesteaded on the northern part of The Plains, were the pioneer ministers who preached in the old Mt. View Schoolhouse.

The schoolhouse was the focal point of the social life in the community.

The Mountain View Literary and Debating Society was organized on December 31, 1901, and perfected on January 7, 1905, when the constitution and by-laws were adopted. They held the meetings every Saturday night which were looked forward to by young and old, alike. Wesley Hill was elected the first president; Milo Gard, Vice President; Harry Gard, Secretary; Miss Addie Jackson, Treasurer; and William Hannon, Sergeant-at-arms. The programs consisted of local talent with almost everyone contributing a part. There were several good entertainers. One of these was Claude Ramsey, who was much in demand for his songs and readings. He had homesteaded in 1903. Lively debates were held on current problems. At one time a joint debate was held with the Mud Springs Debating Society.

A mock trial was carried out in February, 1905, which afforded much merriment and good fun.

One of the most anticipated pleasures in a child's life of the olden days was going barefooted. Shoes came off at the first peep of spring and, oh, what torture was endured when it was necessary to go shod to Sunday school. One young hopeful coaxed his mother until she finally consented to let him go to school prematurely barefooted. She feared that he would rue his impatience and true enough, a good snow fell that day. The boy afforded much amusement to his classmates on the way home by hopping from bunch-grass to bunch-grass for a distance of three miles. He was a chastened little fellow by the time he reached home and was thereafter willing to curb his untimely eagerness.

One of the sports of children on their way to school was the killing of rattlesnakes. They always reported the number of the rattles each possessed. It was an accepted fact in those days that each rattle denoted a year in the age of the rattler. They were plentiful in the rocks and sagebrush and some settlers killed as many as a dozen around their homes. Many dens of rattlers were found in and near the canyons and at times the snakes were seen sunning themselves on warm days. Some dogs were trained to watch for them when with children. They would dash in, grab a snake, and whip it to pieces.

A family one summer was entertaining out-of-state guests. The morning after their arrival one guest, upon reaching into her bag, uttered a loud cry. Lying among the various articles in the bag was a large blow-snake. A few years later a prank was played by a youth in a theatre. He rattled the rattlers from a rattlesnake he was carrying in his pocket and it caused much consternation among the theatre patrons. The prankster was properly chastised and the patrons were assured by the management of no reoccurence of such a mischievous and frightening joke.

The sagebrush was covered with sage ticks, which held to the plants with their front feet. The back feet were extended straight out and when anything brushed against them they would let go with their front feet and adhere to the new object.

Children would get so many on them from running through the sage that they competed to see who would have the most during "tick season". Mothers looked their children over at bedtime to see if any were fastened. If one was attached, a drop of turpentine was generally placed on the tick to induce him to remove his head; otherwise the head would remain in the victim's skin, if extracted by force.

Another great pastime of the younger generation in bygone days was the snaring of sage rats, bountiful in those days, and death on gardens. A boy felt that he was not a real boy unless he owned a long string with a loop at one end tied exactly right. It was his most prized possession. Some girls participated in this sport also. They would wait patiently, sometimes for hours, in the hot sun for a rat to pop his head high enough so a quick jerk of the string would tighten the loop around the rodent's neck. The youngsters carefully kept count of their catches so as to be able to boast of their prowess to their playmates. Sage rats were used in experiments. In 1908 William Harper was in charge of getting the rats gathered up and sent away to be inoculated with a virus.

A rabbit drive was a real spectacle. The extermination of rabbits became necessary, as they were a serious menace to the farming industry. Many a settler's crop was destroyed by these pests. The first rabbit drive held on The Big Plains was on December 14, 1908, with General Paxton in charge. Many other drives followed. First a trap was constructed with quarter-mile wings. The corral, 150 feet in diameter, was made of four-foot wire netting and the wings of two-foot netting. The important factor in a successful rabbit drive is sufficient drivers. The Indians of the Warm Springs were invited to participate. The men formed a half circle, yelling and beating on things to scare the rabbits and get them moving in one direction toward the trap. Thousands would be slaughtered in one day. The Indians would take home hundreds of these slaughtered rabbits for food and dog-food. The squaws, at times, would get so excited killing the rabbits in the pen, that they would frequently whack each other.

Some of the rabbits were shipped to commission houses in Portland where they were sold for 25 cents each. The farmers received 15 cents each. The proceeds were used collectively to purchase ammunition to aid further extermination of these destructive pests.

Regular rabbit hunting was one of the chief pleasures of the young men and boys in the days of long ago. They hunted them on foot and horseback. When the ground was covered with snow and the rabbit trails could be easily followed, the men chased the animal into badger holes. They were then fished out with a wire shaped like a shepherd's crook. The beaten paths seemed to run between badger holes and it was thought that the holes were used for protection against enemies and perhaps for warmth. The rabbits would congregate on these trails to hunt their food and to exercise.

Every June, a Sunday was set aside for the annual Fish Fry. It was held at a site on the Deschutes River. It was the event of the year. Such baking and delightful odors floated from the homes the day before the affair. The trout were fried on the spot. Everyone lined up, and as the veteran cooks fried the fish they would fill the plates with the golden brown delicacy.

South Agency Plains

In the spring when word got around that the river was muddy the men hurriedly shouldered their nets and left, even at midnight, to try their luck at getting a catch of fish. They made a gala occasion of it, although at times it was cold and tiresome work. When a big haul was brought home the women put some of the fish down in brine for future use.

The homestead wife took great pride in becoming proficient in converting the strong twisted cotton warp into intricate loops and knots to fashion a perfect dip net.

The smallpox epidemic was in 1908-1909. Many families were stricken and some were very ill but soon recovered. An elevation of approximately 2400 feet and almost continual sunshine combined to make the high dry plateau of Agency Plains a very healthful climate.

Milo Gard homesteaded in July 1902. On December 31, 1903, his wife Caroline passed away. As there was not a cemetery on Big Agency Plains at this time, Milo donated a tract of land for one, and now, after almost 50 years, it is still the only cemetery on The Big Plains. It is known as the Milo Gard Cemetary. Milo Gard himself passed away on February 13, 1907, and was buried in the cemetery that he had bestowed. He had formerly been a state representative from Clackamas County. Chester Gard, his son, homesteaded on December 6, 1902. He has the distinction of being the only homesteader who still farms and resides on his original homestead.

The first mail came across Agency Plains from Wapinitia, carried horseback to the Warm Springs Agency, thence across The Plains to Madras and elsewhere. One of the carriers was an

Indian called Spotted Jake. He carried the mail from the Agency to Madras—one forgets the year—and he was a very unusual personage. His hands and face were turning white in large spots. The larger the spots became the prouder Spotted Jake became as if he were gradually turning from an Indian to a paleface. He wore gloves to protect and preserve his almost white hands.

When a settler's son became seriously ill in 1906 and all hope for the patient had been given up by the local doctor, Dr. King of Antelope was sent for—a distance of 35 miles. Dr. King sparing no horseflesh in getting to his patient, made the trip in record time and by his skill and God's will the patient often survived.

Frank Elkins, who homesteaded in September 1904 at the head of the River Road, was elected sheriff of Crook County in April 1906, and was reelected in 1908 by a landslide.

In 1905, Jim Stikona, an Indian, was killed near the present site of the railroad depot by Corbett Holt, another Indian. Holt hit Stikona over the head with a bottle and with a rock inside his cap. They had been heard wrangling as they went up the Madras Grade. Both were drunk.

Kutcher Precinct came into existence in 1906, named for Ed Kutcher, a homesteader east of Madras. He had lived in Crook County for over 30 years when he died in March 1909. The Plains plateau was included in Kutcher Precinct, with the polls situated in the town of Madras. In April of 1908 there were 195 registered voters in the precinct, with 143 of them registered as Republicans.

South Agency Plains

Stephan E. Binder, known as Steve, was from the State of Missouri. He homesteaded in April 1902. The Branstetters, also from Missouri, had written to relatives of Mr. Binder extolling the advantages to be found in this "Garden of Eden". Later, he and his son Kenneth, became the biggest farmers on Agency Plains.

Dr. Long was the only doctor on The Plains. He had homesteaded as early as 1901. He assisted at the birth of many of the pioneer babies. It was considered quite a feat when he rode a bicycle across the mountains from a place in the Willamette Valley one fall, to visit his homestead.

A jolly Irishman named Sam Mitchell who filed his homestead claims in November of 1907, brought his bride to share his life on this treeless plain. Both were from Bally Boggy, Antrim County, Ireland.

The settlers strongly resented their urban friends calling The Plains a desert. They thought of it more as a prairie.

The Calvin Fox family homesteaded in March 1902. They were pioneers of the old school, with their latchstring always out to their neighbors. Their son Miles also homesteaded in March of 1902.

In the year 1906 a meeting was called at the Mt. View Schoolhouse for the purpose of selecting a delegate to be sent to Salem in regard to appropriations for well-drilling on Agency Plains. A. P. Clark was selected, but no results were forthcoming from the project.

Another early arrival was William H. Ramsey, who homesteaded near the head of Ferry Canyon on March 28, 1902. This

303

family was from Missouri. They had heard of the new land from Dr. Long who formerly had been a Missouri resident. Mr. Ramsey was one of the first directors of the First National Bank when it was organized in Madras.

The first child born to a settler on The Plains was to Mr. and Mrs. Ramsey on October 8, 1902.

A young man called "Bill"—W. F. Sherrod—made his homestead claims on June 7, 1906, and was married on December 24 of the same year. William Sherrod was the first rural mail carrier on The Plains. The service was inaugurated on September 1, 1911. He held this position for many years.

Martin Pratt was a popular football champion from Portland. Later he became sheriff of Multnomah County for many years. He filed his homestead claims on September 8, 1905.

Don P. Rea dealt in real estate and was one of the influential business men of Madras of that era. He also was U. S. Commissioner of Madras. He homesteaded as early as October 1901. One day Mr. Rea lost his wallet containing valuable papers and around $50 in cash. It was found and returned to Mr. Rea by John Coulter, another early settler.

Then there was Neil Paulsen, hailing from Shaniko, who followed the trade of plumber and tinner. He was a director in the Madras public school.

Harry W. Gard, another entryman, homesteaded on January 23, 1902, at the head of Nigger Brown Canyon on account of a spring that furnished water part of the year. He worked tirelessly for irrigation and sometimes is called the "Father of Irrigation" of this country. He was for 12 years a member of the board of directors of the North Unit Irrigation District.

William C. Moore—known to all of his friends as "Bill"—also homesteaded near the head of Nigger Brown Canyon in September 1904. He and his wife operated the Green Hotel in Madras for many years. Mr. Moore was a very genial host, and both he and Mrs. Moore were excellent chefs.

A young man that liked to sing and would travel far to do so was A. D. Anderson, who made his homestead claim in December 1903. He married Effie Taylor, another homesteader, in 1909. He was active in irrigation work for many years and served as a director.

John H. Jackson of The Dalles homesteaded in 1903. He had served in the Confederate Army during the Civil War. When the town of Madras was incorporated in 1910 he became the first city recorder. He was interested in all civic projects and took an active part. His daughter Addie was married to William Hannon, an early homesteader of 1902, in 1906. Mr. Hannon was a Spanish-American War veteran. May, another daughter, was married to Walter Arney in 1909. A son, John H., known as Tobe, a nickname carried over from childhood days, also was an entryman.

James Hurt made the pilgrimage to this primitive land from Missouri. Jim purchased the meat market from Andrew Larson in early 1908. His brother, George, was a settler on the western part of The Plains.

Another pioneer family of 1902 was the Sam Haberstich family, coming from Iowa, but originally emigrants from picturesque Switzerland.

There was Antone Batalgia, also from Switzerland, as honest

and sincere as the day is long, who filed for his claim in March 1903. He was a director of Mt. View School for many years. His daughter Betty was also a homesteader.

Walter Williams filed for his homestead on January 15, 1902. On December 4, 1910, his only son, eighteen-year-old Wallace, was accidentally killed. In company with V. Z. Branstetter and George Hurt he had been to Trout Creek to shoot ducks. On the return trip Wallace spied a jackrabbit. He hurriedly pulled the gun from the wagon with the muzzle towards him. It was thought the hammer struck the wagon box, thereby discharging the gun.

The settlers, as a whole, were very congenial and worked for the common good of all, but the line fence, that traditional irritant, was a source of trouble to a few, very few, farmers. The first entrymen who fenced their land, naturally expected the adjoining landowner to pay his half of the fence, at and when such time as his neighbor fenced his quarter section. In a few cases, the neighbor did not think it necessary to pay, as the fence was already there when needed. This being the case, some farmers set their fence back a short distance from the line, thereby preventing his neighbor from connecting on to the one already established, if he refused to pay. In some circumstances a settler chose to erect his own fence rather than pay his half. The two fences ran parallel to each other, only a few feet apart, thus forming what was called a "Devil's Lane".

John Burns from Oklahoma homesteaded on March 9, 1902, a very congenial neighbor.

The Heath and McDonald families were also early settlers.

South Agency Plains

The James Watts' family came from Missouri in 1907. Lillian Watts was a teacher at the Mt. View School on the Big Plains for many years. At one time over 80 pupils attended, with Mrs. Watts as the only teacher. It became necessary for her to teach the lower grades in the morning and the upper grades in the afternoon. When the new County of Jefferson was formed, Lillian Watts became the first county school superintendent in 1915, continuing in this office until 1949.

Roscoe Gard, who filed on January 4, 1902, for a quarter section of rich land covered with sage, was one of the first commissioners in 1915 of the newly-organized Jefferson County.

Maude Durham filed on a homestead in 1904. In 1908 she married T. A. Taylor, a noted farmer of the Little Plains.

Another entryman who filed on a homestead at the head of Ferry Canyon near his son, William H. Ramsey, was John P. Ramsey.

Privation and loneliness drove one settler to get a form of persecution complex. He desired to teach at the Mt. View School and in view of that fact had given a large donation towards the school. The directors did not elect him. So in pique he nailed the doors closed and put boards over the windows one night. He came to one settler's home after midnight. After retiring he only remained an hour and left without a word. He became very threatening and the settlers, getting alarmed, went about their duties well armed. Finally he was taken to Prineville for a sanity hearing. He was a very well-educated man and at the hearing appeared completely normal; therefore—the judge released him. He told the board, "If you want to send me any-

307

where, send me to the World's Fair at Chicago." As the time went on he became more aggressive and belligerent and finally it became necessary for a settler to shoot him in self-defence.

Many other settlers contributed to the development of the southern part of Agency Plains. William Zell, Fred Cutendorf, the Pinerton Family all homesteaded in 1904. William Harper and James Chilcote arrived in the early days of 1902, the Charles Hays family came in 1903.

The J. C. Sothman Family, early settlers from Minnesota, farmed at the extreme south end of The Plains. Mr. Sothman was an irrigation director for 12 years. He owned a big steam threshing outfit as early as 1910.

Timothy Brownhill, a homesteader, was the first owner and editor of *The Madras Pioneer,* which came into existence in 1904.

There were the families of Jack Jones, Earnest Smith, John Falkenhagen, Isaac Serier, John Wagonblast, and many other families who endured the hardships of pioneering on Agency Plains. The Mike Braun, the Loving, and Waterhouse families were also early homesteaders on this tableland.

There were a great many old bachelor homesteaders, such as Stanley Grewell, Jean Dubois, a Frenchman, and Tom and Dave Burden. In fact, almost half of the homesteaders were bachelors.

Louis Volrath was another bachelor homesteader on Agency Plains. In the winters he usually made his home with his foster parents, Ed and Sarah Campbell. It was a sight equal to a circus for the children of the community whenever Mr. Volrath came galloping by on his pony with his calico dog perched up behind the saddle.

Volrath spent many of his summers at Silver Lake, working as a camp tender for sheep outfits. One fall after the sheep were brought in from the range to their winter quarters, Volrath started for the Campbell Ranch with his horses and faithful dog.

When Volrath failed to put in an appearance at the Campbell residence during the winter, his foster parents were surprised, and by the time another year had elapsed and still no word from him it became apparent that something was wrong.

Young John Campbell, son of Ed Campbell, took it upon himself to investigate the disappearance of his foster brother. He had no trouble in tracing Volrath from the sheep ranch to a point approximately 50 miles south of Bend near Fort Rock called Horse Ranch where he stopped for the night. He left early the next morning on his saddle horse and leading his pack horse. There the trail ended for man, horses, and dog. They were never seen or heard of again. To this day it is a baffling mystery. One ponders the fate of this oldtimer.

There were the families of Charley Ortman, Dick Dove, and many, many more whose names and activities escape one's memory—but one settler was just as necessary as another in the advancement of this new land, in the common cause of wrestling a living from these arid plains.

They had their pleasures, too, in the olden days. They camped, hunted, fished and went huckleberrying, much as we do today except that there were no down sleeping bags, air mattresses, cars, gasoline stoves, and folding chairs. They frequently picnicked on the Deschutes River on a little island above the ferry.

French fur hunters who came up the Columbia River named the Deschutes River but the Indians called the river Tawah-na-hi-ooks.

A meeting was called at the Mt. View Schoolhouse on March 21, 1908, to organize a branch of the National Farmers Education and Co-operative Union of America. The union was perfected on May 11, 1908, with A. A. Elmore as state organizer and lecturer in charge. The first president of the new organization was H. J. Branstetter; vice-president, William Harper; secretary-treasurer, A. D. Anderson; chaplain, Harry Gard; door-keeper, A. H. Parkey; conductor, William Cook. Mt. Jefferson Farmers' Union organized with 37 members; their meeting nights were the first and third Saturdays of each month.

Fred Zell, a bachelor homesteader, advertised in 1908 for a bride. He wrote that he wanted a wife, "sweet and lovable, between the age of 20 and 24 and a good housekeeper". He received such a quantity of letters that he was heard to remark he wished he lived in Utah so he wouldn't have to disappoint so many fair maidens. Some of the leading papers of that day carried editorials on the request and offered advice.

The first telephone meeting was called at the schoolhouse on April 22, 1911, to formulate plans for the Agency Plains Telephone System connecting with Warm Springs and Mecca. By June of 1911 the first telephone line was installed. Miss Hazel Barnett was the telephone operator in Madras of the Pioneer Telegraph and Telephone Company at this time. This farmers' company continued in service until the middle of 1950 when dial telephones were installed.

South Agency Plains

Agency Plains was practically deserted one day in 1911 when Barnes' Circus came to Madras. The O. W. R. & N. Railroad was the benefactor of this treat to the settlers.

The railroad was a long step toward civilization. As early as 1905 plans were shaping up for the Oregon Trunk and O. W. R. & N. to run lines into the Madras country. By July 1909 the railroad was assured. February 15, 1911, was set aside as a day of rejoicing and celebrating when the first train arrived on the Oregon Trunk Line. It was the greatest event in the history of Central Oregon.

Hope had kept their hearts alive, else the settlers would have despaired of relief for transportation facilities long before. An imposing trestle, or bridge, was built across Willow Creek connecting Big Agency Plains with Little Agency Plains. This bridge, 1050 feet long and 250 feet high, is among the highest of its kind in the United States. It took two months to complete the bridge. It was a rare scenic point for Madras and vicinity. The O. W. R. & N. followed the Oregon Trunk a short time later in 1911. In August of 1911, a railroad depot was constructed on the south end of The Plains. Close by, a 65,000-gallon water tank was filled from a well under the hill, in use by November of that year. The farmers hauled away as much water from the tank as the railroad used, being allowed any amount desired, free of charge. How grateful the farmers felt toward the railroad.

H. N. Waite was the first railroad agent on the Big Plains. He served the people of Central Oregon long and well. The railroad also contributed to the making of good roads for the farmers. Freight roads to its construction camps became roads to be used

311

by the farmers to transport their produce to the railroads. These roads were later turned over to the county.

And now, at long last, the dream of irrigation has become a reality and Agency Plains is a faithful and prosperous country, supporting hundreds of families where only a few years ago it was farmed by a compartively small number.

The settlers did not fully realize, when they made the long trek to this vast plateau, what they must endure, how frugally they must live, but their wants were simple, their hopes high, and their ardor undimmed.

A teeming field of golden grain rippling in the breeze, a meadowlark's sweet trilling, and the joy of progress filled their hearts with serenity and thanksgiving. Even the arrival of a new-born calf could lighten the day's load.

These pioneers of plucky spirit, and yet so humble, who came here in their youth are the embodiment of determination, grit and stamina. They came, they stayed, they endured.

2

ADDITIONAL SOUTH PLAINS HISTORY

By Chas R. Hays

These are memories of 53 years ago. I, like many others, wanting a farm of my own, and I found land in the Yakima Valley selling for $100 per acre. So I began to look for land elsewhere. In 1903 I met a friend of mine who said he had just returned from Central Oregon and that he had filed on 160 acres of land on the Agency Plains. I made up my mind to see

312

Hauling wheat down the Mecca Grade in North Agency Plains, a grade three miles long built by the Oregon Trunk Railroad. Lead wagon driven by Seth Luelling, followed by brother John.

Ellen Luelling watering cows on North Agency Plains, siphoning the water from a wagon loaded with seven 50-gallon barrels.

Finally came organized irrigation. Here the first water contract is being signed by Allie and Ward Farrell. As early as 1913 a permit was asked for 400,000 acre feet of Deschutes water for 100,000 acres.

Madras water festival on May 18, 1946, with thousands present to see the first water deliv
It had been 49 years since the first concerted effort to bring in irrigation water.

the country. In the meantime my friend Fred Hutchison met Dick Anderson in Yakima and had him lined up to go with us.

We three rode that "Narrow Gage" Railroad from Biggs Station on the Columbia River to Shaniko, making about 10 to 12 miles per hour. The nice part of that train ride was that there was no danger of a collison. There was only one train each day. Next day Fred said walking wasn't crowded and we three were on our way, going by way of Antelope.

It was late October and days were growing short and night caught up with us before we reached the Gap. We spotted a large haystack on the V. Z. Ranch and in that we bedded down for a cool night's rest. However, by 3 a.m. we froze out and started on our hike again. We landed at Lou Young's at 2 p.m. and, as he had a little store on his homestead in the Mud Springs district, we did eat some crackers and cheese—first eats since leaving Antelope except for a few apples we had picked up from under a tree on the Schultz Place on Trout Creek. He caught us but welcomed us to help ourselves.

We went on up onto the Agency Plains and the man who had land next to Fred Hutchison sold me his relinquishment, and later Fred Hutchison sold out to Steve Binder.

Dick Anderson and his sister filed on quarter sections west of us, four miles due north of Madras, know at that time as Palmain until the Government made the change in names.

There were a few living on The Plains when we went in. No one had yet grown any crops and, if he had, the terrible hailstorm that hit on The Plains in June 1903 would have destroyed everything. The cabin that was on my place when I bought it had all of the windows knocked out and every shingle split.

Miles Fox and family were there, also his father and mother. Miles was caught out in that storm with a four-horse team and while he was holding onto his lines the hail bruised his hands and head. The only thing that helped him was that the horses stopped running and put their heads to the ground. Miles jumped out and got under the wagon. Later many skeletons of jackrabbits and some coyotes could be seen where they were killed by the hailstorm.

The first winter we were there we had a 14-inch snowstorm. In February rain came on top of the snow and a crust of ice formed on top of all, while my friend Fred Hutchison and I were baching in my cabin. His horses were in my barn but we couldn't get them out to go to town for supplies. The ice would have cut the horses legs to the bone. As something had to be done, we wrapped gunnysacks around our legs and, both arming ourselves with 4-foot clubs we broke the ice ahead of us and walked into Palmain, or Madras as it was named later. One would break the ice ahead until tired and then the other would take over for about a mile. We made it but it took all day.

The snowbirds came into the scene by thousands and my friend Fred said, "Let's have a mulligan stew." I had a good double-barrel gun and it barked twice. We were all day dressing birds but we did have a great stew that lasted three days. Soon a chinook wind came up and melted the snow and we were able to get the horses out on the road again. Never have I killed a snowbird since in order to keep from starving. Homesteading and the hardships we went through are not to be forgotten, even if one lives to be 125.

After we did get our land to growing crops we were pretty well satisfied and for a few years rainfall was sufficient, but then to get wheat to market 45 miles on a three-day trip cost us 25 cents a bushel, not counting our time, and at 65 cents to 70 cents per bushel delivered, one could not get far in a deal like that. After hauling water for domestic and stock use and hauling wheat 45 miles, when can a man find time to farm?

Now times have changed and I am happy to say it's so much nicer for all of us to have modern transportation, and a blessing to our best animals, the horses and mules.

North Agency Plains
And Vicinity

By Cora E. and Chester S. Luelling

The north end of Agency Plains breaks away abruptly, cut off by the canyon of the Deschutes River, which swirls along in its rocky bed nearly a thousand feet below. Two dry canyons lead from The Plains to the river; one, called Frog Spring Canyon, is important for the fact that Fred A. McDonald bought from the Government a tract of 40 acres near the head of the canyon, the first deeded land in this area. A spring outcropped from under a ledge on this land. The other canyon served as an outlet for an access road built from the railroad on the river to The Plains. In this canyon lay the remains of about three thousand sheep belonging to A. W. Boyce; these had perished from hunger and cold when a late spring snowstorm caught them on the range in 1885.

This account covers an area which, specificially, would be designated as Township 9, Range 13, and a portion of Range 14. However, one cannot be specific in relating the growth and development of an area so dependent for existence on the surrounding country. In 1903, when the homesteaders first started moving in, water was hauled from the Basin (later Madras). Lnmber was hauled from a small sawmill at Grizzly

316

and groceries were obtained either from Palmain (now Madras) or the Warm Springs Agency which lay to the west across the river. Several years later a road was built off The Plains to the east, and then water was hauled from Sage Brush Springs or from a well dug by Peter Vibbert at the present town of Gateway.

Prior to the coming of the homesteaders all the area along the river and on The Plains was pastured by wild horses as well as sheep and cattle from Trout Creek. Several well-defined trails led off The Plains to the river, worn by stock going to and from water. Downriver, at the mouth of Trout Creek, lay the farm of a Mr. DeHaven; and on the river upstream, and off the westerly side of this northern Agency Plains area, Cowles had planted a fairly level piece of ground of alfalfa. The first still retained a stand of alfalfa when the railroad was built in 1911. Cowles had irrigated this field by pumping water from the river. Between this field and DeHaven's, a distance of about 10 miles, the river ran in a narrow canyon and could be followed only on foot or by horseback until the railroad was built.

This, then, was the situation viewed by the settlers of 1903 and 1904 who homesteaded practically all the tillable land, and some not so tillable.

Some of the homesteaders sold out as soon as they had proved up, or got a patent for their land. Others stayed until after the building of the railroad in 1911. Those who farmed their land until the ultimate developement of the country were Hiram Links, Charles Klann, John Evick. Seth and John Luelling and

Frank Stangland. However, such homesteaders as Anthony Monner and his sons Nick, George and John; Charles Dillon and his father; Bert Moore, Bert Loomis, Alf Parkey, Hugh Davis and his mother; A. P. Clark and his sons; as well as many others who lived here for a short time, each contributing a share in the clearing, fencing and otherwise developing this area.

Roads were laid out in the beginning on the section lines. Some right-of-ways were acquired by petition, some donated by mutual consent of the adjacent property owners; and some under protest of bitterness and hard feelings between neighbors. This resulted in lanes of various width, ranging generally from 40 to 60 feet. One homesteader contended that each roadway should be wide enough to turn a six-horse team and wagon in. In no case did the roadway amount to more than a fenced lane, with no clearing or grading being done on level ground until in the early 1920s. The traffic of horses and wagons wore off the sagebrush in the traveled portion and, when one set of ruts got too deep for use, the teams merely straddled that set and made new ones, or made turnouts around the rough places. The remaining sage in the lane and fence-rows caught the winter snow blown from the cleared fields, sometimes making the roads impassable in the winter time.

For the first few years there was only one school building on The Plains. This meant a walk of as much as five miles one way for some of the children. In 1906 a school taught by Mrs. Ralph Brown was started on the north end of The Plains, in the homestead cabin of Jessie Mayfield. The following year a schoolhouse was erected on land donated for that purpose by Anthony

Monner, located at the head of Frog Spring Canyon and called Frog Springs School. It was a rough pine-board building, 18 by 24 feet, and of "box construction", that is, there were no studding in the walls. There were only two windows in the east and two in the west walls. The room was heated with a large sheet-iron stove with a heavier cast top. In winter days it was encircled with wet leggings, mittens, and coats.

The desk and benches were hand made, each parent providing furniture for his own children. As a consequence the style and construction were as varied as were the families. This school-house burned down several years later, caused by the metal stovepipe overheating the ceiling and roof. School was then held in the Nick Monner homestead house until the completion of a new and more modern building a couple of years later. There was also provided a teacher's cottage, a stable for saddle horses, and a shed for wood. The school continued to function until the close of the 1930-31 term when it closed finally for lack of pupils, Mrs. William Brownhill being the last teacher.

Sunday school was held in the original school building, with services being conducted by various lay settlers of the vicinity. An organ had been donated by someone, and served to lend harmony as well as melody to the hymns. At times when no organist was present the homesteader's youngsters would watch round-eyed as one of the song leaders who had a tuning fork, would thrust it into his mouth, bite down on it, and then pull it out and wave the vibrating instrument by his ear, humming until he caught the right pitch, then break into song. As the school was by no means mouse-proof the mice found the organ an ideal place to nest. If pumping the bellows with the treadles didn't cause them to abandon, temporarily, their new-found home, the first strains of music would most certainly bring out a few agitated matronly mice. They eventually retaliated, however, by gnawing through the bellows and thereafter, until the fire, led a more tranquil life.

The Plains area continued to develop, reaching a peak shortly after the completion of the railroad. There was a need for more schools, and interest in the formation of a new county was gaining favor. As Frog Springs School served only the north-eastern part of The Plains adequately, a new district was formed and a building completed in 1914 for the northwestern section. This school was called New Era, and first opened in the fall of 1914 with a six-month term taught by Miss Theresa Weaver. School was held steadily in this district until consolidation with District U 9, Madras. The last term was 1948-49, with Mrs Carl Hering as teacher.

Water for stock and household use was a problem here as it was for all the settlers of The Plains, but to the homesteaders on the north end, the greater distance to Madras for water often meant that when their turn came to fill their barrels with water the well would be dry and they would have to wait until more water ran in. It was often late at night before the settler arrived with his precious water. With the completion of the road to Sagebrush Springs, water distance from the north end of The Plains was shortened somewhat but the steep grade on the return trip was a hard pull for the teams. The original Frog Spring came out beneath a rock ledge where sheep and cattle watered during the spring months but it was not possible to drive a wagon beneath the ledge. In the earliest days the settlers drove their wagons above the ledge and filled their barrels by carrying the water in buckets; later the farmers dug wells about a quarter of a mile up the canyon. These wells caught the seepage water, sometimes holding the water until June. It was also the custom to fill the cisterns with snow whenever the snowfall was deep enough to be dipped up in buckets.

After the building of the railroad the farmers were permitted to haul water from the railroad tanks and were thus given their choice of either Madras, Gateway, or Mecca. The haul from Mecca was the shortest but it was also the hardest on the horses.

Clearing the land of sagebrush was a job all the settlers faced.

Some tried plowing the ground first and then pulling the uprooted brush but the light plows of those days often failed to cut the larger roots, making it more difficult to grub the loosened sage and almost impossible to pull by hand. Others tried dragging it out with an iron rail pulled by a team of horses on each end, but the soil held the roots too firmly except in the sandiest places and the brush was too tough to break off. The mattock or grub hoe powered by a pair of strong arms and back proved the most effective means. After being grubbed the brush was piled by hand or by various home-made, horse-drawn rakes and burned. The sage on the sandy knolls near the rim grew larger than average for The Plains, with the trunk and branches often being four or five inches in diameter. Many settlers in the process of clearing their land used this sage for fuel.

The first settlers cut the juniper trees which grew in the canyons, for fence posts. Juniper also grew thick and of good size on a bench extending along the hillside on both the west and east side of Frog Spring Canyon. The bench was about 300 feet below the level of The Plains and a road was built down to it a mile west of Frog Canyon to haul out the posts and wood. In 1904 John Luelling, a bachelor, took this flat as a homestead. He dug a well and got a year-round supply of water sufficient to keep a small band of brood mares from which he raised mules. He later changed to beef cattle. Because of the number of arrowheads found on this bench it is assumed to have been a regular campsite for Indians when hunting or digging camas or "Indian Potatoes" as they were called by the settlers. The elderly squaws continued to dig camas until the coming of the automobile. Wild onions also grew in abundance in certain areas of the wasteland. These onions grew tops similar, though smaller, than the tame onion; with an odor and flavor so strong that it was noticeable in the milk of cows which pastured on the tops. One of the teachers of the Frog Springs School held classes one spring afternoon after her entire flock had made an excursion into the canyon during the noon hour, eating wild onion tops along the way.

The lumber for the homesteader's buildings came from the Grizzly country, but because of the long haul and the scarcity of money, all the buildings were of the simplest construction. In most cases the dwellings consisted of one-by-twelve rough pine boards nailed vertically for the walls, with battons covering the cracks. The floor, which was also of rough boards in some cases, was nailed to two-by-fours set on a loose rock foundation, while the whole building was covered by a roof supported by the walls.

Some of the bachelor's houses consisted of only one room with a lean-to roof. Other homesteaders with larger families built two stories with a peaked roof. Here again it depended on the resources of the settler whether the roof was shingled or made of boards. Some of the houses were papered on the inside with building paper but a number with only newspapers stuck to the walls with flour paste to keep out the draft. After the railroad came and building materials were more readily available there was a noticeable improvement in the houses of those farmers who remained, with plastered houses on concrete foundations being common.

The mail for the homesteaders in the north end of The Plains was brought from the post office in Madras in a large canvas bag put in a house-like box set on posts at the crossroads at the southwest corner of the Charles Klann homestead. It was the custom for anyone going to town to take the mail bag and any outgoing mail it might contain and bring back the mail for any residents of that general area. Any uncalled-for letters or mail gathered dust on the floor of the mailbox until it was returned to the postoffice. It was the duty of the children of the family, if they were old enough to read, to go to this box occasionally and pick out the family mail.

The settlers found the land to be quite productive when

there was sufficient moisture. At first there was constant experimental plantings to find which crops were best suited to the climate, soil, and moisture conditions. Corn, potatoes, watermelons, and garden vegetables grew remarkably well in the weed-free soil. Most settlers set out a small orchard but, although the trees grew slowly and bore fruit, the climate was not suited to this type of agriculture. The trees were gradually winter-killed, and the orchards disappeared. There were no weeds to plague the farmers until the wild morning glory was brought in with seed grain. Russian thistle began to get a foothold but it was not until after the building of the railroad that Jim Hill mustard and china lettuce developed into a real problem for the farmers. Jackrabbits were plentiful and quite destructive to the grain fields. Rabbit drives and the use of a mixture of salt and strychnine controlled them to some extent.

The last two homesteads in this vicinity were taken by the Banna Brothers, Bert and Charlie, who came into the community as laborers on the railroad construction gang. Their claims were on the extreme north of The Plains with most of their acreage laying on the hillside towards the river. Charlie built his cabin beneath the rim and, as the rattlesnakes were quite common in this area, Charlie was not particularly surprised one day upon entering his cabin to find a rattler had moved in during his absence. Thereafter, to the amusement of his neighbors, when Charlie opened his door, he would crouch down before entering and peer under his scant furnishings in the room to be sure there were no snakes present.

The completion of the railroad contributed much to the

permanent development of the community. The Gateway area developed on the railroad to the east. On the west a depot was built in Cowles' alfalfa field by the Oregon Trunk Lines. This depot was named "Mecca" and a road was built by the Oregon Trunk Company up the hill to The Plains. The grade was three miles long and provoked much caustic comment from the settlers because of its crookedness, its narrowness, and its steepness. Wide places were provided occasionally to be used by the teams in passing. These were the days when the automobile was a novelty to the settler and a terror to the horses; so the road was inadequate. However, the road was much traveled with traffic from the Warm Springs Indian Reservation as well as that occasioned by the railroad. Although this road was used from a period of exclusively horsedrawn transportation to completely motorized (1911-1939), only two fatalities occurred from an auto mishap. This was a car of a woman employee and her companion from the Warm Springs Agency which went off the grade and overturned, killing both occupants. Two other cars did leave the road but with no casualties.

At Mecca the Railroad Company built a station, two houses for section hands, and erected a water tank which they filled by pumping water from the river. They also built a "Y" and corrals for handling stock. A ferry was used to cross the river when traveling to or from the Agency, but this was soon replaced with a steel bridge. A store with a postoffice and a dwelling were built by Will See who, previous to this time, also operated a store at the Warm Springs Agency. A grain warehouse and another dwelling were added later to his holdings.

Jefferson County Reminiscences

The Mecca postoffice was established on September 18, 1911, and discontinued on May 31, 1924. Edward Chaloupka, a brother-in-law of Mrs. See, was the first postmaster. Earl Massey later bought an interest in the store and was operator of it and the warehouse at the time of the removal of the railroad in 1924. E. W. Twiss was depot agent at Mecca for quite a number of years. He bought several hundred acres of school land which lay along the hillside and river below Mecca. On a fairly level tract about a mile downstream from Mecca, he set out an orchard and planted a variety of garden produce which he irrigated with a pump. Twiss also kept a small herd of purebred Jerseys and shipped cream to Portland for a number of years. The Mecca flat had been fenced by See and the Railroad Company. Alfalfa continued to grow and was put up for hay until it gradually died from lack of care.

The Oregon Trunk is responsible for the naming of Mecca, and whether they were intentionally prophetic in the choice of name is not known. At any rate Mecca soon became known as the trout fishing center of Oregon. Fishermen from Portland and way-points would charter a pullman coach and leave Portland Saturday evening, arriving at Mecca during the night. Their coach would set on a siding where the occupants would awaken in the morning for a day of fishing. Some would use boats to float down the river to South Junction, fishing on the way. The boats would be shipped back to Mecca during the week for a repeat performance the following weekend. The fisherman and the pullman would be picked up by the train, Portland bound, Sunday night and all would arrive in town in time for their various jobs Monday morning. When the railroad was abandoned in 1924 the farmers from The Plains could no longer see the schools of fish flashing in the clear water, and the surface of the river was no longer broken by feeding trout in the warm spring nights.

Mecca died when the railroad was abandoned, but the grade continued to be used until it was closed by the county in 1939. The railroad lost its franchise on much of its right-of-way, although Mecca flat and the tunnel above Mecca were still retained by the company. Much of the timber in the trestles and ties on the roadbed were salvaged by the farmers of The Plains. The roadbed served as a fisherman's road along the river until the various cuts were closed by slides. The river along the north part of The Plains was once again accessible only to hikers or those on horseback.

By 1912 the farmers had begun to concentrate on the growing of wheat. It was found that oats and barley were an uncertain source of income because there was a lack of spring moisture. An irrigation district was formed as early as 1910 and many farmers were living in the hope that irrigation would someday become a fact. More and more of the land had been coming into production, until by the end of World War I the sage had been cleared from the fields on the northern end of The Plains. In 1927 the domestic water system was completed, thus ending the laborious task of hauling water.

Various makes of farm tractors began to appear on the farms at the north end of The Plains during the 1920's. Combines were being developed at a price within reach of the small farmer, and the stationary thresher and header were fast becoming obsolete.

Then, in the early 1930s, came the drought years and the low prices on produce. Taxes were delinquent on much of the land. The farmers worked on a Public Works Project which was a start of the present Warm Springs Highway. The Federal and State Land Banks foreclosed on various pieces of property. Cash to meet current expenses was again as scarce as in the homesteaders' day.

By the late 30s tractors with rubber tires replaced the more unwieldy iron-wheeled ones. Rotary rod weeders became an efficient tool for working summerfallow, a practice for the conservation of moisture. All combined to enable those farmers who were left to handle more land and to raise the per acre yield.

In 1938 the farmers signed the contract with the Bureau of Reclamation for the construction of the North Unit Irrigation Project. The completion of this was to close one chapter in the growth and development of the northern end of Agency Plains, and with the first delivery of water to the farthermost lateral on July 3, 1948, a new chapter was begun.

Irrigation Of Jefferson County

By Harold J. Eidemiller

Irrigation in Jefferson County begins with the diversion of the waters of Cherry Creek by A. J. Shrum in the year 1872. Cherry Creek arises in the eastern edge of the county on Stevenson Mountain and flows north and east about 15 or 20 miles to the John Day River at what is now known as Burnt Ranch, the original ranch being a couple of miles east of this point and on the east side of the river. Shrum lived on this place until 1916 and died in 1919. This country was right in the midst of the great sheep range; the corrals on Cherry Creek were said to be large enough to hold 1200 head "besides shearing ricks and pens and dipping vats."

About 1890 a great water spout came down the creek and swept the valley clean of buildings and deposited rock and gravel over the irrigated fields. Some of the damage was repaired but the area never was restored to its original condition. This was the first experience of the valley of the waterspouts or cloudbursts which henceforth came almost every year to wash out ditches and diversion dams and make irrigation a hazardous undertaking.

F. D. V. Shrum says that he went to the Willamette Valley to spend the winter of 1872, and that his folks lived on Cherry Creek in a tent and brush house, and that The Dalles was the nearest source of supply. James Cozart was the next water-user, in 1877, selling to James Connolly.

Water records mention George Good, Frank Tompkins and a Blake prior to 1880, but there never was a large flow of water in the Creek other than spring floods, consequently the irrigable land was limited. Mention is made that George Montgomery Wasson operated a toll road in the vicinity and he would stay with the different ranchers, whoever would put him up. This road was probably a short stretch on the bank of the John Day, reputedly built with a wheelbarrow, and was very narrow as late as 1948. Jay Saltzman, who was born at Burnt Ranch in 1870, was a witness in the adjudication proceedings of the waters of Cherry Creek, held in 1921, and in the course of his testimony stated he had fought the Irish for 20 years and would rather ignore them. Jacob Kaser and the Prineville Land and Livestock Company were claimants for the water rights in the adjudication.

Allen Hash initiated the first water right on the headwaters of Willow Creek with a priority date of 1873, according to the evidence secured by Judson Vincent at the time Willow Creek rights were adjudicated. Jud thinks the actual date was 1871, but since the establishment date was sufficient to secure the needed priority, no attempt was made to verify the earlier date. This water was needed on 16 acres a short distance above the mouth of Coon Creek. In 1875, Henry Cleek purchased about 2000 acres of land, including lands adjoining Willow Creek, a small amount of which was irrigated at the time he bought it. Shortly afterwards, Cleek built dams in Willow Creek and used water for the irrigation of what he called the "Natural Meadow" containing about 50 acres. Then in 1885 or 1886 he built a dam and diverted water on both sides of the creek from which he irrigated about 200 acres.

Isom Cleek, son of Henry, was about six years old when the family moved to the Grizzly Basin and, in testimony given by him in a water case in District Court in 1923, he mentions Canada Montgomery as irrigating about a half-acre of garden on the J. M. Blakely homestead prior to 1885. Perry Read, the Sol Woods Place, and the McClure Place were mentioned, and no doubt considerable more history of the area could be written by some of the surviving settlers. Isom Cleek left the area in 1913 and moved to Lebanon.

Land owned at the time of the Willow Creek adjudication by the Grizzly Livestock and Land Company has a water right for 48 acres, dated 1875, and various later rights up to 1905 at which time they were nominally irrigating 477 acres, but of course, most of this area had only spring runoff water in varing amounts, the summertime flow not being sufficient to irrigate more than a few acres. Records show a water right in the name of Antone Fogle as of 1875 on land that was patented to J. K. McClure, the patent being recorded in 1891. The ditch was called the North Side Ditch. It is difficult to find just who the original water user was, since a lot of these lands were farmed by squatters and, in many instances, their improvements were sold to subsequent squatters, and not until a much later date was a formal filing made. Charles W. Palmehn had a Willow Creek right dated 1892 for 61 acres and John W. Dee, 1894, for 45 acres under the North Side and the South Side Ditches. It is to be remembered that the names used here in most cases are those whom the various Adjudication Proceedings allowed a water right, it being impossible within the limited time allotted to search out the original appropriator.

The Deschutes River hearing was held in Deschutes County in 1928 and the transcript of testimony is filed there, and unavailable to the writer, much to my sorrow, since the facts brought out at these hearings are interesting, especially those concerning happenings back in the 70's. We know that many rights listed under the Grizzly Livestock and Land Company and the Baldwin Sheep Company could not have all been initiated by them—since, after all, there were such things as homestead law limitations as to the area of land one person could obtain, although we have heard stories of sheepherders and cowboys filing on homesteads and selling them after proving up, sometimes by prearrangement and many times because the homesteader could not make a go of it. The Cherry Creek history is based upon testimony by the Shrum family and by A. J. Shrum himself by affidavit prior to his death.

The year 1877 is the first date of record of water being used in the Trout Creek watershed in what is now Jefferson County, although the actual first user on that watershed started in 1870 on Antelope Creek just across the line in Wasco County. The 1877 right is in the name of Charles L. Hunter on Wilson Creek, using the Colburn-McPherson Ditch, the name of the ditch indicating to the writer that Hunter was probably not the original user. This same year shows T. S. Hamilton on Trout Creek using the Quinn Ditch. In 1878 John H. Priday was irrigating from Friend Ditch No. 6. In 1879 H. L. Priday was irrigating 98 acres with Trout Creek water from Priday No. 2 and Stewart No. 1 Ditches, and Bostwick No. 4 Ditch on Pony Creek. In this same year the Baldwin Sheep Company established priorities on South, Amity, Beaver, Trout and Foley creeks, with a final priority of 1908 for stock water from Little Willow for the home ranch. Allie Cram was using Trout Creek water through the Bostwick and Ashby Ditch.

Irrigation on the Metolius started in 1885, this being the date of priority on land owned by Alice L. Heising at the time of the adjudication, and indicates the irrigation of 70 acres in that year with water from Jack Creek. In 1887 the land now occupied by the Allingham Ranger Station was irrigated from Lake Creek. Henry L. Corbett, prominent financial personage of Portland, has a right dated 1888 for the irrigation of 60 acres from Jack Creek, using the Corbett Ditch. It is possible this was the beginning of the Camp Sherman recreation area. This same year several Hansens used Lake Creek water for the irrigation of several tracts. In 1897 Isaac New, whose address was Gradview, was using Metolius River water on 12 acres in the river canyon north of Grandview. The ditch was designated the D. W. New Ditch, and the property described in the adjudication proceedings is now known as the Riggs Ranch.

John and Gillis Dizney each filed on water from the Deschutes for the irrigation of six acres each, using waterwheels to lift the water to the land, with the current of the river itself being used for power. This filing was made in 1902 and the location is near the bottom of the old Vanora Road, just below the present highway location.

The first concerted effort to bring irrigation water to the present North Unit Irrigation District was during the year 1897 when a meeting was held to discuss the idea. A. P. Clark, George Gould and Frank Elkins were some of the landowners present at that meeting. About 1902 interest in North Unit land began to increase, and in the next few years most of the desirable acreage was homesteaded and dry farming practiced with varying success. The greatest hardship encountered by these pioneers was the lack of water for household and livestock use, it being found that wells down to as much as 800 to 1000 feet were unproductive and the only alternative was to haul water from the Deschutes River, a very laborious task involving the long road down and up the thousand-foot-deep canyon, or to trek the many miles to Madras where wells were found successful at short distances below the surface. At harvest time it was necessary that each farmer employ someone who spent his full time hauling water for the stock used in the operation.

It is said that each gallon of water used in the household was used many times for successively less sanitary purposes before it reached its final disposition on the rosebush beside the door or to slake the thirst of the poor pig. Small wonder that irrigation was ever present in the mind of everyone.

Dick Anderson tells of meetings as early as 1904 to study the possibilities and in 1913 an application for a permit to use 400,000 acre feet of Deschutes River water yearly for the irrigation of 100,000 acres of land was filed with the state engineer and subsequently set aside for North Unit use. There being no surplus river flow during the irrigation season, this water was all to be stored during the winter months.

At about this time the State of Oregon and the Federal Government entered into a cooperative agreement to survey and study the possibility of irrigation in the Deschutes Valley watershed. In the course of the next few years a very comprehensive report was issued as a result of this survey, with a storage dam to be built at Benham Falls and diversion from the river at Awbrey Falls below Tumalo. The feasibility of the irrigation of four units was explored, with the units being designated South, East, West and North. The South Unit is located east of Bend and around the Powell Butte area, the West Unit being west of Redmond on the west side of the river centering around Cline Falls, and the East Unit east of the river from Bend north to Crooked River. Apparently the North Unit was considered the best, or had more persuasive landowners, since it was chosen for construction.

Efforts were being put forth towards the organization of an irrigation district embracing the North Unit lands. After considerable discussion and several meetings, an election was called and, with a favorable vote, the North Unit Irrigation District became a reality. The first board meeting was held March 27, 1916, in the office of County Judge William Boegli at Culver, then the county seat. The district contained a total area of approximately 133,000 acres. The irrigable acreage within the boundaries was slightly over 100,000, with the expectation that lands east of Willow Creek and on Round Butte would be watered. The board was composed of Harry W. Gard, president; A. D. (Dick) Anderson, secretary; John Henderson, Fred Fisher, and P. N. Vibbert, directors. Harry W. Andrew was named treasurer, and the official place of meeting was to be at Madras. The minutes of the first meetting show concern that at state highway was to run through the Benham Falls reservoir site, and it subsequently developed that the North Unit agreed to pay the Highway Commission $50,000, as shown by a contract dated October 1923, in reimbursement for the extra cost of relocating the survey in order to avoid the reservoir.

Since the infant district had no money and the board must operate on a warrant basis, O. A. Pearce of the Madras State Bank agreed to take any warrants offered at not to exceed five percent discount. In April a group of landowners contested the legality of the formation of the district, the Notice of Contest naming Hiram Links, George Rodman, Perry Henderson, George H. White, Claude G. Ramsey, Walter S. Williams, J. H. Horney, and B. Dombrowe as contestants. L. H. Irving was retained by the board to defend the organization, with I. T. Hinkle hired to assist. Money for defence was obtained by the expedient of the board issuing warrents to whoever would accept them. The recipient would then endorse the instrument and return it to the board which was then able to convert them into cash. The bank thus had double security, that of the district and of the indorser. During the period that the legality of the district was under contest a great number of landowners' names appeared on the records as indorsing these warrants, all of which were issued in $25 amounts. The treasurer on October 3, 1916, reported a balance on hand of 74 cents.

A group of men composed of C. M. Wickham of Boise, D. C. McGilvery of Pocatello, and Charles H. Berryman presented a plan whereby they would construct the irrigation system for the district at a cost not to exceed $55 an acre for the full 100,000 acres. Approval of this plan was expressed by about 40 people present at a board meeting, who requested an opportunity to vote on the proposition. In March 1917 the board agreed to sign a contract with these men and in September of the same year petitions with 176 signatures were filed with the board asking that an election be called on the question of bonding the district for $5,000,000. The election was held on October 29, 1917, with 385 voters present and a favorable majority of 87. Interest in district affairs is evident from the fact of ten candidates for director at the first annual election. But the original board were returned to office. Early, in 1918, negotiations were started toward the purchase of the Central Oregon Irrigation Company rights, culminating in the eventual purchase of these rights for $703,100. The object in buying was to obviate the building of a storage reservoir. Principals of the Central Oregon Irrigation Company were F. S. Stanley, Jesse Stearns, and Denton G. Burdick. In September 1919 the contract was voided by mutual agreement and the deal called off. Also, in 1918, a contract was entered into between the district and John H. Lewis (then state engineer) and Barr & Cunningham for engineering services in connection with project construction, the rate of compensation to be $450 per month. Pursuant to the bond election, bids were called for to be opened on October 22, 1918, but no bids were received.

Beginning with the year 1919 the board was reduced from five to three members by state law. The first mention of the United States Reclamation Service shows in the records that A. D. Anderson was sent to Washington to present the district plea for Federal aid. (We can picture Dick in the effete east wearing his plaid mackinaw). It subsequently developed that the Reclamation Service found the project too costly for the settlers to pay, and nothing came of this first attempt.

At the same time the state supreme court invalidated the bond election, but upheld the formation of the district and thereby opened the way for the board to levy and collect assessments. A second bond election was held with 336 votes cast, and a favorable majority of 136. Validation proceedings were instituted and approval was given early in 1920. Bids were to be received in March, with no response again. It must be remembered that at this time irrigation securities were in very poor repute generally, with a great majority of projects in default. The first assessments made by the board was for the fiscal year 1919-1920. The rate was 17 cents per acre. The warrant indebtedness outstanding at this time amounted to $10,000; the board did remarkably well in holding the indebtedness down to this figure. This money had all to be procured by the warrant-indorser method. In November 1919, the board voted to pay the expenses of Harry W. Gard to Salt Lake City as Oregon delegate to an irrigation conference. This Salt Lake City meeting was the beginning of the National Reclamation Association, and was called by Governor

Irrigation of Jefferson County

D. W. Davis, the governor of Idaho. Irrigation opponents of the district seized upon this trip to censure the board for needless expenditure, a story being prevalent that Gard ran up an expense account of $400, with more to be paid later. A published statement by friends of the board states that Gard received $103.17, of which $66 was for railroad fare. The board was accused of buying a suitcase for A. D. Anderson; the answer was that the controversial suitcase was Anderson's "office", and that "whenever information has been required, the minutes and papers of the District have been easily accessible right in Mr. Anderson's suitcase". Further, Mr. Anderson had worn out his own suitcase in the service of the district. At the election of a director, the incumbent, John Henderson, received 235 votes to his opponent's 89, proving the board had the confidence of the great majority of landowners.

In 1920, C. M. Redfield, irrigation engineer, presented an "Estimate of the Joint North Unit Canal and North Canal Dam to Crooked River". The diversion dam at Bend, now used by the North Unit, was built in 1912 by the Central Oregon Irrigation Company whose rights have all been acquired by the Central Oregon Irrigation District. The proposed canal was to be 25 miles long, and would be built to serve the lands of Bend, and with a surplus to reach the North Unit lands sufficient for their irrigation. In the same year an agreement was entered into with the State of Oregon wherein the State agreed to pay the interest on the district bonds for a period of five years, and John K. Kollock was appointed to represent the board in the matter. With no bids for bonds, the board made a deal with Ralph

339

Schneeloch and Company of Portland to act as "Underwriter" in the organization of a syndicate to purchase the bonds. Schneeloch was immediately to buy $50,000 worth of the bonds for 90 percent of par value, the bonds to bear 6 percent interest. Upon receipt of the report of the engineers, the district was to give Schneeloch a 90-day option to purchase the balance of the bond issue, and to put the district affairs under the jurisdiction of the Underwriting Company. On June 8, 1920, the board formally authorized the sale of the $50,000 bonds to Schneeloch.

Lewis H. Irving resigned as attorney for the board, much to their regret. He had been of inestimable help with their problems, and was still to be so in succeeding years until the project was completed. Director P. N. Vibbert died on June 20, 1920, making the first break in the board personnel since the organization.

A. J. Wiley and F. C. Hermann were employed as engineers to head the project planning program. Wiley was from Boise and Hermann from San Francisco. A contract was made between the district and the State and the United States to purchase for the sum of $35,000 the original field notes of the cooperative survey for the use of the district. In the event the material was returned by January 1, 1925, no payment was to be made. At the present time no trace of this material can be found nor any record of its disposition, and neither was the payment ever made or a request received for the payment. We so find in the minutes of June 5, 1923, a resolution to write Dwight P. Robinson Company, Pos and Allen and John L. Etheridge for the return of such engineering and other data which they might have which belongs to the district. Records show that a surveying crew was in the field for a considerable period of time making reconnaisance surveys with much materials assembled, the work continuing until the available funds were spent. Hermann and Wiley compiled and issued a comprehensive report on the North Unit in April 1921, containing a study and estimate of cost of this project, including the Benham Falls Reservoir, and also containing a detailed study of the water supply. This report was used along with others in a later report compiled by C. C. Fisher in the employ of the United States Reclamation Service.

Upon receipt of the Hermann-Wiley report, a meeting was held in Madras by the landowners and the director of the Reclamation Service to discuss the required terms of the contemplated construction contract. On being advised by the director that the landholders must dispose of their excess holdings over 160 acres, at an appraised value set by the Government board, the Reclamation Plan was informally rejected. This decision was encouraged by the promises of the parties who had purchased part of the district bonds that if the Reclamation offer was rejected, the project would be financed by private funds with no restrictions on land holdings. An appropriation of $500,000 was available at this time to start the project, but the coolness of the landowners at this meeting toward Reclamation law resulted in the appropriation being withdrawn. Schneeloch and Company, due to financial reverses or to other causes, later withdrew their offer to finance the project.

Some consideration was given to the possibility of securing water from Crooked River, with a diversion about 20 miles above Prineville, and a long siphon across the Ochoco Valley to irrigating the Ochoco bench lands, and then down to irrigate some 46,000 acres of North Unit lands, but it was seen that the lands could be more cheaply served from other sources. A. H. Parkey was appointed to fill the unexpired term of P. N. Vibbert, and N. G. Wallace and John K. Kollock authorized to do certain work relative to water rights in connection with adjuducation proceedings then being carried on for the determination of rights to Deschutes River water.

In September 1920, the district purchased the lot and building on the corner of 6th and C Streets in Madras and occupied this as the office of the board until 1946 when the headquarters were moved to the Airbase. The original building was of two stories but was remodeled to the present one story in later years. The property was purchased from the City of Madras, and at one time housed a flourishing saloon which was put out of business with the advent of prohibition.

F. S. Bramwell was appointed as appraiser for the North Unit by the Certification Commission of the State in May, 1921, it being necessary that the State certify as to the worth of any irrigation bonds to be sold. Concern was expressed as to how to attract settlers to the project, and a committee was formed to work along this line with the following members: J. O. Youngstrom, Perry Henderson, Andrew Morrow, C. C. Berkley, Ward Farell, W. G. Moore, Ira P. Holcomb, James Lee and Frank P. Bacon. Judge N. G. Wallace and Attorney L. H. Irving were to advise with the committee.

An elecion was held on January 11, 1921, for the purpose of

changing the name of the district to Jefferson Water Conservancy District with a favorable vote cast. Irrigation district bonds being in disrepute at the time, it was thought that the change in name would make the bond issue more attractive. In December 1921 the board advertised for bids to construct the project facilities, with no bids submitted. Again advertised for bids to be opened January 31, 1922, and again no bids received. On April 15 the board agreed to sell the $4,930,000 balance of bonds to Ryne and Company of San Francisco, and to employ Shattuck Construction Company as general superintendent of construction with the object of constructing project facilities with hired labor directly by the district. However, the succeeding board meeting voted not to complete this deal and the board again dickered with Schneeloch. Apparently the Oregon Irrigation Securities Commission refused to approve the contract with Shattuck. On May 24, 1922, the board agreed to pay Schneeloch 1¼ percent of the five million if the bonds were purchased by anyone other than Schneeloch, or if the project was constructed by other than private capital. This agreement raised a storm of protest from the landowners and Schneeloch and Company voided the deal. Shortly after, J. H. Pos and F. W. Allen of Portland requested to finance the sale of the bonds. The minutes of the meeting say "they were cordially received", but apparently nothing came of this try. January 1923 saw an economy move by the board when the secretary's salary was reduced from $5 to $4 a day. Harry Gard was delegated to attend legislative sessions when necessary to protect irrigation interests. Another $20,000 in bonds were delivered to Schneeloch at this time. In

March 1923, John L. Etheridge proposed to sell the bonds and an agreement was concluded extending to May 16, when it was terminated. In June, Harry Gard resigned the office of president of the board and was replaced by John Henderson. A. D. Anderson quit the post of secretary to be replaced by Gard. Bids for bonds were again requested with the usual results, and in October J. C. Sothman was elected to the board, replacing A. H. Parkey, and, upon taking office, was elected president.

In December it is recorded that H. W. Turner, as treasurer of the Deschutes Project Association, was soliciting funds to defray the expenses of a delegate to Washington, D. C. to interest the United States Reclamation Service in the building of the project. This association embraced the entire Deschutes watershed, and $150 was contributed by the board at this time, with $350 in April of 1924, and $500 in January 1925, to send a delegate to Washington to secure authorization. Apparently the interest of the Reclamation Service was revived, since on July 8, 1925, the board, with L. H. Irving, Howard Turner, Earl Bone, and Ira Holcomb, met with the Secretary of the Interior, Dr. Hubert Work, and the director of the United States Reclamation Service, Dr. Elwood Mead, at Portland to present the needs of the project.

January 1927 brought a delegation of landowners to meet with the board, requesting that the board reduce the salaries and per diem expenses and establish a sinking fund for the retirement of the outstanding bonds now totalling $90,000. This was to the extent of the bond sales, since no further attempt was made to sell the entire issue, and the efforts of the board were

Old Public Library at Madras, the result of activities by 25 or 30 people in 1916.

Architects' drawing of the new Public Library. "On a June day in 1956 one might have seen an odd little procession going along D street, arms full of books, poceeeding from the old library building to a new building a block to the east.... It was the realization of a dream of 40 years."

Maurice Hoover, now with a 29 passenger bus, had one of the first seven-passenger Cadillacs on the Bend-Portland run in 1929— "seven hours, seven dollars."

This way of getting to Jefferson County is a far call from the old horse stages over terrible roads and over streams on rude ferries.

Now over smooth paved thoroughfares without dust and chuckholes—with only one disadvantage: the great powdered peak is not in view so long.

directed henceforth towards the construction of the project by the Reclamation Service. Somewhere about this time the Madras State Bank became insolvent, with the district having $5,000 on deposit, and giving the board a bad time in meeting obligations.

Harry Gard ended 12 years of service on the board in January 1928, being replaced by Cecil Porter. Gard had put the advancement of irrigation above everything else, even to the neglect of his own affairs, and had spent much of his own money for the welfare of the project. Cecil Porter was given the post of secretary. Progress was at a standstill during the years 1928 and 1929. Hiram Links replaced Johnnie Henderson as director in January 1929, with a majority of four votes, ending 12 years for Johnnie. The election in the fall of 1929 was a quiet affair with only 60 votes cast and with incumbent J. C. Sothman reelected. R. W. Sawyer was given $100 to help defray the expense of a trip to Washington, D. C. in the interest of the project in February 1931. Refunding bonds were issued in the amount of $80,000 with none of the original $90,000 being retired. During 1933 a lot of work was done in an effort to secure construction money from the Reconstruction Finance Corporation, and in 1935 application was made to the Public Works Administration. C. C. Fisher was investigating the project for the Reclamation Service, with a dam to be located just below the confluence of the Metolius River. Feasibility of such a prosposition depended upon a market for the incidental power developed, and the idea was abandoned on account of there being no market for the power. Bonneville Dam was being built at the time, and was ridiculed for the same reason. Howard Turner replaced J. C.

Jefferson County Reminiscences

Sotham in January 1936, ending 12 years board service for him.

On October 23, 1937, an election was held to determine whether to sign a contract with the Federal Government whereby the project would be built by the Bureau of Reclamation. The vote was 179 yes, and 10 no, to agree to repay up to $8,000,000 in 40 years after construction was completed, thus ending 20 years of heartbreaking disappointments and efforts by the board of directors and friends of irrigation for the North Unit. Much delay was still to be encountered before the dreams of the pioneers were to be realized, with World War II delaying the work for a considerable time. Feasibility of the project was made possible by the use of CCC boys in the construction of the dam at Wickiup and the main canal from Bend north, the value of their work amounting to $850,000. They were replaced by a Concientious Objector group during the war who contributed an additional labor value of $450,000. Actual construction of the project began on July 21, 1938, with crews working on Wickiup Dam and Reservoir. The contract for the outlet gates was awarded in November. By 1940 the boys had opened up 21 miles of main canal and completed 12 miles, and had cleared a dense stand of jackpine from 700 acres of Wickiup Reservoir area, in addition to placing 107,000 cubic yards of impacted earth in the embankment.

At the December 1938 board meeting Cecil Porter presented his resignation as director, which was not accepted until the June meeting. His health failed rapidly until his death in August. Cecil Porter had also devoted 12 years of his life to the promotion of irrigation of the North Unit, and unquestionably

346

undermined his health in the process. H. Ward and Allie M. Farrell signed the first contract for the sale of excess lands on August 20, 1938. In 1941 the board was considering the acquisition of the Odin Falls water right, but the matter was subsequenly dropped, and the right was later obtained by the Central Oregon Irrigation District. At this time it is considered of little value. Harry W. Gard died in 1941, ending his long years of unceasing service to the cause of irrigation.

In February 1942, the contract was let for the tunnels in the Smith Rock area, and it was proposed to dismantle some railroad trestles in California for the purpose of fluming the canal across Crooked River.

A clipping from the Redmond *Spokesman* dated September 3, 1942, states that Hans Kjar, director of the Central Oregon Irrigation District, sought support of the Redmond Chamber of Commerce in a movement to force abandoment of the North Unit irrigation project on the grounds it would ruin the upper projects by taking water needed by them. The Madras Chamber of Commerce resolved at their next meeting that the Central Oregon Irrigation District "Investigate the possibility and urge action on the part of the directors in eliminating admitted heavy loss of water in their canal system". "Classify lands under the C.O.I. and other projects in terms of duty of water required to the end that all lands requiring nine to fifteen acre feet be required as submarginal land". It is noted that J. F. Short was named chairman of a committee of the Redmond Chamber to study the matter, and on September 17 the Redmond *Spokesman* denied that the chamber had taken a stand. In spite of the fact that the upriver districts were offered first chance at storage rights to be developed and had refused, there remains a feeling even yet that the North Unit deprived them of some of their water. Many were skeptical that the North Unit would ever deliver any water, due to the thinking that all would be lost by seepage in the main canal.

Percy A. Cupper, lawyer and civil engineer, was retained by the board as advisor in April 1933, and served continously until his death on June 20, 1943, while enroute home from Washington where he had been on district business. His services to the district were of inestimable value; considering his ability both as a lawyer and as an engineer, the board could not have made a better choice. State engineer from 1918 to 1922, prior to that state water superintendent and assistant state engineer from 1907 to 1916, Cupper drew up Oregon's Water Code which was later enacted into law and which is considered one of the best water codes of any western state.

In 1944 the board discussed the advisability of hiring a full-time secretary; planned for the sale of "excess" land; and acknowledged the inadequacy of the domestic water system in view of the expected increase in population. The Bureau of Reclamation studied the situation and made a report on the rehabilitation of the water system, but due to the estimated cost the idea was abandoned at the time to be revived later. Mrs. Beatrice Bryant was employed as the first full-time secretary, and shortly thereafter C. A. Lyman, Bureau of Reclamation auditor, came to the district and set up the system of bookkeeping and made a record of ownership of project lands. Lyman spent six months on the job, with the result that the district has as near a perfect record system as can be had.

The last of the $90,000 of bonds were retired in 1944, and the authorization for the balance of the $5,000,000 was voided.

The first water was delivered to project lands on May 20, 1946, with thousands of people here for the celebration. Of the board of directors who took office in 1916, two, Johnnie Henderson and Dick Anderson, were left to be present at the successful termination of their many years of struggle and disappointment.

The history of irrigation in Jefferson County is a volume in itself, and the foregoing is only the highlights. Each happening had many interesting facets that should be made of record, and of the hundreds of people who played an important part only a few have been mentioned. Judge Sawyer of Bend had a part, even to the extent of defending the North Unit editorially against older rights when such a position must have been very unpopular. We note, too, that Howard Turner was generally among those present from the start. Lewis (Turk) Irving contributed much. It should be mentioned that, although there were always pros and cons, personal enmity never arose to serious proportions, and the battle was of principles rather than of personalities.

Transportation

By Mrs. William Brownhill

The part of Oregon comprising the present Jefferson County was little known for a great many years because of the rugged terrain. The early explorers made slight mention of this territory except as camping-spots as they passed through. Peter Skeen Odgen was the first man to make a recorded trip up the Deschutes River into Central Oregon. The Peter Skene Ogden State Park which encompasses the Crooked River bridges in southern Jefferson County commemorates one of his camping-spots while on that trip.

There were no roads into Central Oregon until 1862, when a crude one was made up the McKenzie River and eastward. However, in 1859 cattle were driven over the area. In 1861, at least one packtrain crossed on the rugged McKenzie Trail enroute to Idaho and Eastern Oregon because of the mining excitement.

In 1867 a caravan of wagons, with soldiers as guards, came out of the north to blaze the present route of U. S. Highway 97 into the Klamath Basin. That was the wagon train that carried supplies from Fort Dalles to the Klamath Indian Reservation. The Barlow Pass was the route chosen. After a wagon road was slashed southward through the jackpine forest, there was a heavy movement of travelers south through the Deschutes

350

country. The crossing of the Crooked River was at Carmichael, and from there the road led into the Hay Creek-Trout Creek area. At the foot of Cow Canyon the north-bound traveler had the choice of going up through Antelope Valley to The Dalles-Canyon City route, or of continuing up Cow Canyon where Charles Haight collected toll.

The mail was carried in early days by Pony Express. Ed Campbell was one of the early mail carriers. This route was from The Dalles via Dufur, Wapinitia, Simnasho, Warm Springs, across a ferry on the Deschutes near the Ed Campbell place, across the Agency Plains to Hay Creek, and on to Prineville. The first settlers on the Agency Plains had one large box in the middle of the plains into which the mail carrier put their mail, thus saving them a trip to Warm Springs. The early settlers respected each other's rights and property and, so far as is known, nobody ever disturbed their mail, and nothing was ever pilfered.

After the railroad was extended to Shaniko in 1900, the mail was routed through Cow Canyon to Heisler Station, and on to Prineville. Later, a carrier brought the mail to Young's Post Office at Sage Brush Springs from Heisler Station.

Establishment of roads was a major problem for the early settlers, as the fencing of homesteads made it impossible to take short-cuts across the country, as formerly. It was not unusual, but nonetheless disconcerting, for a homesteader upon making a trip to town, to find on his return, that a barbed wire fence had been erected, closing the road which he had traveled that very morning when he left home. So roads were mapped out, of travel.

and petitions circulated and presented to the county court at Prineville, by public spirited volunteers, to legally establish lanes

Because of the rugged terrain, it was necessary to carve roads in the sides of hills and mountains in many places, and bridges had to be built to span the streams. Instead of a highway department to attend to this work, much of it was accomplished by donated labor, and later the county court appointed road supervisors in various prescribed districts to handle the work. Funds were obtained from a poll tax, as well as from a property tax. Some of the early road supervisors were Perry Monroe, William Brownhill, William Farrell, and D. V. McBrain. At the present time, the county court maintains a road crew with the necessary equipment to build and maintain roads, in cooperation with the State Highway Commission.

In 1906 the first automobile to come into Central Oregon was a 2-cycle high-wheeled Holsman, being transported from The Dalles to Bend to be used by the Deschutes Telephone Company. The roads were totally unsuited to motor cars—narrow and rutted—used previously only by horse-drawn vehicles. Fuel for the auto had to be stationed along the line of travel, and was in five-gallon cans. The car moved up Rattlesnake Canyon through Moro, and finally reached Cow Canyon at night. The car moved slowly down the rugged canyon, with the driver picking the trail by the dim illumination of the primitive headlights. As the grade narrowed, fenders on one side of the car were ripped and dented. And, in going through a narrow cut, fenders on the opposite side were torn. By the time the car reached the bottom of the grade, it's fenders were scraps of metal. They were taken off at the pioneer Heisler Stage Station on Trout Creek, and remained there a relic for years.

Even in 1910 horse-drawn vehicles had the right-of-way over automobiles. Goggled motorists in dusters were forced to draw to the side of the road, shut off their engines, and permit the freight outfits to pass.

Freight was moved into Central Oregon via Cow Canyon by 4-6-8-horse teams from the railroad station in Shaniko. Merchants in Madras, Prineville, Bend, and Redmond, had their regular freighters to haul for them, but there was such a demand for merchandise as the county settled up that almost anyone who had an outfit could get a load of freight from the warehouses in Shaniko to supply the needs of the interior. Freight outfits and stage coaches enroute to Bend crossed over Crooked River between the present high bridge on U. S. Highway 97 and Smith Rocks, dipping to the bottom of Crooked River gorge over a narrow grade. It was in 1927 that the present high bridge was completed over Crooked River, and the route of Highway 97 established. The Prineville cut-off, branching off Highway 97 south of Madras, and extending in a southeasterly direction, is a link in U. S. Highway 26, and was completed in 1950.

When the railroads were extended up the Deschutes River Canyon in 1911, the mail was brought into Central Oregon by rail. Rural carriers served the interior points. Many of these rural post offices have long since gone out of existence. Such names as Kilts, Maud, Youngs, Heisler, Grandview, Hay Creek, Horse Heaven, Willowdale, Opal City, Grizzly, which once were post marks on letters, are now only memories to the pioneers.

The coming of the railroads into Central Oregon, up the Deschutes Canyon, was of such major importance to this area that it merits a story all its own.

Hitherto this part of the state was little known, and stock raising was about the only profitable industry because of the distance to markets. Wheat raising increased as the homesteaders settled down to the business of carving a living out of the 160-acre homesteads of sagebrush and bunch grass. The first crops had to be hauled the long, dreary miles to Shaniko for shipment to market but, with the advent of the railroads into Central Oregon, warehouses were built at Gateway, Paxton, Madras, Metolius, Culver and Opal City, for housing and shipping the grain. As this is written, motor trucks are bidding fair to replace the railroads in handling farm produce, including livestock.

When established, the O-W R & N railroad had a passenger train leaving Bend for Portland in the morning, and one arriving in Bend from Portland in the evening. This line came from The Dalles, following the Deschutes River to South Junction, then leaving the river to come up the canyon through Gateway, on through Paxton, and climbing to the Agency Plains where the present Madras depot now stands. Then, crossing Willow Creek Canyon over the high bridge, on to Metolius, Culver, Opal City, and southward to Bend. It is said that this line would have been extended through the City of Madras, but greedy property owners, with a get-rich-quick attitude, put such high values on the land needed for a right-of-way that the officials by-passed the city by way of retaliation.

The O-T, or Hill line, crossed the Columbia River near the

354

mouth of the Deschutes River, following the canyon wall on the river side opposite the O-W, to North Junction. There it crossed the Deschutes River and the two railroads shared a joint track as far as South Junction. From here the O-T continued to occupy the Deschutes Canyon to the north of Willow Creek Canyon, which it traversed as far as Madras, where a depot was erected on a spot southwest of the high school. From Madras the rails were extended to a point north of Metolius, where the two lines again merged and continued on to Bend on a joint track. This line carried passengers to Portland, leaving Bend in the evening, arriving in Portland via Vancouver in the morning. A train left Portland in the evening, arriving in Madras in the small hours of the morning, and on to Bend. These trips by rail were rough and tiresome and usually boring after the "new" wore off, as the walls of the canyon did not offer much in the way of variety of scenery. However, the trip was not always wholly uneventful, as there were times when a large rock, tumbling down from the canyon wall, would land squarely in the middle of the track, and the train would be stalled until the rock was removed. The railroad companies have always kept men employed as "Track Walkers" to keep the way cleared for the trains, but even this precaution could not always keep a mishap from occurring. On one trip which my husband made from The Dalles to Gateway, on the O-W train, a rock about the size of a man's head, came plunging down the canyonside, crashed through the window, and onto the seat directly in front of him. Fortunately, the seat was not occupied, so the only casuality was a broken window.

The primary purpose of the railroads was to carry freight, and it was evident that the passenger service was secondary and inadequate.

Before the coming of the railroads into Central Oregon, stage lines operated between Shaniko and Prineville, and also to Bend. Among the early operators was Mack Cornett, whose stage line carried passengers from Shaniko to Prineville. The Wenandy Stake line ran between Shaniko and Bend, via Trail Crossing over Crooked River. As soon as roads were conditioned for motor cars, more and more people chose this method of travel to and from interior points.

Rays and Hammond operated the first auto stake line, making regular trips from Bend to Portland by way of The Dalles, as there was no surfaced road over the mountains at Government Camp at that time. The wagon road over the Barlow Pass had been traveled many years, but motorists found it rough and dusty, quite unsuited for automobiles.

However, one day in 1929, when Myrl Hoover stopped at a service station in Redmond, enroute to Portland in a Model A Ford, he found four persons who had missed the regular bus to Portland. He asked them if they would care to take a chance and travel with him over the old Barlow Trail, to which they agreed. It was on this trip that his idea was born for starting bus service between Bend and Portland over the Barlow Trail. While in Portland he traded his Model A Ford coach for a 1926 7-passenger Cadillac sedan, and filed for a PUC license to operate stage service on alternate days between Bend and Portland. Myrle and Maurice Hoover officially started the Mt.

Transportation

Hood Stages, Inc., on June 24, 1929. They advertised a trip to Portland "in 7 hours for 7 dollars." In 1933 William Niskanen joined the system as one of the owners of what we all know now as "Pacific Trailways, The Friendly Line."

The first trip which the busses made over the Warm Springs cut-off was May 28, 1950, thus bringing Central Oregon only two to three hours away from Portland. What a contrast to early day travel!

Jefferson County Schools

By June Fisher and Ethel Hofstetter

In May, 1915, when the first county superintendent of schools, Lillian Ramsey Watts, took office, there were 35 school districts in Jefferson County. By 1921 the districts numbered 43, although some of the original number, by then, had been consolidated with others. Each area had its own little white school house. The now familiar yellow school bus was unknown and would have had difficulty traveling the roads which traversed Jefferson County during those years.

In March 1957, there were seven districts in which school was held. Some others still exist but send their children away by arrangement with other districts. There are two Class One districts, Madras and Madras Union High School, and one unified school at Culver, with both elementary and high school in the same system.

For a number of years Metolius maintained a high school but some years ago joined the Madras High School district.

During the years which saw these changes the "little white school houses" with their water pails and dippers, their "Waterbury Heaters," and their sonorous bells, began to disappear. Gone now are the outdoor privies, the horse sheds, the tobacco and lard-pail lunch buckets. No corner of Jefferson County nowadays but is reached by the yellow school bus or has its own modern building, with electricity and running water, shining floors and walls of windows.

Happy memories remain, however, of the school days spent in those little schoolhouses. Meadowlarks' songs, fragrance of yellow bells, the sight of sage-rats scurrying through the brush, bring to many a rush of nostalgic recollections.

If one person could be chosen to symbolize the schools of Jefferson County that person would be Lillian Ramsey Watts, who served as superintendent of schools for 34 years. Mrs. Watts took office by appointment in May 1915, "Until they could get some one else," she humorously states. Elected at the first general election held in Jefferson County, she served continuously until her retirement on July 1, 1948.

Mrs. Watts was succeeded in office by Wayne Foster, who served by appointment until June 1950. Walter Shold then took office and served, also by appointment, until June 1952. Mr. Shold was succeeded by Asa T. Eaton who was elected to the office in 1953. These men have done well during a period in which their task has been made difficult by the problems attendant upon an increasing school population and a changing economic picture in the county.

Jefferson County had just been organized when Mrs. Watts took office. She had taught almost continuously, however, from her arrival in Oregon in May 1905. Born in Chariton County, Missouri, and educated at Salisbury Academy, Lillian Ramsey began to teach in that state when she was 18 years old. She was married in 1898 to James J. Watts and came with him and their two small sons, Carl and Ross, to Oregon. Her daughter Edna (Mrs. Harl VanNoy) and son James were born in Oregon.

The shortage of teachers in 1905 in this new country impelled Mrs. Watts to begin teaching here. She taught in residences, and

359

in one vacant saloon building. One term, on the Agency Plains, in the old Mountain View school house, she had 70 children in all eight grades, the first appearance here of the "staggered school day."

The first year or so of her service as superintendent Mrs. Watts made her semiannual visits to the schools by horse and buggy driven by Mr. Watts. With the acquisition of a shiny new "Reo," Mr. Watts became the "chauffeur." He was a familiar figure and welcome visitor to the schools with Mrs. Watts until a few months before his death in 1933.

A book could be written of the interesting, humorous, sometimes pathetic experiences encountered by Mrs. Watts on those semiannual visits. She knew every school child in the county by name and sight. Among her cherished souvenirs are letters, pictures, and gifts from her "youngsters" now scattered. She has listed in her "little notebooks" every student who received an eighth grade diploma while she was superintendent and can tell many amusing anecdotes about them. It was a source of great satisfaction to her that her eldest son Carl, who died tragically in 1934, had become a teacher.

Who's Who in the Pacific Northwest has listed her interests as flower raising, collecting arrow-heads, camping, and fishing. Those who know Mrs. Watts feel she failed to mention her chief and abiding interest, love of children.

Many of Jefferson County's leading women came here to teach in our schools, and remained to marry local men. Many local girls have also become teachers and returned to live and teach in Central Oregon.

Jefferson County owes much to the public-spirited men and women who have served through the years on local school boards, budget committees, and other groups dedicated to the betterment of schools.

Library Association And Pioneer Association

By Helen Hering

1

On a June day in 1956 one might have a seen an odd little procession going along D Street in Madras. Boy Scouts, arms full of books, were proceeding in an orderly way from the old library building to the new building a block to the east.. In a fairly short time the contents of the old shelves were transferred by the boys and arranged by the librarian in the new building.

It was an interesting activity even to a casual observer. To many people of Madras, it was the realization of a dream 40 years before.

On July 25, 1916, a group of 25 or 30 people met in the old Athletic Hall in northwest Madras to discuss ways and means of providing library service for the people of the town and vicinity.

Lewis H. Irving was the presiding officer. A committee on permanent organization was appointed, and officers were elected. —Lewis H. Irving, president; Fanny J. Kane, vice-president; Mrs. L. E. Hyde (Forrest Clover), secretary.

Mrs. Hyde resigned in a few months when her husband, a Pacific Power and Light employee, was transferred to another area. Mrs. W. H. Snook took her place as secretary-treasurer, a position which she held for 16 years. Mrs. Snook also served faithfully as a volunteer librarian, and as a member of many different committees over a period of many years until the death of her husband, pioneer doctor William H. Snook, and her own departure from the community.

Mrs. Kane served in one capacity or another until she left Madras. Howard Turner and Milton G. Pillette took active parts at this first meeting as did Wade Siler and Mr. Black.

At the second meeting, held on August 3, a constitution and by-laws were adopted. A membership committee was appointed and the name chosen for the organization. Mrs. J. Lee DeHuff, Mrs. John McTaggert, Mrs. W. A. Ellis, and Howard Turner were the members of this committee.

Arrangements were made to secure books from various sources. The first books were given to the library by Mrs. J. Jerro. Mrs. G. V. Stanton gave a stove. Other gifts, whose donors were not mentioned, served to stock the shelves and to help furnish the first library quarters. Mrs. Leslie Ramsey (Lela Gard) and Mr. and Mrs. J. W. Warren are mentioned among those who helped.

During the first part of October 1916, the library began to function in rooms on the lower floor of Odd Fellows Hall. This space was used, free of charge, for over a year. For a part of this time the space was shared with the county school superintendent, Lillian Ramsey Watts.

When the Madras City Hall, now the Jefferson County Courthouse, was finished, the library moved into the new building.

Many members joined the Association and many gifts of books, magazines, furniture, and money were received in these early years.

The list of volunteer librarians for this period reads like a roster of the women who were interested in every phase of wholesome civic development.

In 1920 the Association purchased a small building and moved it to the lot now occupied by the Shangri-La Cafe. This property then belonged to Howard Turner, who permitted the building to remain in that location, free of charge, until the lot was sold in 1944.

As the city had promised to house the library whenever space was available, the council then permitted the building to be moved to the city lot just west of the Free Methodist Church, on D Street. Here it stood until it was moved again to permit erection of the new library building which was dedicated in August 1956, almost 40 years, to the day from the first meeting of the group which organized the Jefferson County Library Association.

The first funds for operation of the library came from dues for membership in the organization and gifts from persons interested in the project.

In December of 1917 the Jefferson County Court appropriated $250 for upkeep of the library and purchase of new books. This sum was appropriated nearly every year until 1930. During part of this time a small sum was additionally appropriated by the city of Madras.

Early in the forties the Jefferson County court began to budget the sum of $50 per year, for library use. The city of Madras too, began again to give a small sum for library support. Both of these sums have been substanially increased during the last few years.

During the "depression decade" the membership drive was the only source of income for the library. Any expenses not covered by these funds were paid by individuals interested in keeping the library operating or by funds raised from benefit programs of one sort or another.

Many methods have been used to raise funds. For several years annual dances were given, pleasant social affairs largely attended.The annual membership tea was given each spring for many years. Mrs. W. H. Snook, Mrs. Andrew Morrow, Sr., Mrs. B. N. Conroy, Mrs. Snowden White, and Mrs. W. E. Johnson (May B.) were among the hostesses for these affairs. Bazaars, food sales, and rummage sales have all been utilized as means for raising funds.

Many will remember the famous Needlecraft Club. This organization, which met weekly at the homes of members, was a friendly sewing group. Practically every woman in Madras belonged, or attended at one time or another, during the time this organization existed. There was no age limit. Grandmothers and granddaughters, children and babies, were all welcome. And sometimes they were all there at the same time!

This group did a good deal to help the library. One year the club made a beautiful appliqued quilt which was sold. Mrs. Andrew Morrow Sr. received the quilt and still displays it with pride. Some of the fine applique and quilting was done by Mr. and Mrs. W. A. Ellis, at whose home several quilting parties were held while the quilt was being made.

Library Association and Pioneer Association

Many amusing incidents will be recalled, many friendly faces remembered, at the thought of those quilting parties and other meetings of the Needlecraft Club.

An original play, written by Pearl Dutt Coy, was produced one year, and the proceeds used to buy books. Mrs. Coy was the primary teacher at the Madras grade school for many years. This play, *The Enchaned Worms,* called for some very interesting costumes and stage effects. Some of our leading younger citizens will recall wearing green "worm" costumes and crawling across the stage on hands and knees to be transformed into beautiful butterflies. The Grant boys, Dale and Erwin, made a huge airplane, remarkably like a Piper Cub, of scrap lumber and muslin, for one of the scenes in this play. Their mother, Mrs. Dayton Grant, who was a volunteer librarian for many years, welcomed this outlet for the boundless energies of her two inventive sons.

Mrs. J. A. Toothman, another faithful librarian, designed the costumes and also made many of them for this production.

Two operattas were given to raise funds and provide a summer activity for children of the community.

The Children of Mother Goose was produced in August 1938, under the direction of Mrs. Dale Osborn (Wilma Osborn). This was so well received that *Rip Van Winkle* was given in 1939. Mrs. John L. Sheythe (Dorothy Sheythe) was the director, assisted by Mrs. Charles A. Bay as dance director, and Mrs. Truman Hofstetter as accompanist. Mrs. J. A. Toothman designed the costumes and the scenery, assisted with the scenery by her son Joe. Mrs. Carl Hering was the general chairman of the production.

365

This was one of the most successful money-making projects, involving, as it progressed, almost every child in Jefferson County, and necessitating many costumes and stage effects. Mrs. Toothman evolved some beautiful and unusual costumes, using odds and ends from many attics, and many households were strewn with pink, blue, and white material as the Dutch costumes for some 50 children were fitted and finished.

Mr. Charles A. Bay, at that time publisher of the *Madras Pioneer,* printed programs, which are still treasured items in many albums.

The Library Association, and the community, owe much to Mrs. Osborn, Mrs. Sheythe, Mrs. Bay, and the others who gave a great deal of time to projects planned to afford children an opportunity to take part in dramatic experiences, as well as to raise money for library use.

Many amusing incidents will be recalled by the people who participated in these productions, some of whom came from Trout Creek, Metolius, and Culver.

Mention of later affairs to raise money should include the tea given in the spring of 1955, at the Madras high school by the Library Association. The feature of this affair was a book report by Father Rene Bozarth, witty and renowned traveler and commentator. The book he reviewed was Pearl Buck's *My Several Worlds.* Music by local people and an attractively decorated tea table helped to make this a pleasant and successful affair.

The Library Association has from the first taken an active part in sponsoring social and community affairs.

The Pioneer Associatian and the group responsibile for the

writing of the history of Central Oregon were both outgrowths of Library Association activities.

Book Week has been observed in many different ways. For several years a children's parade was featured with costumes and prizes.

Poster contests have been held, with children from all over Jefferson County exhibiting their handiwork. Several business firms have given window space for the exhibition of the posters.

Much credit should be given to Jefferson County teachers for their help in these contests. The *Madras Pioneer* has always cooperated to the fullest extent in giving publicity to the contests and other library activities. The winners have been awarded prizes, usually in the form of books.

During the depression period the library had an especially difficult role to fill. To provide reading material for an increased number of people, from a non-existent budget, was not an easy assignment. With the help of the State Traveling Library and contributions of books, magazines and jig-saw puzzles from many people, a devoted staff of volunteer workers kept the library open.

Another especially difficult period came during World War II. With the influx of workers for building the airport, in the fall of 1943, all of the facilities of the community were crowded to the utmost.

On their way from Trailer Town, on the fair grounds, to the shopping district, many of the worker's families stopped at the library for reading material and a chat with the librarians. Crowded into the limited space, drying their wet wraps by the

367

tiny stove, many of these people expressed theeir gratitude for the loan of books and the friendliness shown to them.

That was the winter that it rained almost daily from October until March. The crowded condition, the mud, the worry caused by the war, all united to create an atmosphere of uncertainty and excitement among permanent residents as well as the transient workers.

The Library Association is proud of the fact that with the help of the State Traveling Library and a staff of volunteer librarians, our little library was able to provide a cheerful meeting place and good reading material for the airport workers as well as for its regular patrons.

Many people have helped with the upkeep of the little frame libray building. Painting was done by several, among them Fred Green, Mr and Mrs. Arthur Lierman, and Walter McCaulou. At least one reshingling was necessary: Carl Hering, Harl VanNoy, and W. A. Ellis, assisted by a group of Boy Scouts, were responsible for one such repair job. Mr. and Mrs. Charles Classen and Frank Graham have helped with cleaning and repairing.

When the building was moved in 1944, Lewis H. Irving, in addition to paying for the moving, had a concrete foundation put under it. Mr. and Mrs. Fred Green offered to furnish the lumber and labor to build on another room during the depression period but no funds were available at that time to finance the small amount which would have needed to finish the building. The Sahallee Club has often assisted the library. Mrs. W. R. Cook and Mrs. Gillis Dizney each sponsored projects.

In addition to serving as volunteer librarians for many years,

Library Association and Pioneer Association

Mrs. Dayton Grant, Mrs. J. A. Toothman, and Mrs. Carl Hering scrubbed and scoured the dusty little building many a time. One such cleaning took place before the momentous occasion when the State Librarian, Eleanor H. Stephens, came to spend a day advising and arranging during World War II. A spring dust-storm had made a thorough cleaning a necessity. The aroma of soapsuds and furniture polish pervading the little building was referred to, in her sparkling way, by Miss Stevens in her account of the visit at several later meetings with her.

In 1947 a partial reorganization of the Library Association took place. Under the leadership of Mrs. J. H. Ross, a campaign was begun to modernize and enlarge the book collection and to provide more adequate library service. Mrs. Max Ricker, Mrs. Bruce Stewart, Mrs. Lloyd Root, and Mrs. Paul Jones were of great assistance to Mrs. Ross in organizing, selecting, and cataloging the books during this period. Mrs. William Wiese and several others served as librarians for many months.

With Mrs. Ross at the helm, a small group of enthusiastic and determined members initiated a campaign to secure a new building. Walter McCaulou was especially active in this campaign. In the spring of 1955 the members of the Kiwanis Club pledged their assistance toward the erection of a building. A drive for funds was conducted by the Library Association. With the funds secured from various sources, and those pledged by the city and county, construction was begun in August of 1955. Kiwanian Adrian Smith was appointed "clerk of the works" to supervise and coordinate the volunteer labor. Much credit is due Mr. Smith for his intense interest and faithful continuation of this job.

Jefferson County Reminiscences

Miss Eleanor Ebert, from the Oregon State Library, said that it was greatly to the credit of citizens of Jefferson County that their volunteer labor program was continued to the last and the building finished without delay. There have been some such community undertakings which started out in full swing and then bogged down because help became scarce.

On August 9, 1956, the new building was dedicated, having already been in use as a library for several months. It is located on D Street, between Sixth and Seventh streets, in downtown Madras, and has an attractive entry with librarian's desk, book sections for children and adults, and toilet facilities. Appraised at $16,000 recently, the building represents an outlay of more than $10,000 for construction and basic furnishings. The city of Madras gave $1,500 and the lot on which the structure is located. Jefferson County gave several thousand dollars. Individuals contributed generously. Warm Springs Lumber Company and many local firms and individuals donated materials. Labor was provided by county residents, members of the Kiwanis Club providing the major portion.

One Kiwanian, Sumner Rodriquez, might be cited as an example of a family's continuing interest in the library. His parents, Mr. and Mrs. S. R. G. Roderiquez, took an active part in library affairs during the time they spent in Madras years ago. Mrs. S. R. G. Rodriquez was among the many faithful volunteer librarians at that time. Sumner himself worked many hours to help insure the completion of the new building on schedule.

Amos Fine and Everett VanWert also worked long hours,

370

spearheading a group whose personnel varied from day to day. Especially faithful were E. W. Mason, W. J. Stebbins and Howard Turner, a trio whose interest in library affairs dates back to the beginning of the Library Association.

The library is now open conveniently, with a paid librarian, and two assistants. Cataloguing, book mending, making inventory, and other services are still done by volunteed labor provided by a group of enthusiastic and loyal women.

Without the assistance of the Oregon State Library it would have been impossible to maintain library service in Jefferson County, especially during the depression years. Special loans of books at critical times, special help with cataloging and selection problems, and visits from State Library personnel, are among the many helpful services which have been provided to our local library.

Seldom, until the new building was in use, had there been a paid librarian or paid janitor service. The hours of volunteer help in the library constitutes an unforgettable contribution to the community by a group of people far too numerous to mention here. The service they have given will never be forgotten by those who believe that a free public library is one of the bulwarks of a free citizenry.

2

The Pioneer Association was organized on Sunday, May 25, 1952, at an informal picnic at the Cove. A group of pioneers, members of a committee for the writing of a history of Jefferson County, were discussing the need for an organization.

Mrs. H. Ward Farrell, the chairman of the history committee, called the group together after the dinner and appointed Mrs. L. M. Horney as presiding officer. The officers elected at the meeting were president, Retta Horney; vice-president, Fred Rodman; secretary-treasurer, Evada Power. A committee, consisting of Howard W. Turner, T. A. Power, and Mrs. Fred Rodman, was appointed to draw up a constitution and by-laws for the organization.

The group in attendance at this picnic became the first charter members of the association.

In June 1953, the first annual Pioneer Picnic was held at the Cove. In a colorful and picturesque ceremony Mrs. Howard W. Turner (Pearl Read) was crowned queen. She was very appropriately dressed in a beautiful costume of the pioneer period, a custom which has been followed by succeeding "royal ladies."

Mrs. L. M. Horney (Retta Peck) became queen in 1954, followed by Mrs. S. E. Gray (Viola Isham) in 1955, and Mrs. John Helfrich (Minnie McCoin) in 1956.

Fred Rodman became president in 1954, with Howard W. Turner as vice-president and Mrs. T. A. Power as secretary-treasurer.

In 1955, Howard W. Turner became president, Winifred Osborn vice-president, and Mrs. Power secretary-treasurer.

Winifred Osborn was elected president in 1956. Gus Ramsey vice-president, and Mrs. Power was re-elected as secretary-treasurer. In 1957 Gus Ramsey became president, Vern Merchant vice-president, and Mrs. Power continued as secretary.

Membership in the Pioneer Association is considered a privilege and an honor. One must have come to Central Oregon prior to 1914 or be the child of parents who did so.

It is the purpose of the organization to keep alive the pioneer spirit and to honor the memory of those sturdy individuals who settled Jefferson County.

Warm Springs Indian Reservation

By Ralph M. Shane, Copied by Helen Wing

As a preface to this story Howard Turner wrote:

"The following is a chronological history of the Warm Springs Indian Agency from the first treaty to the present time.

"As a person long interested in Indian history and lore, I find it specially interesting to recall the events during the 50 years that I have been acquainted with this reservation and many old timers whose relatives are now a part of the increasing population of the Indian Tribes. Some tribes have diminished and others have increased so that the population at this time is approximately 1200.

"Fifty years ago it was all horse and buggy times. The writer has seen many families with all of their belongings in all kinds of rigs, with several head of horses, kids riding bareback on the horses, dogs trailing along over the dusty roads. How different now their riding along in ease and comfort in late model automobiles. And in their homes, where formerly there was only an open fire for light as well as for cooking their food after dark, with occasionally a lantern, and now electricity and many of the latest conveniences of the white man.

"We wonder at the evolution during the past 50 years and whether or not it is conducive to a better life for the Indians.

I believe that it is, though I do feel that they had many old ideas that were good.

"The white man's new way of living has penetrated into the old traditions and superstitions. Now the younger generation is trying to live as the white man. For one thing now there are clocks and calendars, while in the early days the old boys merely looked at the sun to tell the time and to the 'moons' when they desired to say they would see you in 30 days or a month.

"The writer has seen much development in the agricultural, economic home life in the last half century on the reservation. I happened to be called in by the Indian Commissioner in Washington to sit in with two other men to map out some of the developments. We spent considerable time on the reservation and made an extensive report on conditions. Improvements included additional equipment in many departments, new building to take the place of fire-traps in the dormitories and other buildings, new and better water supply, improved roads, irrigation and the general building up of the agricultural possibilities.

"New roads and highways have been constructed, better farming and livestock practices, use of water by irrigation and many other innovations have all been carried on so that the present generation of Indians are to a great extent keeping pace with the white man. Their timber is being manufactured into lumber. And now with power generated at the dams on the Deschutes River, the Indian population will enjoy a perpetual income from their natural resources which will in a way offset the poor lands."

Warm Springs Indian Reservation

CHRONOLOGY OF WARM SPRINGS HISTORY

1825—Peter Skene Ogden beaver-hunting expedition crossed area that is now the reservation.

1834-35—Nathaniel J. Wyeth trip of exploration across the reservation and back.

1843—John C. Fremont exploration from Columbia River to Fort Sutter in California crossed the present reservation.

1848—Office of Commissioner of Indian Affairs, Oregon Territory, was established with a sub-agency at The Dalles to handle affairs of the Columbia River Indians. Robert Newelle, superintendent, took charge at The Dalles on August 17.

1849—Department of the Interior created and the Bureau of Indian Affairs transferred to the new department, from the War Department. J. L. Parrish appointed superintendent on December 18.

1850—Elias Wampole appointed superintendent on September 24.

1852—Elkanah Walker, superintendent on March 11.

1853—J. M. Garrison, superintendent on March 22.

1854—J. L. Parrish reappointed superintendent on January 11. Increasing conflict between Indians along the Columbia River and the white settlers infiltrating the Oregon frontier. Nathan Olney became superintendent on November 2.

1855—(June 25)—Treaty of 1855 creating the Warm Springs Reservation. Henry L. Abbot surveyed for the Pacific Railroad across the reservation.

1857—A. P. Dennison became superintendent. The Dalles band of Wascos and a large part of the Upper and

375

Lower Deschutes bands of Walla Wallas (about 500) were removed to the new reservation.

1858—The remaining bands of Wascos were removed to the reservation.

1859— (March 8) Ratification of the Treaty of 1855. August—Heavy Snake raid drove employees from Agency back to The Dalles, and also a large number of the Indians. September—Detachment of U. S. Dragoons stationed at Agency.

1860—Sawmill put in operation at the Agency.

1861—Three white men murdered on Barlow Road by Indians. Four Indians hanged for the murders on November 8. Wm. Logan became superintendent on June 13.

1862—Detachment of U. S. Dragoons withdrawn from the Agency. Headquarters of the Agent for Warm Springs Agency changed from The Dalles to Warm Springs.

1865—John Smith became superintendent on November 14. Supplemental Treaty of 1865 negotiated with Warm Springs Indians on November 15. Indians unknowingly relinquished fishing rights.

1866—Act of Congress authorized recruiting of Warm Springs Scouts for campaign against the Snake Indians of Southeastern Oregon.

1868—Close of the Snake campaign—end of the Snake raids on the reservation. First religious services conducted for the reservation Indians by Agent Smith and his staff of employees.

1869—Capt. W. W. Mitchell appointed superintendent on June 21.

1871—T. B. Handley made first surveys of reservation

boundary. John Smith reappointed superintendent on May 7.

1872—Malheur Reservation established for Snake or Piute Indians.

1873—Warm Springs Scouts took part in Modac Wars in the Lava Beds.

1874—First Indian boarding school established at the Agency.

1875—Deschutes Ferry rebuilt, probably at Cowles Ranch—Mecca.

1877—Epidemic of typho-malaria with high mortality to both whites and Indians.

1878—Rev. R. N. Fee, first appointed missionary, (United Presbyterian), and wife arrived from Nez Perce Reservation. Part of Piutes from Malheur Reservation joined the Bannocks in war—all Indians left the Malheur Reservation.

1879—First group of Piute Indians brought to Warm Springs Reservation from Vancouver Barracks where they had been held as prisoners of war.

1880—New sawmill on Mill Creek 14 miles from Agency. (Not old Mill).

1882—Retracing of Handley-Campbell Survey by Rumsey. First Church building constructed at the Agency. Malheur Reservation restored to public domain.

1884—Indian Appropriation Act (July 4, 1884) carried $50,000 for survey of Indian Reservation boundaries. Chief Oitz and his band of Piutes brought to Warm Springs Reservation from the Yakima Reservation. Supt. John Smith died on January 18. Alonzo Gesner appointed superintendent on March 1.

1885—First group of Warm Springs Indian students to Salem Indian School returned to reservation. Jason Wheeler superintendent on October 1.

1886—Resurvey and remarking of lines and corners of surveys of Warm Springs Reservation authorized by Congress.

1887—McQuinn-Campbell survey of Reservation North Boundary made. W. W. Dougherty became superintendent on January 1.

1888—Report of investigating committee (Special Agent of Indian Service and Special Agent of General Land Office) favored Handley Survey Line. Henry Heth, superintendent on September 8—stayed one day. Daniel W. Butler, superintendent on September 17.

1889—James C. Luckey, superintendent on July 17.

1890—Commission of 1890 for review and survey of boundary dispute. (Fullerton, Dufur, and Payne).

1893—Lt. E. E. Benjarmin appointed superintendent August 10.

1894—Permanent Act of Congress fixed North Boundary on Handley Line. John A. McQuinn, U. S. deputy surveyor, contracted to survey West Boundary of reservation. Lt. C. W. Farber, superintendent on November 1.

1896—Lt. Farber died on June 12. Peter Gallagher appointed superintendent on June 13. James L. Cowan appointed superintendent on December 19.

1897—New Boarding School building completed and school opened in September with Mr. and Mrs. Nardin as first superintendent of schools and matron respectively.

Warm Springs Indian Reservation

1900—Albert O. Wright, superintendent July 1 to August 7. James E. Kirk appointed superintendent on August 8.

1905—Claude C. Covey appointed superintendent on July 29.

1911—Oregon Trunk Line Railroad opened to Mecca.

1912—Steel Highway Bridge over Deschutes at Mecca was built. Peter Wadsworth, superintendent May 21 to September 5. Gilbert L. Hall appointed superintendent on September 6.

1915—Seekseequs and He-He Sawmills built. A. M. Reynolds superintendent on July 1.

1917—Fred Mensch, U. S. surveyor, retraced surveys of boundaries and reported in detail—recommended cash payment on ceded lands and a change of Northwest and West Boundary.

1918—Omar L. Babcock appointed superintendent on September 27.

1921—General Council of Warm Springs Indians for consideration of Mensch recommendation.

1922—Chas. W. Rastall appointed superintendent on July 1. Beginning of timber cruise and classification survey.

1924—J. B. Mortsolf appointed superintendent on March 1.

1926—Completion of timber cruise and classification survey.

1928—Fred Perkins appointed superintendent on October 1.

1930—Enabling Act (public law no. 552) passed by Congress, authorizing Indians to submit boundary claims to U. S. Court of Claims.

1932—Judge Whaley of U. S. Court of Claims took testimony on Reservation in boundary case.

379

1933—Fred Boyd appointed superintendent on December 1.

1934—New Highway Bridge built over Deschutes River on State Highway 50.

1936—J. W. Elliott appointed superintendent on October 1.

1938—Warm Springs Indians vote to accept the Indian Reorganization Act. New hospital for Indians completed at the Agency and put into use. New boarding school and dormitories completed.

1941—Opinion handled down by U. S. Court of Claims on Warm Springs Boundary case. Opinion stated Warm Springs Indians entitled to recover approximately 80,000 acres of land on North and West Boundaries.

1942—Sale of Schoolie Timber Contract sold to Warm Springs Lumber Company.

1947—Whitewater Timber Sale contract sold to Tite Knot Pine Mill at Redmond.

1948—Public Law 894 passed by the 80th Congress awarded proceeds of sales from disputed area in Mt. Hood National Forest to Warm Springs Tribe.

1949—Simnasho Timber Sale Contract sold to Philip Dahl of Tite Knot Pine Mills at Redmond. Opening of Warm Springs Cut-off, State Highway from Portland to Central Oregon, in November.

Index

Agates, 85, 103, 255.
Alfalfa, 11-12, 16, 21-22, 209.
Allingham log drives, 223.
Amusements, 179, 211, 245, 269, 287, 295, 299, 309.
Antelope, 106.
Ants, 216.
Applegate Trail, 1.
Artesian Well, 177.
Ash Butte, 98.
Ashwood, 82, 96-113.
Ashwood gold rush, 99-101, 256.
Automobiles, 29, 73, 114, 130-132, 151, 181, 352.
Axchandle Springs, 110.

Baby Roy, trotting horse, 268.
Backwash of immigration, 98.
Bake Oven, 23, 24.
Baldwin Sheep & Land Company, 11-21, 332, 333.
Banks, 149.
Bannock War, 11.
Baptising, 65.
Baseball, 207.
"Basin", first name of Madras, 114.
Beavers, 87, 93, 221, 236.
Bells, frieghters', 259-260.
Bicycle across the Cascades, 303.
Blacksmiths, 57, 146-147.
Blizzard Ridge, 46-53.
Blue Mountains, 20, 38, 81, 92, 103.
Bridges, 78, 230, 354, 380.
Bunch grass, 10, 70, 92, 240.
Butchering, home, 76, 293.

Camp Polk, 226.
Camp Sherman, 221, 234-238.
Candles, 181.
Cascades, 38, 90, 189.
Cattle, 10, 43, 85, 97, 109, 119, 209, 220, 224, 252.
Cattle drives, 87, 93-95.
Cave dwelling, 167.
Cemeteries, 4, 33, 214, 301.
Centenarian Pioneer, 119.
Central Oregon Irrigation Company, 337.
Chinees laborers, 234.
Chinook wind, 289.
Churches, 74, 86, 161, 212-213, 257, 273.
Circle M Dude Ranch, 237.

Circus, first, 155.
Clark Brothers, largest wheat growers, 278.
Coal oil lamps, 196, 271.
Columbia Southern Railroad, 130.
Combs of chickens frozen, 210.
Conscientious objectors at work, 346.
Corvallis & Eastern Railroad, 234.
County seat removal, 133-138.
Cove Palisades, 59.
Cow adventure, 41.
Cow Canyon, 22, 24.
Coyote Mountain, 113.
Coyotes, 77, 200, 210, 249, 260, 285.
Craig, John snowshoe mail-carrier over McKenzie Pass, 226.
Crook County, 1, 5, 6, 108, 114, 119, 134, 140, 147, 254, 262, 302.
Crooked River, 56, 58, 77, 246, 347, 351.
Crooked River Bridge, once third highest, 78.
Crooked River Laundry, 246.
Culver, 54-80.

Dams, 25, 55, 119, 207-208, 254, 345, 374.
Dances, 50, 52, 65, 178, 180, 245.
Deer, 92, 220.
Dentists, 180, 222, 248.
Deschutes River, 151, 209, 222, 229, 310, 316, 342, 353.
Doctors, 124-126, 222.
Donnybrook, 109.
Double winter, 57, 163, 204, 224.
Drouths, 7, 32, 183, 252, 328.
Dugout house, 72.
Dust storms, 162-164, 289.

Eastern Oregon Land Grant, 228.
Eggs, packed in rolled barley, 181.
Electricity, 66, 250, 268.
Ex-pugilist teacher, 175.

Falls into canyons, 79.
Farmers Union, 273-274, 310.
Fence fights, 306.
Ferries, 197.
Ferry across the Deschutes, 199, 201-202.
Fever, typhoid, 212.
Fires, 141-145, 182, 256.

Fish fry, 121, 129, 202, 300.
Fishing, 93, 158, 220, 234, 235, 326-327.
Floods, 295, 329-330.
Flour mills, 145, 293.
Fog, 288.
Fossils, 190.
Freighters, 30, 64, 77, 98, 129, 177, 181, 194, 196, 217, 243, 260-261, 353.
Fremont, John C., "The Pathfinder", 90, 105-107, 219, 225, 375.
Frog Springs Canyon, 316.
Fruit, 74, 294.
Fruit peddler, 73.
Fuel, 64.
"Fuzz-tails", pioneer horses, 265.

Game, 10, 58, 200.
Gardens, 75, 211, 216, 229-230, 294.
Gateway, 184-197.
Geology of Jefferson County, 188-191.
George, Chief, 25-26.
German Colony, 211-215.
Grandview, 228-230.
Grange, 180, 274-277.
Grater Hotel, 99.
Grizzly, 1-8.

Hailstorms, 294, 314.
Harriman, E. H., 13, 144.
Hay Creek, 9-45.
Homesteading, 2, 7, 35, 61, 151, 283-284, 290, 317.
Horse Heaven Creek, 7.
Horse Heaven Mines, 102.
Horse thieves, 39.
Hotels, 83, 122-124, 142, 156, 233.
Houses, 13, 39, 55, 57, 209, 252, 267, 323.
Huckleberries, 237.
Ice, packed for summer, 77.

Indians, 56, 68, 92, 107, 111, 225, 238, 247, 295, 302.
Irrigation, 72, 119, 224, 253, 304, 312, 328, 330-349.

Jackrabbit Drives, 197, 210, 249, 260, 299-300.

Jefferson Mountain, 54, 188, 239, 284.
Jim Hill mustard, 324.
John Day River. 108, 329.
Jump-off Joe, 45.
Juniper Butte, 54.
Junipers, 55, 64; largest juniper forest in world in Jefferson, Crook and Deschutes counties, 192-193; 242, 282, 322.

Kibbe, Guy, movie actor, nephew of Blizzard Ridge settler, 51.
Killing of prisoner, 251.
Kilts Post Office,113.
Krug, Robert H., murdered, 227.
Kutcher precinct, 302.

Lamonta, 174-186.
Lava beds, 31, 91, 97, 189.
Library Association, 361-371.
License plate road markers, 221.
Lightening, 174, 207, 288-289.
Literary societies, 245, 269.
Livery barns, 120, 122.
Livestock, 62, 71, 109.
Lower Desert, 228.
Lumber, 47, 52, 128, 203, 212, 218, 223, 241, 322.

McKenzie Pass, 9, 91, 226.
Madras, 46, 114-173, 285.
Madras pioneers, list of 171-173.
Madras *Pioneer*, newspaper, 165, 166.
Mail, 32, 44, 73, 88, 116-117, 151, 175, 182, 192, 206, 244, 256, 272, 304, 351.
Marginal land, 183, 252.
Maupin, Howard, killer of Chief Paulina, 97, 104.
Mercury mining, 96, 101-102.
Metolius, 209-216.
Metolius Rim, 230.
Metolius River, 219, 220, 230, 237, 238, 333.
Military Road, 112.
Mountain View Debating Society, 270, 297.
Motion pictures, first, 156.
Mud Springs Valley, 259-281.
Mules, 292, 293.
Murders, 158-160, 227, 302.
Mushroom project, 202.

Index

Negro Brown, 206.
New Culver, 61.
Newly-married bachelor's long hike for pepper, 29.
Nichols, Lyn, from chore boy to foreman of Haycreek Ranch, 17-18.
North Agency Plains, 316-328.
Northeastern Jefferson County, 107.
Northern Pacific Scrip, 151.
North Unit Irrigation Canal, 253.

Ogden, Peter Skene, 375.
Oil, drilling for, 177.
Old Culver, 243, 247.
Old Maid's Canyon, 121,
Old Spot, famous cow, 43.
Opal City, 239-252.
Opal Springs, 63, 69, 164, 215, 250.
Orchards, 51, 177, 324, 326.
Oregon Trunk Railroad, 78, 121, 125, 153-154, 207, 274, 325, 354.
Organ salesman, 72.

Packtrains, 112, 350.
Palmehn or Palmain, second name of Madras, 114-115, 117-119, 316.
Paulina, Chief, 16.
Peter Skene Ogden State Park, 79.
Petrified Corpse, 33.
Photographer, first, 129.
Pictographs, Indian, 241.
Pioneer Association, 371-372.
Pittock, H. L., 15.
Poems, long ones recited, 270.
Pony Butte, 254-258.
Post cards, scentic, 129.
"Poverty sop" or grease gravy, 267.
Primeval forests, 191.

Race track, 237.
Railroads, 60, 66, 77, 125, 141, 144, 152, 283, 311, 317, 354.
Railroad race, 36, 151, 153, 249, 277, 298.
Range wars, 6.
Rattlesnake Canyon, 352.
Rattlesnakes, 77, 195, 249, 298, 324.
Red Rock District, 54.
Rimrock Springs, 174.
River log-drives, 204.
Roads, 22-23, 45, 48, 58, 79, 91, 235, 311, 318, 351.

Sagebrush, 192, 240, 255, 266, 282, 285, 298-299, 307, 318.
Sage rats, 210, 299, 359.
Salmon hatchery, 232.
Santiam Toll Road, 229.
Saloons, 110, 141, 143, 149.
Sawmills, 30, 42, 46, 71, 163, 176, 203, 218, 219.
Scalp of Chief Paulina, 105.
Schools, 3, 23, 31, 63, 132-133, 175-176, 182, 187, 191, 195, 214, 221, 244-245, 263, 279, 280, 307, 318-320, 358-360.
Shaniko, 18, 23; once world's largest wool-shipping point, 98; 129, 259-260.
Sheep, 7, 11-20, 98, 309.
Sheep sale to Soviet Government, 27.
Shorthorn cattle, 82.
Sidesaddle, 71.
Skyline of Jefferson County, 55.
Skull Hollow, 111.
Smallpox, 160.
Snake Indian uprising, 25, 376.
Snowbirds, 314.
Snowstorm of 1884-1885, 204.
Soap, home-made, 75.
Soda pop drinking ponies, 235.
Soda Springs, 223.
Sour dough bisquits, 44, 231.
South Agency Plains, 282-315.
Springs, 26, 231, 259, 304.
Spring snowstorm, 316.
Springtime flowers, 255.
Squaw Flat, 228.
Squaw trouble, 40-41.
Stills, 141, 203.
Summer homes, 238.
Sunday schools, 213, 254, 258, 296.

Telephones, 65, 89, 133, 144, 310.
Teller Flats, 28.
The Dalles, 2, 91, 108, 261.
Three counties, living in, in same house, 84.
Three-toed horse, 192.
Threshing, 68, 180, 196, 210, 229, 256.
Toll roads, 83, 86, 185, 226, 229.
Trail Crossing District, 70-80.
Transportation, 350-357.
Trapping, 249.
Trout Creek, 81-95, 317.
Tumbleweeds, 211, 239.

Jefferson County Reminiscences

Union Pacific Railroad, 13, 120, 186.
Upper Soda Springs, 233.
U' Ren, W. S., (noted Initiative and Referendum crusader) attorney for Madras in county seat removal from Culver, 136-137.
U. S. Highway 97, 24, 186, 194.
U. S. marshal arrested pro-German, 140-141.
U. S. Reclamation Service, 344, 346, 348.

Vanora, 198-208.
Various nationalities in Jefferson County, 112, 305.
Veterans' State Aid Commission, 224.
Vibbert, Noah, in double missing adventure, 184.
VZ brand, still used, 87, 313.

Warm Springs Indian Reservation, 282, 317, 325, 373-380.
Wasco County, 9.
Water, scarcity of, 69, 75, 120, 126-127, 146, 147; "More Water for Washday" platform of woman candidate for mayor of Madras, 148; 197, 199, 210, 231, 240, 247-248, 254, 264, 271, 286-287, 296, 321, 327.
Waterwheels, 333.
Wells, 126-127, 165, 231, 240, 248, 334.
Wheat, 197, 273, 315, 327.
Whitman Massacre, 12.
Wildcat adventure, 200.
Wild horses, 63, 285-291.
Wild parsnips, 63.
Wife-wanted advertisement, 310.
Willoughby Post Office, 3.
Willow Creek, 1, 3, 4, 10, 23, 35, 74, 330.
Windmill feed grinder, 177.
Winter storms, 4, 16, 51, 83, 204-206, 280, 287-288.

384

SURNAME INDEX

Abbot, Henry L., 375
Achey, Arthur, 174
  Bill, 174
  Earnest, 174
  Jerry & Mary Russell, 174
  Nora, 174
Adams, Amanda, 59
  Walter, 179
Akeson, Marvin, 194
  Monte, 194
Alderdyce, Tom, 240, 248
Aldrich, John, 28
  John & May Lippe, 29
Alexander, Ernest, 85
Allen, Alf, 85
  C. W., 221
  Ed, 34
  Mr/Mrs. Edwin D., 34
  F. W., 343
  Hardy, 224
  Williamson G., 10
Allingham, Athey, 229
  Carter, 223
  Daisy, 221
  David, 232
  David Warren, 238
  Lou, 223
Aldrich, John, 16
Anderson, Mr/Mrs
    Andy, 34
  A. D., 262, 265, 310, 339
  A. D. "Dick," 336
  A. D. & Effie Taylor, 305
  Dick, 313, 334, 349
Andrew, Harry W., 335
Andrus, Mr/Mrs. H. P.,
  267
Arensmeier, Daniel, 214
  Louis, 214
  Louie H., 213
Arensmuir, Louis, 212
Armstrong, Bob, 180
Arney, Walter D., 171
  Walter & May Jackson,
  305
Atteburg, John, 102
Auberry, Marsh, 224
Babcock, Omar L., 379
Bacon, Frank, 247
  Frank P., 342
Baily, Curtis, 222

Baldwin, Dr.,26
  Dr. D. M., 10
Bales, Joe & Irene, 178
Banks, Jerry, 175
Banna, Bert, 324
  Charlie, 324
Banta, Abe, 71
  Bill, 324
  John, 71
  M. Martha, 56
  R., 34
Barber, Bill, 245
  William, 241
  W.C., 66, 136
Barker, Nora, 178
Barlow, Adie, 265
Barnes, Al G., 155
  Edgar, 73, 175
  Irene, 176
  Sue, 73
Barnett, Benjamin, 59
  Bobbie, 137
  Dave, 171
  David W., 59
  Elijah, 62, 243
  Elijah & Elanor, 59
  Hazel, 310
  Margaret, 59
  Robert, 171
  Viola, 59
Barnstetter, Edith, 296
  George, 296
  Henry, 296
  V. Z., 306
  William, 296
Bartlett, Dr. J. A., 171
Barton, Fannie, 171
  Jim, 196
Basey, Irvine, 178
Bagatia, Antone, 305
Bateson, Ed, 178
Bay, Mrs. Charles A., 365
Bean, Jim, 223
  Laurie, 223
Beddingfield, Joe, 171
Beeman, Ben, 55
  Esther, 55
Belknap, H.A., 60
Bell, H. L. Rev., 296
Belnap, Harley, 3
Belshe, C.L., 234

Hansen, 236
Henrich, 236
Benefield, Tom 180
  Willis, 178
Benjarmin, E.E. (Lt), 378
Bennett, M. W., 171
Berkley, Charles, 29
  C. C., 342
Berryman, Charles H., 337
Bettis, Jim, 178
Betts, Robert, 102
Bigelow, Mike, 178
Billips, Mrs. John Sr., 257
Binder, Kenneth, 278, 303
  Leita, 278, 280
  Stephan E., 303
  S. E., 261,274,
  Mr/Mrs. S. E., 278
Black, Ad, 50
  Ira, 141, 180
  Logan & Laura McCoy,
  50
  Ronald, 53
  Stanton & Elizabeth
  Boyd, 53
Blackley, James, 140
Blackwell, Harry E., 4
Blair, Dr. Harry, 125
  Hubert, 245
  Ruth, 194
  William, 192
Blakley, James, 331
  J. M., 331
Boegli, William, 135
  William & Amanda
  Adams, 58
  William, 335
  Wm., 67
Bolter, Edward, 84
  Elwood, 176
  John, 84
  John E., 84
  J. E., 84
  Kate, 84
Bone, Earl, 344
Boone, Luther , 62
Booth, Bob, 228
  Frank, 228
Borden, Myrtle, 159
Bowman, Alvin, 44
Boyce, Alonzo, 205

385

A.W., 171,316
Mr/Mrs. A. W., 130
Mary J. (Brown) Weber, 114
Boyd, Elizabeth, 58
Fred, 380
Boylen, Tom, 17
Bradon, Irwin, 178
Bramer, Charles, 35
Brammer, Charles, 34
Brannon, Joe, 109
Branstetter, Anna, 171
George, 171
H. J., 310
William, 171
W. J., 171
Braun, Mike, 308
Breedens, Joe, 60
Breeding, Joe, 175
Breen, Gladys, 176
Brewster, W. K., 129,171
Brock, Bill, 218
Brogan, Celia, 110
Dan, 110
Jack, 110
John C., 107,111
Phil, 110,188,194
Brooks, Frank J., 140,146
J. F., 171
Brown, Billy, 220
Edith, 263
Fate, 1
I. D., 273
Ralph, 186
Mrs. Ralph, 318
T. J., 100
Warren 3, 63, 175
Willis, 186
Brownhill, Ada, 263
Timothy, 165, 171,308
William, 352
Mrs. William, 319
Bruns, John, 238
John & Ruth, 236
Bryan, Moses, 178
Buchanan, John, 229
Bullard, Ava, 176
Burden, Dave, 308
Tom, 308
Burdick, Benton 236
Denton G., 237
N.A., 79
Burdin, Dave, 172
Tom, 172

Burgess, Martha, 73
Simon Peter, 73, 245
T., 29
Burns, John, 306
Butler, Clay, 179
Daniel W., 378
Dick, 179
Bye, Charles E., 133
E. C., 148
Cadanaugh, Avis, 176
Cain, Squire, 176
Cake, Ralph, 232
Campbell, Ed, 295, 351
Ed & Sarah 308
Edward, 151
John, 172,296, 309
John E., 152,199,205
Judge, 21
May, 198
Ruby, 20
Carney, Ed, 232
Carson, Addie, 56, 53
Kit, 90
Lew, 180
Carter, Ava, 279
Cartwright, C.M., 12, 100
Caslioet, O. G., 180
Chaloupka, Edward 326
Champion, Art, 101
Chilcote, James, 308
Christian, Carl, 193
Church, Jack, 5,16, 28
Cilgore, Charles E., 280
Clark, A. P., 196, 303, 318
Bert, 53
Dolph, 278
Harold (Dr.) 172
J. N., 104
Matt, 78, 151, 251
Roth, 278
Clarke, Bert, 44
Day, 44
Jim, 43
Ora, 44
Clarno, Francis, 176
Classen, Mr/Mrs.
Charles, 368
Cleek, Henry, 6, 330
Isom, 199, 33
Alfred & Martha 226
Fanny, 226
John, 226
Newton, 226

Otto, 226
Coburn, Alice, 194
Ester, 194
Cochrane, Myrtle, 247
Cockerham, J. C., 66
Coleman, Henry, 72, 87, 93, 98, 102
Coles, Ase, 72
U. S., 186
Colliver, O. G., 88
Orace G. & Maggie Barnett 59
Orace G. & Virginia B. 59
Colman, Johnnie, 179
Compton, Sam, 4
Conklin, J. M., 150,172, 147
Connelly, Jim, 34
James, 112, 330
Conroy, Mrs. B. N., 364
John, 166, 172
Simon Peter, 128, 144, 148
Simon P., 172
Bill, 172
Riley, 175
William, 310
Cook, William R., 133
W. H., 147
W. Riley, 147
W. R., 161, 172, 275
Mrs. W. R., 368
Cooper, Charles, 46
Corbett, Harry, 221
Harry & Ruth, 238
Henry L., 333
H. L., 232
Corey, Jim, 178
Cornett, Max, 60
Corruthers, J. C., 150
Corwan, James L., 378
Cottenjin, Arthur, 196
Coulter, John, 304
Counsel, Dan, 229
Cover, Lee, 220
Covey, Claude C., 379
Cowan, Florence 182
Frank & Lillian Frogge, 182
Hazel, 182
Maude,182
Myrtle, 182
M. T., 152, 175, 180,182

Index

Cowles, Julian, 121
  Morris, 121
  U. S., 203
Cox, James, 102
  Oscar, 177
Coy, Pearl Dutt, 365
Coyne, John, 35
Cozart, James, 330
Craig, Charlie, 193
  John, 226
Cram, Allie, 333
  Bidwell, 86,255
  Bidwell & Kate Bolter, 84
  Robert, 84,89
Cramer, Jerry, 132,172
Crawford, Seth, 72
Creegan, John, 110,112
Crissman, Preston, 159
Criswell, Mr/Mrs. N.S.
  & children, 261
Crocket, Tobe, 50
Crook, General George, 89
  Major General, 114
Crosby-Robinson, Ina, 172
Crosswhite, Windom, 27
Crowfoot, Charles, 132
Crowley, Dan, 110
  Ellen, 110
  Elvie, 110
  Hazel, 110
  Ruth, 110
Culp, Austin W., 172
  Austin (city marshal) 147
Cummins, Zelma, 287
Cunning, Max, 79
Cunningham, Bob, 267
  Mr/Mrs. Bob &
    children, 262
  Ray, 272
Cupper, Percy A., 348
Curtis, Cal, 178
  Jim, 178
  Lee, 178
Cutendorf, Fred, 308
Cyrus, Dean, 179
  Evick, 179
  George, 179
  Mrs. Melvin, 177
  Omar, 179
Daly, Charles, 191
  Dorothy, 191
  John, 191

Darling, Ralph & Estella, 113
Darrar, W. C., 279
  Mr/Mrs. W. C. &
    children, 261
Daugherty, Lew, 1
  Wm., 1
Davis, D. W., 339
  Fred, 116
  Hugh, 318
Dawson, Abraham, 176
Deal, Joe T., 93
Dean, Ed, 13, 15
Dee, Elizabeth, 35
  George, 128, 144, 148
  Jack, 4, 46, 51, 185, 241
  John W., 332
Degner, Dewey, 113
  Elizabeth, 213
  Herman, 211
  Julius, 214
  Mrs. Julius, 213
DeHaven, Milt, 186
DeHuff, Mrs. J. Lee, 362
Deitzel, Henry, 172
DeLude, William, 34
Dennison, A.P., 375
DeShazer, Rev. Jacob J., 267
Dietzel, Henry, 128, 144, 148
Dillon, Charles, 318
Dinwiddle, Charles, 175
Dizney, Gillis, 333
  Mrs. Gillis, 368
  John, 333
  John T., 198
  Marie Galloway, 118
Doak, Eva Dunham, 30
Dobkins, John 180
Dodd, Eva, 176
Dodson, George, 72
Dombrowe, B., 213, 336
  O., 215
Dougherty, W. W., 378
Dove, Dick, 309
Drake, A. M., 219
Drexel, Godfred, 128
Droblitz, Mr/Mrs. Endre, 216
Dubois, Jean, 308
Duchein, A. G., 34
Duffy, Judge T. E. J., 136

Duling, Clara, 272
  C. V., 264
  Mr/Mrs. C. V. &
    children, 261
  Mrs. C. V., 273
  LeRoy, 272
Dunham, Amos, 31
  Mr/Mrs. Amos, 24
  Claude, 24, 26
  Eva, 30
  Lydia, 51
  Preston, 34
  Vina, 31
  Charles, 46, 128, 162, 203
  Claude, 26
  Maud, 215
  Maude, 307
  William, 215
Dussault, Henry, 141
  Julie Hobson, 144
Eades, Dell 113
  Dessie, 110
  Gertie, 110
  Howard, 110
Eagen, James, 61
  Sarah Ellen, 61
Eagon, John 178
Eaton, Asa T., 359
Ebert, Eleanor, 370
Edmonson, Bill, 229
Edwards, Jack, 100
  Jack Griffith, 12
  J. G., 19, 100
  Lord, 21
  William, 276
Ekerson, Mont 194
Elkins, Arthur, 47
  Cora, 47
  Eunice, 47
  Frank, 140, 302, 334
  Marvin, 49
  Marvin & Ora Clark, 44
  Milo, 46, 51
  Roy, 47
Elloitt, J. W., 47
Ellis, Mr/Mrs., 364
  William, 172
  Mr/Mrs. William A., 161
  Mr/Mrs. William, 123
Elliott, W. A., 368
  Mr/Mrs. W. A., 216
  Mrs. W. A., 362
Elmore, A. A., 310

Enderud, Louis, 13, 15
Etheridge, John L., 340, 344
Evans, John B., 10, 92
  Jones, 62
  Louella, 52
  Sam, 178
  Thomas J., 10
Evick, John, 317
  Mrs. J. E., 274
Fagan, Pat, 112
Falkenhagen, John, 308
Farber, C. W. (Lt), 378
Farquarson, Charles, 34
Farrell, H. Ward & Allie M., 347
  Mrs. H. Ward, 371
  Philip, 195
  Ward, 195, 254, 352
  William, 121, 196, 352
Fee, Rev. R. N., 377
Ferguson, Jack, 178
Fields, Sanford, 175
Filey, Harvey, 120, 128, 172
Fine, Amos, 370
Finlayson, Sandy, 110
Fisher, C. C., 341
  Fred, 172, 336
  Mr/Mrs. Fred, 123, 268
Fleck, James, 196
  Jim, 196
Flenner, Colby, 73
Floyd, Bill, 178
  Charlie, 178
  Noah, 178
Forest, Frank, 177
Foster, Mr/Mrs. C. H., 233
  Della, 176
  Evelyn M., 235
  Mr/Mrs. R. C., 235
  Wayne, 359
Fox, Calvin, 303
  Mr/Mrs. Edward, 34
  Miles, 303, 314
  Mr/Mrs. Miles & children, 279
  Dr. T.. 172
Franks, George, 178
  John, 178
  Lou, 178
  Oscar, 178
  Walter, 178

Fraylic, Daniel, 161
Freeman, Charles, 178
  J. M., 141
Freenias, Charles, 175
Freitas, Tony, 112
Fremont, John C., 90, 105, 375
  Captain John, 219, 225
Friend, Alex, 50
  Byron, 97
  Columbus, 97
  Mrs. Columbus, 48
Frogge, Dick & Lillie, 178
Fulgham, Rev. W. I., 196
Fuller, Dick, 234
Fullerton, Augusta, 227
  Inez, 227
  Mr/Mrs. Walter, 229
  Mrs. Walter, 226
Fulton, Glen, 85,
  P. C., 132, 172
Gailbraith, Mrs. Russell, 177
Gale, Dr. J. H., 172
Gallagher, Peter, 378
Galloway, Mr/Mrs. Frank, 34
  Marie, 118,296
Galloway-Dizney, Marie 172
Gamble, Horace, 111
  Simon, 111
Gard, Bern, 141
  Chester, 301
  Edna, 253
  Harry, 67, 248, 295, 297, 310, 343, 345
  Harry W., 304, 336, 338, 347
  H. W., 263
  Jesse J., 149
  Lela, 287
  Milo, 295, 297
  Milo & Caroline, 301
  Roscoe, 135, 307
Garet, Dick, 24
Garett, Clayton, 27
  Harlan, 36
  James, 167
  Jim & Leona O'Kelly, 35, 50, 53d
Garrison, J. M., 375
Gates, William H., 87
Gay, Clyde, 50

  David, 35
  Mary, 35
George, Chief, 25
Gesner, Alonzo, 377
Gibeon, Z. T., 176
Gibson, Chartles, 34
Gilbert, Clarence, 250
  Victor, 14
Gill, Frank, 16, 27, 274
  Ray, 276
  W. A., 130
Gills, Ballard, 180
  Joe, 180
Glass, Floyd, 277
Glover, Bob 230,
  Buzz, 230
  Frank, 230
  Henry, 230
  Luis, 230
Goff, Gene, 34
  Ray, 34
Goldsmith, Barney, 87
Gomer, Henry, 211
  William, 211, 214
Gould, George, 334
Grady, Bruce, 172
Graham, Ed, 164
  Frank, 368
  Mr/Mrs. Glen, 216
Grant, Dale, 365
  Mrs. Dayton, 365, 369
  Erwin, 365
  Jimmie, 174
  John, 174
  Mason, 174, 179
Grater, James M., 103
  Jim, 102
Gray, LaVelle, 124
  Samuel E. 115
  Mr/Mrs. Samuel E., 123
  S. E., 147, 172
  Mrs. S. E./Viola Isham, 372
  Wendel, 124
Green, Fred, 16
  Mr/Mrs. Fred, 161, 368
  Mr/Mrs. Wm., 279
  Mrs. W. I., 34
Grewell, Stanley, 308
Grey, Mattie, 176
Grimes, Florence, 17
Grittan, Bill, 214
Grout, Elon, 164
Gulliford, Jake, 9

388

Index

Haberstich, Fritz, 34
Sam, 305
Hahn, Joshua P., 88, 116
Daisy, 201
Joshua & Lula, 122
J. P., 148, 156, 172
Haight, Lige, 84
Haights, Charles, 22
Haile, Dr. Homer B., 125
Dr. H. B., 172
Hale, Aaron, 82, 97
Orla, 164
Orlie, 60
Mr/Mrs. W. S., 60
Hall, Art, 47
Gilbert L., 379
Will, 49, 97
Hamilton, Beth, 97
George, 5
Joea, 97
Lou, 5
Mary, 53a
Reppa, 53
Thomas S., 97
Thomas (Uncle &
Mother), 256
Tom, 81
T. S., 333
Hammers, W. F., 180
Hammond, A. E., 115,
130
Handley, T. B., 376
Haner, J. H., 134
Hannagin, George 234
Hannon, William 297
William & Addie
Jackson, 305
Hansen, Martin, 232,
234, 238
Harbin, Ed, 144
Harbison, Sadie, 257
Charles S., 10
Harper, Bogue, 139
William, 299, 308, 310
Harriman, E. H., 13, 144
Harrington, Elmer, 244
John, 240
Harris, Winifred Windom,
179
Harter, Jess, 220
Hartnagel, Theo, 212
Harvey, Laura, 110
Hash, Allen 330
Martha, 180

Hatfield/McCoy, fued, 88
Hauley, John, 176
Hawkins, Halbert, 113
Hayes, C. C., 102
Mr/Mrs. Marion, 265
Hays, Charles, 308
Daisy, 201
Healey, Mr/Mrs. J. H., 60
Healy, Clara, 26
Healy, Jeff, 180
Heath, Frank M., 205
Heising, Alice L., 333
Dan, 237
Mr/Mrs. Dan, 217
Dorsey, 217
Harry, 217, 236
Helfrich, Ben, 179
John 179
Katie 175
Mrs. John/Minnie
McCoin, 372
Walter, 179
Helm, Elizabeth Sager,
12, 37
Henderson, John, 241,
252, 336, 339, 344
Johnnie, 345, 349
Perry, 32, 264, 265,
336, 342
Perry & Blanche, 265
Mr/Mrs. Perry, 274
Mrs. Perry, 276
Hendrick, George, 178
Walter, 230
Henneman, Albert, 211
Clara, 211
Kate, 211, 215
Henske, Frederich, 213
Hering, Carl, 368
Mrs. Carl, 320, 365, 369
Hermann, F. C., 340
Hershner, Blanche, 263
Joyce, 263
Hershy, Kenneth, 191
Herst, Elden, 228
Hess, William H., 172
Higdon, Charles, 157,
172
Hill, James J., 144
Josephine, 34, 263
Sam, 13
Wesley, 297
Hindman, Charles, &
Martha Cobbs, 226

Hinkle, I. T., 336
Hinton, Claude, 50
Hobbs, Harry, 247
L. L., 73, 247
Hobson, Charles 123
Julie, 144
M. A., 172
Hockett, John & Lucy, 178
Hoefeld, Otto, 196
Hoffman, Frank/Addie
Carson Jenkins, 56
John, 214
John A., 115, 210, 213
John A. & Clara
Hennenan, 211
John, Sr., 210, 213
Hofstetter, Mrs.
Truman, 365
Holcomb, Ira, 344
Ira P., 141, 342
Holdship, Eva F., 266
Holmes, Gus, 172
Priday, 226
Holt, Corbett, 158, 302
Nannie, 170
Hood, Douglas, 128,
145, 166, 172
Hoover, Maurice, 344,
356
Myrl, 356
Horigan, Lester, 86,88
Horney, Eunice, 175
J. H., 336
Mrs. L. M.\Retta Peck,
372
Houk, Alex, 180
Houston, Joseph, 250
Howell, Jim, 34
Hubbard, Mr/Mrs. Carl,
223
Hunter, Bill, 62
Charles L., 332
Frank, 62
Lloyd, 148, 172
Wiley, 62
Hurst, Emery, 178
Walter, 178
Hurt, George, 306
James, 305
Hurt-Huntington,
George, 159
Huston, Dean, 51
Wade, 51
Hutchison, Fred, 313

Hyde, Mrs. Forrest Clover, 361
Hype, Frank, 178
Irving, Lewis H., 143, 340, 342, 361
L. H., 172, 336
"Turk," 202, 349
Isham, John, 172
Viola, 372
Jackle, John, 186
Jackson, Addie, 297, 305
Bill, 234
John H. 115,140,172
John H. "Tobe," 305
J. H., 147, 159, Mae, 305
Jenkins, Aaron, 56
Aaron Thomas & Addie Carson, 56
Aaron Thomas & Mary Melinda, 55
Alvin, 55
Delbert, 55,178
John, 55, 178
Tom, 55
Virgil & Martha Banta, 55
Jennings, Harry, 172
Neil S., 172
Jerro, Mrs. J., 362
Johnson, Bob, 179
David, 254
Dick, 247
Joea, 256
Joea Hamilton, 97
William E. & May B., 65,354
Jones, Ben, 172
Jack, 308
Johnny, 44
Lem, 10
Mrs. Paul, 369
Rube, 120
Wilfred, 250
Jubbard, John, 99
Julseth, Mr/Mrs. L. T., 216
Kaas, N. C. B., 216
Tom, 28
Kamper, Albert, 88
Godfried, 88
Kane, Fanny J., 361
Jesse, 224
Kaser, Jacob, 112, 330
Katch, Mr/Mrs. Leo, 88

Kaufman, Mrs. Ben, 279
Keaton, Grover, 101
Keckler, Billy, 72
Keegan, Charles R., 103
Mrs. Chas., 176
Keenan, James, 6
Keeney, H. E., 274, 276
Kelley, Captain E. W., 102
Kelsay, Lester N., 113
Kemp, Mr/Mrs. Harvey, 34
Kennedy, Chester, 86
Kesner, Joe, 228
Keys, Harry G., 123
Harry & Myrtle, 129
Kibbee, Gus, 51
Gus & Elizabeth Dee, 35
Guy, 51
Horace, 35
Kickler, Bill, 179
Kilts, Floyd, 113
Jesse, 113
King, Arthur, 222
Carl, 180
John M., 135
J. M., 67,180
Merle, 180
Pauline Windom, 179
Kirby, John, 99
Kirk, James E., 379
Kitcher, Ed, 196
Kjar, Hans, 347
Klann, Charles, 317, 323
C. F., 275
Knight, John, 100
Knorr, Lee, 177
Kollock, John K., 339, 342
Kongrasky, Agnes, 176
Kosteliz, John, 34
Kraut, John, 17
Krug, Robert H., 227
Kutcher, Ed, 302
Lagursie, Pete, 167
Laird, Hazel Windom, 179
Lamb, Lena M., 148, 172
Lambert, Nick, 216, 230
N. J., 224
Thompson, 224
Lampson, Ward, 63
Lamson, Charles, 240, 243
Claud, 240, 244, 248
Henry, 240
Jim, 240

Paul, 244
Ward, 240
Lance, Guy, 224
Landis, Grace, 176
LaNell, Theresa, 179
Larkin, Ben 173
Larson, Andrew, 175, 296
Joe, 178
Pete, 216
Laughlin, Emma, 196
George, 196
LaVein, Mr/Mrs. Harry, 34
Lawrie, Harold, 66
Leach, Jeanette, 279
Tom, 179
Lee, Bill, 265
Bill & Adie Barlow, 265
Mr/Mrs. Isaac, 265
James, 342
Mr/Mrs. & children, 261
John & Etta Richardson, 265
Mr/Mrs. John, 274
Leithauser, Frank, 234
Leuddemann, Max, 128
Lever, Henry, 86
Lewis, John, 5
John H., 337
Liermann, Mr/Mrs. Arthur, 368
A. F. & Bonnie Thompson, 279
Sophia, 258
Limbaugh, Andrew, 62
Lincoln, Abraham, 58
Links, Hiram, 317, 336, 345
Roscoe & Aural Moore, 280
Lippe, Charles, 35
May, 29
Lithgow, Walter, 175
Livingston, Joseph W., 121
J. W., 128, 173
Lochard, John, 120 152,192
Logan, Wm., 376
Loneoy, H., 12
Long, Elizabeth, 194
Lex, 28
T. A., 147
Dr. T. A., 124, 173
Loomis, Bert, 318
Looney, Russell, 263

Index

Loose, Mrs. Fred, 231
Loring, Charles, 73
Lott, Charles, 180
Loucks, Kyle, 173
  M. L., "Tice," 148, 173
Love, Ed, 178
Loveall, J. E., 173
Loveland, Frank, 62,
  173, 177
Loving, Mr/Mrs. S. P. &
  dau., 262
Lowther, Charles, 113
Lowthers, C. L., 72
Lucas, Frank, 131
Luckey, James C., 378
  John, 199
Lueddemann, Max, 46,
  99, 165, 173
Luelling, Ellen, 312
  John, 317, 322
Lundgren, Leonard,
  230, 223
Lyle, Al, 185
  W. H., 86
Lyman, C. A., 348
Lytle, George, 30
  Purl, 169
Mack, H. L., 220
Maddox, Lila, 176
Madsen, Mr/Mrs.
  Barney, 232
  Barnhart, 238
  Barry, 220
Magness, James, 171
  James & Myrtle
    Borden, 159
  Mina, 263
Mailing, Charles, 4
  Mr/Mrs. Charles, 46
  Mrs. (nee Dee), 46
  C. C., 4, 88
Malloy, J. T., 294
Maloy, Mr/Mrs. Tom,
  122
Marnach, Joe, 214
Martin, Anna, 73
  A. T., 196, 263
  Mrs. Glen, 279
  Helen, 279
  Isaac, 73
  John, 34
  Myrthena, 263
Mason, Archie, 122,
  130,171

Ed, 171
E. W., 371
M. C., 140, 171
Massamore, G. W., 34
Massey, Earl, 326
Masterson, Addie, 112
  Sol, 204
Matson, Ernie, 5
Maupin, Howard, 16,
  96, 97, 105
  Perry, 11, 16, 83
Mayes, Mr/Mrs. John, 170
Mayfield, Jessie, 318
Mays, Grant, 111
  John, 171
  Polk, 111
McBrain, D. V., 352
McCallister, Ferd, 177
  T. F., "Ferd," 58
McCalou, Walter, 46
McCarthy, Dan, 104
McCaulou, Walter, 132,
  369
McClure, J. K., 331
McCoin, Julius, 179
  Minnie, 179, 372
  Numa, 179
  Walter, 179
McCollum, Joel, 157
  Joel & Lydia Dunham,
    51
McCorkle, Chester, 199
  Chet, 48, 50
  Chuck, 53
McCormack, Patrick, 171
  Tom, 171
McCoy, George, 50
  Laura, 50
McCrudden, Matilda, 158
McCue, Charles, 34
  Mrs. Charles, 12
McDonald, Alex & Beth
  Hamilton, 97
  Beth, 256
  Fred A., 316
  Ronald, 82, 256
  Thomas, 256
  Tom, 82
McDougal, Emily G.,
  158, 176
McFaffery, Neva
  Weigang, 176
McFarland, George, 191
McGee, Floy, 181

McGhee, Carl & Florence
  Cowan, 182
  Floy, 176
  J. J. Thomas, 179
McGilvery, D. C., 337
McInnis, Mr/Mrs.
  Martin, 34
McKenzie, Cecil, 5
McLauthlin, Hap 137
McLennan, John, 111
  "Red Alex," 104
McLennon, Mr/Mrs. D.,
  216
McMean, Charles, 5
  Jim, 69, 178
McMeen, Nora Ackey, 174
McMullin, Bud, 232
McNemar, Mr/Mrs.
  Delbert, 216
McPherson, Mr/Mrs., 32
  Mrs. Colburn, 168
McQuinn, John A., 378
McTaggart, John, 116,
  133, 148
  Mrs. John, 362
Mead, Dr. Elwood, 344
Meek, Joe, 178
  Stephen, 90
  William, 178
Meloy, Thomas P. 171
  Mr/Mrs. Tom, 156
  T. J., 126, 144, 148
Mendenhall, Abijah, 244
  Joe, 241, 245
  Joseph, 252
  J. W., 216, 244, 245, 250
  Michael, 241
  Ruth, 244
  Walter, 241
Menefee, E. B., 15
Mensch, Fred, 379
Merchant, Abe, 240
  Anna Lee Martin, 73
  Nina, 244
  Vern, 244, 372
Merrill, Jake, 179
Messinger, Kelly &
  Clara, 180
Meyers, W. P., 136
Miller, Dave, 229
  Everett, 179
  Frank, 179
  George, 179
  Mildred, 176

Milligan, Neil, 179
Minger, Fred, 180
Mingers, Fred & Maud
 Cowan, 182
Mishler, Asa, 178
Mitchell, Billie, 247
 Henry, 180
 Mr/Mrs. J. L., 216
 Sam, 275
 Mr/ Mrs. Sam, 303
 Capt. W. W., 376
Moerhing, Rev/Mrs., 214
 Marie, 214
Monner, Anthony, 318
 George, 318
Monner, John, 318
 Nick, 318
Monroe, Flossie, 272
 Myrtle, 272
 Perry, 352
 Tom, 119
 T. P., 263
 Mr/Mrs T. P. &
  children, 261
 Mrs. T. P., 265
Montgomery, Canada,
 331
 E. A., 233
 George, 330
 Hattie Ellen, 2
 H. O., 73
 Joe, 5
 Kennedy, 1
 Mrs. Velotis, 231
Moore, Albert, 178
 Aural, 280
 Bert, 318
 Lee, 178
 Ralph, 27, 30
 Seth Wallace, 30
 Mr/Mrs. William C.
  "Bill," 305
 W. G., 171, 342
Moorehead, Rev. G. R.,
 296
Morfiett, William, 250
Morford, Lynn, 178
Morgan, Mr/Mrs. Frank,
 256
 J. R., 110
 Lucille, 176
Morris, Frank, 256
Morrisey, Dan "Pegleg,"
 113

Morrow, Andrew, 6, 171,
 342
 Andrew & Emily G.
  McDougall, 156,
  176
 Mrs. Andrew, Sr., 364
 Millie, 148
Morse, Mrs. Bill, 174
Mortimore, Olive, 176
 Oliver, 263
Mortsoft, J. B., 379
Moyes, James M., 171
Munz, Alfred, 249
Nartz, J. Willis, 254
Negas, George Ragner, 177
 Joe, 177
 Luther Melton, 177
 Myrtle Markee, 177
 Simon, 177
Nesbitt, Jean, 176
Neu, Bob, 216
 D. W., 333
 Isaac, 224
Newbill, Carl & Nova, 5
Newell, L. A., 166
 Roy, 16, 28, 36
 Roy & Clara Healy, 28
 Sam, 28
Newelle, Robert, 375
Nichols, Lou, 175
 Lyn, 16
 Lyn & Florence
  Grimes, 17
 L. L., 73
Nickles, Joe, 60
Niskanen, William, 357
Nisson, H. K. W., 133
 J. K. W. "Baldy," 171
Noble, Earle, 63
Noonan, Charles, 113
Northy, Otto, 172
Ogden, Peter Skeen, 79,
 350, 375
Oliver, Mr/Mrs. &
  children, 261
Oller, Andrew, 113
Olney, Nathan, 375
Olson, Alice, 279
 R. T., 144, 148, 150,
  172
Orfitt, A. B.,102
Ornduff, Ross C., 234
Ortman, Charley, 309
Osborn, Clair, 56

Dale & Wilma, 365
Dan, 169
Dan's father, 169
Osborn, Fannie, 56
 Floyd, 56
 Frank, 56, 172
 George, 69
 George & Ella Rogers,
  56, 58
 Gertrude, 56
 Lois, 56
 Lula, 56
Osborn, Maude, 56
 Rex, 56
 Robert, 56
 Winnifred, 56
Oswald, Joe 194
Overturf, Jim, 219
O'Kelly, Bart, 53a, 53b
 Birdie, 53a
 Georgina, 53a, 53b
 Grover, 53a
 John, 50 62
 John Harrison, 53a
 Jonnie, 53a
 Martina, 53a, 53b
 Mr/Mrs., 35
 Leona, 35, 50, 53a, 53d
Palmahn, John, 172
 Charles W., 331
 John A., 114
Palmer, A. C., 26
Parkey, Alf, 316
 Alfred, 137
 A. H., 310, 342
Parks, Ed, 221
Parrish, J. L., 375
 Mr/Mrs. Orlando 12
 Rolla, 26
 Walter, 28
Patterson, Lou, 179
Paulina, Chief, 16, 97
Poulsen, Neil, 304
Paxton, Charles, 176
 G. A., 278
 Mr/Mrs. Hull, 279
 Ira, 176
 L. P., 262
Pearce, Mrs. Charles, 32
 John, 168
 Joshua, 32
 Orin A., 136,150, 172
 O. A., 336
 Vine W., 165

Index

Peck, Dave, 57,61,65
  Euretta, 57
  Hattie, 57
  Jack & Pearl Tucker, 61
  John, 57
  Lee, 57
  Lee & Francis Tucker, 61
Peck, Ralph, 57, 65, 73, 175
  Retta, 372
  Vena, 57
  William, 62, 69, 176
  William & Mollie, 57, 61
Pederson, Mr/Mrs.
    Fred, 34
Peetz, Lou, 234
Percival, Sydney D., 166,
    172
  Sidney D. & Alice
    Renolds 187
Perkins, Fred, 379
Philipi, Hill, 228
Philips, Jim, 44
Phillipi, King Louis, 19
Phillips, A. S., 172
Pierce, Sam, 180
  Walter M., 275
  Governor Walter, 67
Pike, Aaron, 63
  Ed, 63
Pillette, Effa, 159
  Milton G., 172, 362
Pinkerton, N. H., 287
Pittock, Henry L., 15
Pitzer, Harry, 34
  Jack, 34
Porter, Cecil, 345
  Cecil & Anna
    Branstetter, 214
  Johnson D., 151
Pos, J. H., 343
Post, T. M., 228
Powell, Roy, 34
Powers, Evada, 372
  T. A., 16, 35, 372
  Mrs. T. A., 372
Pratt, Martin, 304
  Martin H., 172
  Martin T., 116
Prentiss, Virginia B., 59
Preston, Mr/Mrs. B. F.
    & child, 261
Priday, Albert, 85
  Albert James, 32
  A. J., 85

H. L., 255
John, 83
John H., 333
Leslie, 32, 85, 88
Mr/Mrs. Leslie, 167
Warren, 84
Pringle, Sanford, 174
Pummell, Lester, 150
Putz, Max, 128, 144,
    148, 172
Quaaly, P. J., 100
Quinn, Joe & Hattie, 178
Ragan, William, 105
Ragsdale, Bill, 234
Ralston, Clifford, 241, 244
  Earl, 244
  Wannie, 244
  William, 241
  Willia, 242
Rammin, Mrs Hans, 279
Ramsey, Bernice, 287
  Claude, 297
  Claude G., 336
  D. R., 231
  Ethel, 263
  Gus, 372
  John P. 307
  Mrs. Leslie/Lela Gard,
    362
  Lillian, 359
  William, 295
  William H., 303, 307
  W. H., 363
Randal, Ray, 34
Randolph, B. O., 172
Rankin, George, 148, 172
Rastall, Chas. W., 379
Ray, Pat, 34
Rea, Don, 130, 132
  Don P., 115, 150, 172,
    304
  Robert, 130, 132
Read, James P., 60
  Jim, 65
  Lillie, 175
  Lilly, 132
  Lilly May, 60, 132, 372
  Pearl, 60, 132, 372
  Perry, 1, 88, 132, 172,
    331
  Perry & Hattie, 60
  Perry & Hattie
    Montgomery, 2
Reardon, Bessie, 176

Redfield, C. M., 339
Reichen, John, 214
Reilly, Tom, 108
  Mrs. P. L., 232
Renolds, Mable, 30
Retzloff, Julius, 177
Reynolds, Alice, 187
  A. M., 379
  Frank, 247
Rheinhardt, Phil, 44
Rhodes, Dusty, 150
  Ora, 172
Rice, James, 148, 172
  Joe, 214
  Walt, 175
  Walter, 172
Richards, Bill, 62
  G. E., 45
  G. W., 44
  Harold, 244
Richardson, Bert, 34
  Etta, 265
  Mr/Mrs. George, 267
  G. W., 265
  John, 87
  Leita Binder, 280
  Vance, 267
Ricker, Mrs. Max, 369
Rideout, Edith, 176
Ridgeway, Charlie, 174
  George, 174
  Glen, 174
  Glen & Grace
    Robinson, 73
  Mrs. Glen, 179
Riebhoff, Ann, 176
Riggs, Alvin, 221
  Dave, 224
  J. C., 220
  Perl, 222
Ringo, Frank, 287
Ritterspacher, Kate
    Henneman 215
Roba, Henry, 179
Roberts, Dwight, 72,
    175, 244
Robinson, Dwight, P. 340
  Grace, 73
  James, 148
  Jim, 179
  John, 148
  John W., 99
  J. W., 127, 172
  M. A., 127

Rodgers, Bill, 174
Bob, 180
Ida, 73
Rodman, Adrian, 61
Dorothy, 61
Frank, 63
Fred, 372
Mrs. Fred, 372
George, 53d, 336
George Jr., 61
George & Sarah Ellen
Eagen, 61
Geo., 63
Iva, 61
Lelia, 61
Millard, 61
Wm. H., 61
Rodriguez, Sumner, 370
Mr/Mrs. S. R. G., 370
Rogers, Bill, 58
Clark, 57, 61
Dave, 58, 61
Ella, 58
May, 58
Romo, Anthony, 113
Root, Mrs. Lloyd, 369
Ross, Mrs. J. H., 369
Rott, Fred, 247
Roush, Chester E., 130,
148,172
Rowan, Mr/Mrs. Sam, 216
Ruble, Mr/Mrs. Andrew,
71
Claude, 71
Katie, 71
Lucy, 71
Walter, 71
Rufner, Fred, 5
Rush, Benjamin, 183
John, 175, 180, 183
Martha J., 82
Russell, Mary, 174
Sager, Elizabeth, 12, 37
Saltzman, Jay, 330
Sanderson, W. U., 15, 27
Sandvig, Sam, 256
Sanford, Alfred C., 148,172
A. C., 144
Sann, Bill 176
Sawyer, R. W., 345
Saxton, George, 241
John, 241
Roy, 244
Scates, Jim, 34

Schanck, R. F., 207
Schneeloch, Ralph, 340
Schooling, Jerry, 13, 15,
22, 34, 52
Jerry & May Rogers, 58
Schreiber, Carl, 73
Schriber, Carl, 245
Schrum, Volney, 112
Schultz, Mr/Mrs.
Sanford, 84
Schwartz, Al, 221
Scott, Felix, 91, 97
Felix & Marion, 9, 167
Marion, 10, 91, 97
Presley, 10
Seal, Emery, 180
Seales, Emery, 178
Seals, Albert, 179
Jim, 152
See, Will, 325
Seethoff, Henry, 145
Sellers, S. J., 143, 172
S. J., "Beany," 154
Selman, Frank, 231
Serier, Isaac, 308
Shane, Ralph M., 199
Shawe, Bruce, 34
Sherar, Joseph, 106, 112
Sherrod, W. F. "Bill," 304
Sheythe, John L. &
Dorothy, 365
Shold, Walter, 359
Short, J. F., 347
William H., 181
Shrum, Andrew Jackson,
111
A. J., 329, 332
F. D. V., 329
Shugert, A. F., 141, 172
Grace, 148
Shutt, I. F., 172
Sights, Doc, 177
Siler, Wade, 172
Siment, Hester O., 176
Simpson, Darrell, 5
Harmon, 87
Roy, 5
Slobig, Clarence, 113
Smith, Adrain, 369
A. J., 15
Bud, 5
C. F., 130
Earnest, 308
Elizabeth Justice Bell, 13

Elva, 222
Elva J., 133, 172
Ethel, 175, 244
Grace, 296
Jennie, 172
John, 35,
Levi, 207
Lynn, 181
Robert, 199
T. M., 175
Viola, 191
Warren, 147, 172
Snook, Dr. W. H., 124,
172, 243, 246
Mrs. W. H., 361, 364
Snyder, Alta, 175
Sotham, J. C., 345
Sothman, Mr/Mrs. Jerry,
216
J. C., 274, 275, 308, 344
South, Jesse, 73
Perry, 220
Sparks, Lige, 226
Spaulding, Henry, 9
Speaker, Gus, 241
Springer, Guyon, 60, 63,
176, 179
Crook County Judge, 136
G., 69
Stacks, Willis, 178
Stangland, Frank, 139, 318
Stanley, F. S., 337
Stanton, G. V., 146, 172
Mrs G. V., 362
Vern, 160
Stats, Billy 219
Stearns, Jesse, 337
Steavens, Johnny, 228
Stebbins, Winstead J. & Eva
F. Holdship, 265
W. J., 265, 371
Mr/Mrs. W. J., 274, 276
Stephens, Eleanor H., 369
Stevans, George & Fanny
Cobbs, 226
Carl, 62
George, 132, 172
John F., 153
Stewart, Mrs. Bruce, 369
Delta, 176
Stikona, Jim, 302
Stockton, Glenn, 44, 145
Stollicker, Herman, 194
Stolte, Emil, 34

Index

Stonehocker, Mr/Mrs.
  W. H., 262
Storts, Katy, 50
Stout, Harry, 222
Straight, Martha Hash,
  180
Stranahan, Charles, 178
Strand, Jake, 179
Strasser, Conrad, 210, 213
  Reinhard, 213
Stricklin, Henry, 228
Striebel, Paul, 236
Stuart, Joe, 89
  John, 85
Summers, Jack, 133
Summerville, John, 21
Sumner, Mr/Mrs. Wesley,
  280
Swanson, John F., 153
  Lavoy, 254
Swartz, Al, 232
Sweeting, Della, 172
Swift, Dan 66
Talbert, I. A., 73
Tandy, Margaret, 34
Tate, Dick, 56
Taylor, Effie, 265, 305
  Effie T., 263
  Mr/Mrs. Henry K., 215
  Joe, 177
  M. W., 130
  T. A., 184
  T. A. & Maud Durham,
    215, 307
  Zachary, 16
Teal, Joseph, 93
  Joseph N., 87
  Colonel Joseph, 87
  J. N., 193
Teegarden, Hattie, 273
Tellefson, Mr/Mrs.
    Andrew, 279
  Martin, 265
  Martin & Joyce
    Hershner, 265
  Orpa & Fern, 279
Terrill, Nellie G., 176
Thacker, John, 44
Thielman, Roy, 172
Thomas, Grace, 184
  Jim, 5, 178, 276
  John, 184, 196
  Lena, 5
  Lorenzo, 178

Lulu, 184, 194
Martha Short, 181
Nick, 184, 194
W. S., 100
Thompson, Bonnie, 279
  Bud, 25, 31
  Charlie, 72
  Duovery, 11
  Earl, 67
  George, 25, 31, 166
  Martha, 279
  Millard, 178
  Owen, 235
  S. G., 11
  William "Bud," 11
  Colonel William "Bud,"
    166
Thornburgh, Tom 247
Thornton, Henry W.,
    254, 257
  Ward, 258
Thronson, Thron, 99
Tipton, Al, 17
Todd, John C., 21, 23
  John V., 228
  John Y., 21, 93
Tompkins, Frank, 330
Tompson, Bud, 26
Toothman, Joe, 365
  Mrs. J. A., 365, 369
Topping, H. C., 141
Traglis, J. E., 213
Trahansham, Tony, 228
Travis, Dave, 270
Trolan, Dan, 45
  Selma, 263, 276
Tucker, Francis, 61
  Pearl, 61
  Thomas B., 147
  Tom, 165, 207
  T. B., 147, 172
Turner, Bert, 34
  H. W., 344
  Howard, 16, 77, 175,
    203, 345, 349,
    362, 371, 373
  Howard W., 51, 115,
    138, 140 148,
    151, 165, 172
  Howard W. & Pearl
    Read, 372
  Mayor Howard W., 147
  Lilly Read, 175
Twiss, E. W., 326

Updike, Earl, 221
  George W., 232
U'Ren, Charles P., 166,
    172
  W. S., 136
Van Houten, C. C., 12
  J. P., 12
Vandervert, Bill, 218
VanHorn, Nella, 263
VanMeter, Mr/Mrs. &
    children, 261
VanNoy, Clark, 263
  Mrs. Harl/Edna Watts,
    359
  Harl, 368
  Helen, 263
Van Tassel, Grace, 244
  Merrill, 241, 244, 252
  Ora, 172, 198
VanWert, Everett, 370
Veazie, A. L., 86, 167
  Edmund F., 86
  P. L., 91
Versaw, Glen, 44
  Harrison, 44
Vibbert, Andrew, 184
  Noah, 184
  Peter, 184, 317
  P. N., 336, 340, 342
Vincent, Judge, 5
  Judson, 330
Volrath, Louis, 308
Wadsworth, Peter, 379
Wagonblast, John, 30,
    308
Waite, H. N., 311
  Oren, 176
Walker, Elkanah, 375
Wallace, N. G., 342
Wallen, Capt E. H., 106
Wampole, Elias, 375
Wanberg, Ben, 196
Warren, J. W., 272
  Mr/Mrs. J. W., 362
  Robert, 3
  Willis, 272
Waterhouse, Charles,
    173
Watson, John, 192
Watts, Carl, 263, 359
  Clarence, 173
  Edna, 359
  F. H., 32
  James, 173, 307, 359

James J. & Lillian Ramsey, 359
Mrs. James, 161
Lillian, 263, 307
Lillian Ramsey, 358, 362
Ross, 359
Wawrinfosky, Chas., 214
Charles, 210
Edwin, 211
Waymire, Frederick J., 114, 120
J. C., 17,
Webber-Boyce, Mary, 173
Weber, E. W., 123
Weigand, Ernest, 176
Jack, 176
Joe, 177
Joseph, 176
Neva, 176
Norman, 177
Pearl, 176
Rolla, 177
Weigle, Lee, 199
West, Governor Oswald, 135
West, William, 34
Weston, A. J., 139
Wever, Theresa, 320
Wharton, Fenton, 112
Wheeler, Mancel, 173
Mrs. Mancel, 173
White, Ed, 73
Edward, 247
George, 196
George H. 336
George, Jr, 279
Mr/Mrs. George, 279
Mrs. George, 268
Harry, 73
Mary J., 196
Nancy, 273
Mr/Mrs. Snowden & children, 261, 266
Mrs. Snowden, 364
Whiting, Ray Jr., 101
Wible, Jerry, 173
Perry, 129

Wickham, C. M., 337
Fred W., 15
Wiese, Mrs. William, 369
Wild, Fritz, 196
Wiley A. J., 340
Williams, Richard M., 87
Wallace, 306
Walter, 306
Walter S., 336
Williamson, E. W., 85
Volney, 215
Wilsie, Reverend, 26
Wilson, Charles P., 173
Mr/Mrs. Charles, 251
Charlie "High Pockets," 60
Dr. Clarence True, 236
C. P. "Doc," 157
Wilson, Ethel, 244
Francis, 251
Frank, 251
Jay, 241
Mr/Mrs. Lewis, 216
Max, 118, 173
Nellie, 244
Nettie, 244
Oscar, 241
Ruby, 244
Stella, 118
Windom, Alonzo, 68
Carl, 69
Harry, 69, 179
Hazel, 69, 179
Hen, 60, 62
Henry, 60, 63, 176, 179
James Henry & Rebecca Leach, 68
Jess, 68
Jesse, 179
Jim, 179
Lance, 179
Lant, 60
Pauline, 69, 179
Winifred, 69, 179
Winslow, Clifford, 34
Winters, Charles, 150, 213

Wood, Harvey, 84
James, 82
James & Addie, 98
Lee, 82
Whitfield T., 99
W. T. & Martha J.Rush, 82
W. T., 100
Woods, Erskine, 221
Wool, General John E., 90
Work, Dr. Hubert, 344
Wrenn, Edtta, 89
Wright, Albert O., 379
Flether, 178
Colonel George, 90
Harold Bell, 236
Wurtzweiler, Bill, 224
Wyeth, Nathaniel, 105
Nathaniel J.,375
Yancer, Pete, 180
York, Frank, 43
Harry, 28
Yost, John Sr, 45
Young, A. C., 136
Jerry, 228
Lewis A., 152
Lou, 294
Louis, 192
Mr/Mrs L. A. & children, 261
Mr/Mrs L. A., 266
Mabel, 194
Young/Moung?, L. A., 262
Youngs, Gomer, 62
Lou, 313
Youngstrom, J. O., 342
Zehntbauer, John, 220
Zeigler, Al, 163
Zell, Fred, 173, 310
William, 308
Zemke, Albert, 214
Albert F. 213
A. F. 213
Emil, 210, 213
Gustaf, 213
Zumwalt, Mrs Frank 238